Presented to: _____

_____

By: _____

_____

On: _____

_____

_____

2000   1500   10

Connections Bible

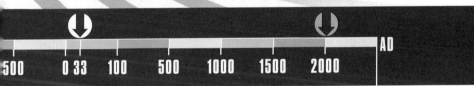

| 500 | 0 33 | 100 | 500 | 1000 | 1500 | 2000 | AD |

Table of Contents

OLD TESTAMENT STORIES

NEW TESTAMENT STORIES

THE OLD TESTAMENT

»»» AND SO LIFE BEGINS «««

Introduction

Every story has a beginning. That's what the word *Genesis* means—"beginning." But the one that started all beginnings is this one—the creation story. Moses, one of the greatest leaders of all time, wrote the story of God's creation of an entire universe out of nothing. Can you imagine the universe without a sun, planets, stars, or even without you? Come, take a look at how everything began . . . in the beginning.

Genesis 1:1–2:3, NLT

In the beginning God created the heavens and the earth. The earth was empty, a formless mass cloaked in darkness. And the Spirit of God was hovering over its surface. Then God said, "Let there be light," and there was light. And God saw that it was good. Then he separated the light from the darkness. God called the light "day" and the darkness "night." Together these made up one day.

And God said, "Let there be space between the waters, to separate water from water." And so it was. God made this space to separate the waters above from the waters below. And God called the space "sky." This happened on the second day.

And God said, "Let the waters beneath the sky be gathered into one place so dry ground may appear." And so it was. God named the dry ground "land" and the water "seas." And God saw that it was good. Then God said, "Let the land burst forth with every sort of grass and seed-bearing plant. And let there be trees that grow seed-bearing fruit. The seeds will then produce the kinds of plants and trees from which they came." And so it was. The land was filled with seed-bearing plants and trees, and their seeds produced plants and trees of like kind. And God saw that it was good. This all happened on the third day.

And God said, "Let bright lights appear in the sky to separate the day from the night. They will be signs to mark off the seasons, the days, and the years. Let their light shine down upon the earth." And so it was. For God made two great lights, the sun and the moon, to shine down upon the earth. The greater one, the sun, presides during the day; the lesser one, the moon, presides through the night. He also made the stars. God set these lights in the heavens to light the earth, to govern the day and the night, and to separate the light from the darkness. And God saw that it was good. This all happened on the fourth day.

And God said, "Let the waters swarm with fish and other life. Let the skies be filled with birds of every kind." So God created great sea creatures and every sort of fish and every kind of bird. And God saw that it was good. Then God blessed them, saying, "Let the fish multiply and fill the oceans. Let the birds increase and fill the earth." This all happened on the fifth day.

And God said, "Let the earth bring forth every kind of animal—livestock, small animals, and wildlife." And so it was. God made all sorts of wild animals, livestock, and small animals, each able to reproduce more of its own kind. And God saw that it was good.

Then God said, "Let us make people in our image, to be like ourselves. They will be masters over all life—the fish in the sea, the birds in the sky, and all the livestock, wild animals, and small animals."

So God created people in his own image;
God patterned them after himself;
male and female he created them.

God blessed them and told them, "Multiply and fill the earth and subdue it. Be masters over the fish and birds and all the animals." And God said, "Look! I have given you the seed-bearing plants throughout the earth and all the fruit trees for your food. And I have given all the grasses and other green plants to the animals and birds for their food." And so it was. Then God looked over all he had made, and he saw that it was excellent in every way. This all happened on the sixth day.

So the creation of the heavens and the earth and everything in them was completed. On the seventh day, having finished his task, God rested from all his work. And God blessed the seventh day and declared it holy, because it was the day when he rested from his work of creation.

Take ANOTHER LOOK

Obviously, David, the Bible hero, wasn't around when the world was created. But he could still write a song, or psalm, to show his appreciation for God's awesome creation. Here's part of a psalm that he wrote. As you read it, think about what you would do to show your appreciation for God's creation.

Psalm 19:1-4, NLT

The heavens tell of the glory of God.
　The skies display his marvelous craftsmanship.
Day after day they continue to speak;
　night after night they make him known.
They speak without a sound or a word;
　their voice is silent in the skies;
yet their message has gone out to all the earth,
　and their words to all the world.

Here's What I Think

Julie, age 18

The creation story might be something you've heard so often that you'd like to skip it. But guess what! This short little passage of Scripture is loaded with a huge lesson. Clearly and powerfully, it shows that God is *all-mighty.* When he was making different aspects of the universe, all he had to do was *speak.* "And God said, 'Let there be (fill in the blank)' . . . and it was so."

How comforting to know that our God is capable of creating everything and anything—simply by his words! Why is that fact so comforting? Because it means I don't need to worry. If God can create the universe, he can certainly give me wisdom and confidence before a big presentation or test in school. It's easy to worry about schoolwork or get nervous about speaking in front of the class—but I can look back at this story and know God is big enough to help me.

Julie

Trust in the one who created everything.

OFF TO A BAD BEGINNING

Introduction

In our next story, we discover another beginning: the start of sin, or wrongdoing. Moses, the writer of the first five books of the Bible, describes how the first people, Adam and Eve, broke the only rule that God gave them. Their actions affected every person born on the earth—including you. Instead of living happily in the peaceful, perfect garden, Adam and Eve would be separated from God. But God had a plan. One day, a Savior would make things right. But that Savior wouldn't arrive on Earth for many, many years.

Genesis 2:15–3:21, NLT

The LORD God placed the man in the Garden of Eden to tend and care for it. But the LORD God gave him this warning: "You may freely eat any fruit in the garden except fruit from the tree of the knowledge of good and evil. If you eat of its fruit, you will surely die."

And the LORD God said, "It is not good for the man to be alone. I will make a companion who will help him." So the LORD God formed from the soil every kind of animal and bird. He brought them to Adam to see what he would call them, and Adam chose a name for each one. He gave names to all the livestock, birds, and wild animals. But still there was no companion suitable for him. So the LORD God caused Adam to fall into a deep sleep. He took one of Adam's ribs and closed up the place from which he had taken it. Then the LORD God made a woman from the rib and brought her to Adam.

"At last!" Adam exclaimed. "She is part of my own flesh and bone! She will be called 'woman,' because she was taken out of a man." This explains why a man leaves his father and mother and is joined to his wife, and the two are united into one. Now, although Adam and his wife were both naked, neither of them felt any shame.

The Man and Woman Sin

Now the serpent was the shrewdest of all the creatures the LORD God had made. "Really?" he asked the woman. "Did God really say you must not eat any of the fruit in the garden?"

"Of course we may eat it," the woman told him. "It's only the fruit from the tree at the center of the garden that we are not allowed to eat. God says we must not eat it or even touch it, or we will die."

"You won't die!" the serpent hissed. "God knows that your eyes will be opened when you eat it. You will become just like God, knowing everything, both good and evil."

The woman was convinced. The fruit looked so fresh and delicious, and it would make her so wise! So she ate some of the fruit. She also gave some to her husband, who was with her. Then he ate it, too. At that moment, their eyes were opened, and they suddenly felt shame at their nakedness. So they strung fig leaves together around their hips to cover themselves.

Toward evening they heard the LORD God walking about in the garden, so they hid themselves among the trees. The LORD God called to Adam, "Where are you?"

He replied, "I heard you, so I hid. I was afraid because I was naked."

"Who told you that you were naked?" the LORD God asked. "Have you eaten the fruit I commanded you not to eat?"

"Yes," Adam admitted, "but it was the woman you gave me who brought me the fruit, and I ate it."

Then the LORD God asked the woman, "How could you do such a thing?"

"The serpent tricked me," she replied. "That's why I ate it."

So the LORD God said to the serpent, "Because you have done this, you will be punished. You are singled out from all the domestic and wild animals of the whole earth to be cursed. You will grovel in the dust as long as you live, crawling along on your belly. From now on, you and the woman will be enemies, and your offspring and her offspring will be enemies. He will crush your head, and you will strike his heel."

Then he said to the woman, "You will bear children with intense pain and suffering. And though your desire will be for your husband, he will be your master."

And to Adam he said, "Because you listened to your wife and ate the fruit I told you not to eat, I have placed a curse on the ground. All your life you will struggle to scratch a living from it. It will grow thorns and thistles for you, though you will eat of its grains. All your life you will sweat to produce food, until your dying day. Then you will return to the ground from which you came. For you were made from dust, and to the dust you will return."

Then Adam named his wife Eve, because she would be the mother of all people everywhere. And the LORD God made clothing from animal skins for Adam and his wife.

Take ANOTHER LOOK

This single mistake caused everyone to be born with the desire to sin. But God had a solution, his Son, Jesus. Jesus was a "second Adam"—the man who came to fix what the first Adam messed up. That's the idea behind this passage from Paul's letter to the Christians of Rome.

Romans 5:12-15, NLT

When Adam sinned, sin entered the entire human race. Adam's sin brought death, so death spread to everyone, for everyone sinned. Yes, people sinned even before the law was given. And though there was no law to break, since it had not yet been given, they all died anyway—even though they did not disobey an explicit commandment of God, as Adam did. What a contrast between Adam and Christ, who was yet to come! And what a difference between our sin and God's generous gift of forgiveness. For this one man, Adam, brought death to many through his sin. But this other man, Jesus Christ, brought forgiveness to many through God's bountiful gift.

Here's What I Think

Verity, age 13

Every day we are faced with choices—how we're going to act, what we're going to say. The biggest choice is whether to follow God, or to do things our own way. For example, my temper is my worst struggle. I always get frustrated at people in school, at home—anywhere! If things don't go my way, I get angry and bothered. Like if my mom starts talking a lot and I'm not in the mood, I will just completely ignore her. Not such a good choice, is it? Constantly, I have to remind myself that God is there, too, so I try to be more patient.

So much of the time I act just like Adam and Eve—ignoring what God wants and doing what I want instead. When I do that, there are definitely consequences—just as there were for Adam and Eve. That's when I need to remember—his way *is* best.

Verity

Choose today to go God's way—not your own.

»»» THE GREAT FLOOD «««

Ôntroduction

Long after the deaths of Adam and Eve, people continued to do wrong. At one point, the people's behavior was so bad God decided that enough was enough. He would send a flood that would cleanse the world. This flood would be unlike anything that had ever happened on Earth. It would start with rain—something that also had not occurred before. But all of life wouldn't end. God would save one family—the family of Noah. Why Noah? Because he was a good man in a bad world.

Genesis 7:11–8:19; 9:8–13, NLT

When Noah was 600 years old, on the seventeenth day of the second month, the underground waters burst forth on the earth, and the rain fell in mighty torrents from the sky. The rain continued to fall for forty days and forty nights. But Noah had gone into the boat that very day with his wife and his sons—Shem, Ham, and Japheth—and their wives. With them in the boat were pairs of every kind of breathing animal—domestic and wild, large and small—along with birds and flying insects of every kind. Two by two they came into the boat, male and female, just as God had commanded. Then the LORD shut them in.

For forty days the floods prevailed, covering the ground and lifting the boat high above the earth. As the waters rose higher and higher above the ground, the boat floated safely on the surface. Finally, the water covered even the highest mountains on the earth, standing more than twenty-two feet above the highest peaks. All the living things on earth died—birds, domestic animals, wild animals, all kinds of small animals, and all the people. Everything died that breathed and lived on dry land. Every living thing on the earth was wiped out—people, animals both large and small, and birds. They were all destroyed, and only Noah was left alive, along with those who were with him in the boat. And the water covered the earth for 150 days.

The Flood Recedes

But God remembered Noah and all the animals in the boat. He sent a wind to blow across the waters, and the floods began to disappear. The underground water sources ceased their gushing, and the torrential rains stopped. So the flood gradually began to recede. After 150 days, exactly five months from the time the flood began, the boat came to rest on the mountains of Ararat. Two and a half months later, as the waters continued to go down, other mountain peaks began to appear.

After another forty days, Noah opened the window he had made in the boat and released a raven that flew back and forth until the earth was dry. Then he sent out a dove to see if it could find dry ground. But the dove found no place to land because the water was still too high. So it returned to the boat, and Noah held out his hand and drew the dove back inside. Seven days later, Noah released the dove again. This time, toward evening, the bird returned to him with a fresh olive leaf in its beak. Noah now knew that the water was almost gone. A week later, he released the dove again, and this time it did not come back.

Finally, when Noah was 601 years old, ten and a half months after the flood began, Noah lifted back the cover to look. The water was drying up. Two more months went by, and at last the earth was dry!

Then God said to Noah, "Leave the boat, all of you. Release all the animals and birds so they can breed and reproduce in great numbers." So Noah, his wife, and his sons and their wives left the boat. And all the various kinds of animals and birds came out, pair by pair.

9:8-13

Then God told Noah and his sons, "I am making a covenant with you and your descendants, and with the animals you brought with you—all these birds and livestock and wild animals. I solemnly promise never to send another flood to kill all living creatures and destroy the earth." And God said, "I am giving you a sign as evidence of my eternal covenant with you and all living creatures. I have placed my rainbow in the clouds. It is the sign of my permanent promise to you and to all the earth."

Take ANOTHER LOOK

Jesus often used Old Testament stories to help the people understand truths about God. Jesus frequently told his disciples that he would die, rise again, and return to heaven. But someday, Jesus would return to Earth to collect his people. Yet he warned them that his second coming to Earth would be just as sudden as the flood during Noah's time. Check out what he had to say:

Matthew 24:37-39, NLT

When the Son of Man returns, it will be like it was in Noah's day. In those days before the Flood, the people were enjoying banquets and parties and weddings right up to the time Noah entered his boat. People didn't realize what was going to happen until the Flood came and swept them all away. That is the way it will be when the Son of Man comes.

Here's What I Think

Jammeshia, age 17

Many times I look to people who promise me things, but they always seem to break their promises at some time or another. There was a time when one of my friends promised to be at my basketball game. I waited and waited, but that friend never showed up. I was very disappointed. That's when I realized that I was putting too much trust in people who would let me down.

Through this story we can see that God will never break his promises. It's awesome that I serve a God who makes promises he won't break. This story helps me remember not to look to people who will let me down, but to a God who will never let me down. So every time I see a rainbow I remember the promises God has made to me and will never break.

Jammeshia

Look to God—the real promise-keeper.

>>> THE TOWER OF BABEL <<<

Introduction

Even though the flood brought a new beginning, some things didn't change. People continued to do wrong. Many years after the flood, the people decided to worship their own greatness, instead of God. But God stopped their plans in a unique way. God scattered the people by giving them different languages so they couldn't understand each other anymore. Imagine the confusion! It must have sounded like a bunch of nonsense. That's how the town got its name—Babel.

Genesis 11:1-9, NLT

At one time the whole world spoke a single language and used the same words. As the people migrated eastward, they found a plain in the land of Babylonia and settled there. They began to talk about construction projects. "Come," they said, "let's make great piles of burnt brick and collect natural asphalt to use as mortar. Let's build a great city with a tower that reaches to the skies—a monument to our greatness! This will bring us together and keep us from scattering all over the world."

But the LORD came down to see the city and the tower the people were building. "Look!" he said. "If they can accomplish this when they have just begun to take advantage of their common language and political unity, just think of what they will do later. Nothing will be impossible for them! Come, let's go down and give them different languages. Then they won't be able to understand each other."

In that way, the LORD scattered them all over the earth; and that ended the building of the city. That is why the city was called Babel, because it was there that the LORD confused the people by giving them many languages, thus scattering them across the earth.

Long after Jesus returned to heaven, the apostle John saw a vision. In this vision of heaven people from every nation were joined together in worship. They didn't worship themselves like the tower of Babel builders— they worshiped God. As you read this passage, think about which crowd you would want to be among: the crowd at the tower or the crowd at the throne of heaven.

Revelation 7:9,10, NLT

After this I saw a vast crowd, too great to count, from every nation and tribe and people and language, standing in front of the throne and before the Lamb. They were clothed in white and held palm branches in their hands. And they were shouting with a mighty shout, "Salvation comes from our God on the throne and from the Lamb!"

Here's What I Think

Daniel, age 15

When I think I'm doing well, my pride almost always sneaks up on me. I begin to think, *Hey, I'm OK. I can do this. I don't need anyone.* And I forget all about God. Kinda like those people at Babel. At times, my ego can be very subtle, so I always have to be on guard. Pride left unchecked can cause pain just as all sin does.

Our pride is a lot like the law of gravity. I call it the Law of Pride and the Over-Inflated Ego—what goes up must come down. As Proverbs 29:23 puts it, "Pride ends in humiliation, while humility brings honor." The people's pride dishonored God, so God allowed them to be humiliated. On the flip side, if we put God and others first by taking on a humble spirit, God will honor us. And that's better than honoring ourselves.

Daniel

Want to honor God? Check your pride at the door.

ABRAM'S BIG ADVENTURE

Introduction

The world was full of people. But one family takes center stage in the book of Genesis. That family belonged to a man named Abram, who was a descendant of Noah's son Shem. At a time when many people today are retired, 75-year-old Abram and his 65-year-old wife Sarai were just beginning a new adventure. They didn't know where they were going or what life would be like when they arrived. All they knew was that God told them to go. Abram's nephew, Lot, went with them.

Genesis 12:1-8, NLT

Then the Lord told Abram, "Leave your country, your relatives, and your father's house, and go to the land that I will show you. I will cause you to become the father of a great nation. I will bless you and make you famous, and I will make you a blessing to others. I will bless those who bless you and curse those who curse you. All the families of the earth will be blessed through you."

So Abram departed as the LORD had instructed him, and Lot went with him. Abram was seventy-five years old when he left Haran. He took his wife, Sarai, his nephew Lot, and all his wealth—his livestock and all the people who had joined his household at Haran—and finally arrived in Canaan. Traveling through Canaan, they came to a place near Shechem and set up camp beside the oak at Moreh. At that time, the area was inhabited by Canaanites.

Then the LORD appeared to Abram and said, "I am going to give this land to your offspring." And Abram built an altar there to commemorate the LORD's visit. After that, Abram traveled southward and set up camp in the hill country between Bethel on the west and Ai on the east. There he built an altar and worshiped the LORD.

Take ANOTHER LOOK

Maybe you won't have to move to a strange land like Abram did. But there may be times when you need to take a step of faith. That can be scary! But, like Abram, you don't have to take a step by yourself. God promises to direct the steps of those who believe in him as this passage from the book of Psalms declares. Are you willing to trust the Lord like David, the writer of this psalm?

Psalm 37:3-5, NLT

Trust in the LORD and do good.
  Then you will live safely in the land and prosper.
Take delight in the LORD,
  and he will give you your heart's desires.
Commit everything you do to the LORD.
  Trust him, and he will help you.

Here's What I Think

Janna, age 14

Sometimes it's hard for us to trust God. We want to do things our own way. But God has a perfect plan for us. In this passage, Abram demonstrates complete trust in God. God told him to leave his home and go into a new land. Abram did it without even hesitating!

As Christians, we need to be open to what God wants for us in our lives. A few years ago, my dad became the minister of a new church. I was not happy at all. I didn't want to leave our old church. It was hard to accept what God had planned for me. I realize now that I should have trusted like Abram did. We should never hesitate to do what God wants. He loves us, and he knows what is best for us.

Janna

Believe that God has good plans for you . . .
like he did for Abram.

»»» THE PROMISED SON «««

Introduction

Both Abram and Lot soon had many sheep, cattle, tents, and other possessions. Being so wealthy caused problems between their servants. So, Abram and Lot decided to go their separate ways. Soon after that, God established an agreement with Abram. One day, this childless man would be the father of a nation. As a sign of this agreement, God changed his name to Abraham (which means "father of many"). His wife Sarai would be called Sarah (which means "princess"). But many years passed before God's promise came true.

Genesis 15:1-6; 17:1-9; 21:1-7, NLT

Afterward the LORD spoke to Abram in a vision and said to him, "Do not be afraid, Abram, for I will protect you, and your reward will be great."

But Abram replied, "O Sovereign LORD, what good are all your blessings when I don't even have a son? Since I don't have a son, Eliezer of Damascus, a servant in my household, will inherit all my wealth. You have given me no children, so one of my servants will have to be my heir."

Then the LORD said to him, "No, your servant will not be your heir, for you will have a son of your own to inherit everything I am giving you." Then the LORD brought Abram outside beneath the night sky and told him, "Look up into the heavens and count the stars if you can. Your descendants will be like that—too many to count!" And Abram believed the LORD, and the LORD declared him righteous because of his faith.

Abram Is Named Abraham, 17:1-9

When Abram was ninety-nine years old, the LORD appeared to him and said, "I am God Almighty; serve me faithfully and live a blameless life. I will make a covenant with you, by which I will guarantee to make you into a mighty nation." At this, Abram fell face down in the dust. Then God said to him, "This is my covenant with you: I will make you the father of not just one nation, but a multitude of nations! What's more, I am changing your name. It will no longer be Abram; now you will be known as Abraham, for you will be the father of many nations. I will give you millions of descendants who will represent many nations. Kings will be among them!

"I will continue this everlasting covenant between us, generation after generation. It will continue between me and your offspring forever. And I will always be your God and the God of your descendants after you. Yes, I will give all this land of Canaan to you and to your offspring forever. And I will be their God.

"Your part of the agreement," God told Abraham, "is to obey the terms of the covenant. You and all your descendants have this continual responsibility."

The Birth of Isaac, 21:1-7

Then the LORD did exactly what he had promised. Sarah became pregnant, and she gave a son to Abraham in his old age. It all happened at the time God had said it would. And Abraham named his son Isaac. Eight days after Isaac was born, Abraham circumcised him as God had commanded. Abraham was one hundred years old at the time.

And Sarah declared, "God has brought me laughter! All who hear about this will laugh with me. For who would have dreamed that I would ever have a baby? Yet I have given Abraham a son in his old age!"

Take ANOTHER LOOK

Abraham's faith not only pleased God, but it also made him right (in good standing) with God. Abraham didn't have to "see" in order to believe. (Maybe that's why Hebrews 11:1 tells us that faith is "the evidence of things we cannot yet see.") As you read the passage below, you can decide whether you will believe God like Abraham did. Will you trust in God's promises even if you can't see the results?

Romans 4:1-3, NLT

Abraham was, humanly speaking, the founder of our Jewish nation. What were his experiences concerning this question of being saved by faith? Was it because of his good deeds that God accepted him? If so, he would have had something to boast about. But from God's point of view Abraham had no basis at all for pride. For the Scriptures tell us, "Abraham believed God, so God declared him to be righteous."

Hebrews 11:8-12, NLT

It was by faith that Abraham obeyed when God called him to leave home and go to another land that God would give him as his inheritance. He went without knowing where he was going. And even when he reached the land God promised him, he lived there by faith—for he was like a foreigner, living in a tent. And so did Isaac and Jacob, to whom God gave the same promise. Abraham did this because he was confidently looking forward to a city with eternal foundations, a city designed and built by God.

It was by faith that Sarah together with Abraham was able to have a child, even though they were too old and Sarah was barren. Abraham believed that God would keep his promise. And so a whole nation came from this one man, Abraham, who was too old to have any children—a nation with so many people that, like the stars of the sky and the sand on the seashore, there is no way to count them.

Here's What I Think

Faith, age 14

God sometimes puts us in situations that challenge our faith, like he did with Abraham. God had promised Abraham as many grandchildren as stars in the sky—but he didn't even have a son. That required a lot of faith on Abraham's part. It looked like an impossible situation to Abraham, yet God was able to make it happen. That's true in my life too. When I put my trust in God, he can do amazing things.

A few months ago, I hurt my knee really bad while playing soccer and I eventually had to have surgery. I got depressed and discouraged because my knee was healing so slowly. I thought I'd never play soccer again. Finally, I decided to just put the situation into God's hands and trust him that he knew best. Sure enough, my knee started to heal. After many months of patiently trusting God, my knee healed completely, and I was back to soccer!

Faith

Put your faith in the God of the impossible.

THE BIG TEST

Introduction

Imagine getting what you've always wanted only to be told to give it up. Abraham had waited 25 years for God to keep his promise and give him a son. God was true to his word and gave the 100-year-old man a son—Isaac. But now God told Abraham to take that son and sacrifice him on a mountain. What's a father to do?

Genesis 22:1-19, NLT

Later on God tested Abraham's faith and obedience. "Abraham!" God called.

"Yes," he replied. "Here I am."

"Take your son, your only son—yes, Isaac, whom you love so much—and go to the land of Moriah. Sacrifice him there as a burnt offering on one of the mountains, which I will point out to you."

The next morning Abraham got up early. He saddled his donkey and took two of his servants with him, along with his son Isaac. Then he chopped wood to build a fire for a burnt offering and set out for the place where God had told him to go. On the third day of the journey, Abraham saw the place in the distance. "Stay here with the donkey," Abraham told the young men. "The boy and I will travel a little farther. We will worship there, and then we will come right back."

Abraham placed the wood for the burnt offering on Isaac's shoulders, while he himself carried the knife and the fire. As the two of them went on together, Isaac said, "Father?"

"Yes, my son," Abraham replied.

"We have the wood and the fire," said the boy, "but where is the lamb for the sacrifice?"

"God will provide a lamb, my son," Abraham answered. And they both went on together.

When they arrived at the place where God had told Abraham to go, he built an altar and placed the wood on it. Then he tied Isaac up and laid him on the altar over the wood. And Abraham took the knife and lifted it up to kill his son as a sacrifice to the LORD. At that moment the angel of the LORD shouted to him from heaven, "Abraham! Abraham!"

"Yes," he answered. "I'm listening."

"Lay down the knife," the angel said. "Do not hurt the boy in any way, for now I know that you truly fear God. You have not withheld even your beloved son from me."

Then Abraham looked up and saw a ram caught by its horns in a bush. So he took the ram and sacrificed it as a burnt offering on the altar in place of his son. Abraham named the place "The LORD Will Provide." This name has now become a proverb: "On the mountain of the LORD it will be provided."

Then the angel of the LORD called again to Abraham from heaven, "This is what the LORD says: Because you have obeyed me and have not withheld even your beloved son, I swear by my own self that I will bless you richly. I will multiply your descendants into countless millions, like the stars of the sky and the sand on the seashore. They will conquer their enemies, and through your descendants, all the nations of the earth will be blessed—all because you have obeyed me."

Then they returned to Abraham's young men and traveled home again to Beersheba, where Abraham lived for quite some time.

Take ANOTHER LOOK

Sometimes, being a Christian is like being in school—you have to take a test. God doesn't test people because he likes to see us suffer. He tests us to measure how much faith we have in him. But God already knows whether or not we'll pass any test he gives. Hard times are some of the "tests" or "trials" we might have to endure. That's why Peter, one of Jesus' disciples, encourages us to persevere through any trial. God wants our faith to be solid gold!

1 Peter 1:6,7, NLT

So be truly glad! There is wonderful joy ahead, even though it is necessary for you to endure many trials for a while. These trials are only to test your faith, to show that it is strong and pure. It is being tested as fire tests and purifies gold—and your faith is far more precious to God than mere gold. So if your faith remains strong after being tried by fiery trials, it will bring you much praise and glory and honor on the day when Jesus Christ is revealed to the whole world.

There are many times when I find that I put other things before God—my friends, school, sports, and even homework. At the time those seem really important, but in the long run they are the things that fade away. God is always with us, he never leaves, and he wants nothing more than our full attention. Abraham had only one son, but when God told him to sacrifice Isaac on the altar, Abraham didn't hesitate. He was prepared to give all he had to God.

Is there something that you are withholding from God? What is it that you need to sacrifice to him? Maybe it's your favorite TV show, or that video game that you spend hours playing, or even some of your time spent with friends? I know there are things in my life that I need to give up. And as hard as that is, I also know that if we obey God and not withhold anything from him, he promises to bless us richly!

Kali

Don't hold back—give it all to God.

JACOB AND ESAU

Introduction

Years later, Sarah died. Isaac grew up and married Rebekah, the daughter of his uncle Laban. Soon after that, Abraham died. More grief came when Isaac learned that Rebekah could not have children. But he knew someone who could help—God. So Isaac prayed. One day, Rebekah gave birth to twin sons, Esau and Jacob. These weren't just ordinary kids. They would someday be the fathers of two nations, the Edomites and the Israelites. Just as the brothers were often at odds with each other, these nations would be at war with each other.

Genesis 25:19-34, NLT

This is the history of the family of Isaac, the son of Abraham. When Isaac was forty years old, he married Rebekah, the daughter of Bethuel the Aramean from Paddan-aram and the sister of Laban. Isaac pleaded with the LORD to give Rebekah a child because she was childless. So the LORD answered Isaac's prayer, and his wife became pregnant with twins. But the two children struggled with each other in her womb. So she went to ask the LORD about it. "Why is this happening to me?" she asked.

And the LORD told her, "The sons in your womb will become two rival nations. One nation will be stronger than the other; the descendants of your older son will serve the descendants of your younger son."

And when the time came, the twins were born. The first was very red at birth. He was covered with so much hair that one would think he was wearing a piece of clothing. So they called him Esau.

Then the other twin was born with his hand grasping Esau's heel. So they called him Jacob. Isaac was sixty years old when the twins were born.

Esau Sells His Birthright

As the boys grew up, Esau became a skillful hunter, a man of the open fields, while Jacob was the kind of person who liked to stay at home. Isaac loved Esau in particular because of the wild game he brought home, but Rebekah favored Jacob.

One day when Jacob was cooking some stew, Esau arrived home exhausted and hungry from a hunt. Esau said to Jacob, "I'm starved! Give me some of that red stew you've made." (This was how Esau got his other name, Edom—"Red.")

Jacob replied, "All right, but trade me your birthright for it."

"Look, I'm dying of starvation!" said Esau. "What good is my birthright to me now?"

So Jacob insisted, "Well then, swear to me right now that it is mine." So Esau swore an oath, thereby selling all his rights as the firstborn to his younger brother. Then Jacob gave Esau some bread and lentil stew. Esau ate and drank and went on about his business, indifferent to the fact that he had given up his birthright.

Take ANOTHER LOOK

Esau didn't understand how valuable his rights were as the firstborn son. Some items, like birthrights, are too valuable to give up. Jesus told several parables, stories that teach a lesson about God, that helped explain the true worth of the kingdom of heaven. In these stories, Jesus meant that knowing God was more valuable than anything.

Matthew 13:44-46, NLT

"The Kingdom of Heaven is like a treasure that a man discovered hidden in a field. In his excitement, he hid it again and sold everything he owned to get enough money to buy the field—and to get the treasure, too!

"Again, the Kingdom of Heaven is like a pearl merchant on the lookout for choice pearls. When he discovered a pearl of great value, he sold everything he owned and bought it!"

Mike, age 19

A lot of times in life I feel as if God has cheated me out of something. Perhaps a girl I have liked for a long time suddenly takes an interest in my best friend. Or some other person gets the summer job I really wanted. Imagine how Esau must have felt when his younger brother tricked him to swap his birthright, his future, for a bowl of stew and some bread. I'm sure he must have felt cheated big time.

The truth is that God doesn't cheat anyone. Jacob was given the birthright because it was God's intention to build the foundation of his chosen people upon Jacob's family. So when something goes wrong in my life, it is encouraging for me to remember that God has a reason for all the events that happen—even if I do not understand them at the time.

Mike

God will always give you his best—
count on it!

JACOB'S DREAM

Introduction

We've already seen how Esau sold his rights as firstborn for a bowl of stew. To make doubly sure that Esau's rights would be given to Jacob, Rebekah and Jacob hatched a plan. Jacob would wear some of Esau's clothes and put hair on his arms to convince the nearly blind Isaac that smooth-skinned Jacob was his hairy brother Esau. Well, the plan worked only too well. Jacob received a blessing from Isaac that was meant for Esau. Esau, in anger, vowed to kill his brother. To save her favorite son's life, Rebekah warned Jacob to run away to her brother's relatives. This is where the story begins.

Genesis 28:10-22, NLT

Meanwhile, Jacob left Beersheba and traveled toward Haran. At sundown he arrived at a good place to set up camp and stopped there for the night. Jacob found a stone for a pillow and lay down to sleep. As he slept, he dreamed of a stairway that reached from earth to heaven. And he saw the angels of God going up and down on it.

At the top of the stairway stood the LORD, and he said, "I am the LORD, the God of your grandfather Abraham and the God of your father, Isaac. The ground you are lying on belongs to you. I will give it to you and your descendants. Your descendants will be as numerous as the dust of the earth! They will cover the land from east to west and from north to south. All the families of the earth will be blessed through you and your descendants. What's more, I will be with you, and I will protect you wherever you go. I will someday bring you safely back to this land. I will be with you constantly until I have finished giving you everything I have promised."

Then Jacob woke up and said, "Surely the LORD is in this place, and I wasn't even aware of it." He was afraid and said, "What an awesome place this is! It is none other than the house of God—the gateway to heaven!"

The next morning he got up very early. He took the stone he had used as a pillow and set it upright as a memorial pillar. Then he poured olive oil over it.

He named the place Bethel—"house of God"—though the name of the nearby village was Luz.

Then Jacob made this vow: "If God will be with me and protect me on this journey and give me food and clothing, and if he will bring me back safely to my father, then I will make the LORD my God. This memorial pillar will become a place for worshiping God, and I will give God a tenth of everything he gives me."

Take ANOTHER LOOK

The habit of giving a king a tenth started with Abraham, the grandfather of Jacob and Esau. After rescuing his nephew Lot from an enemy army, Abraham gave Melchizedek, the king of Salem, one tenth of all that he gained through winning the battle.

Genesis 14:20, NLT

Then Abram gave Melchizedek a tenth of all the goods he had recovered.

Hundreds of years later, the people of Israel were commanded to give God one tenth of their crops. This commandment was part of the rules for living that God gave to Moses. God didn't need the crops for himself. He wanted his people to show their love and respect for him by their habit of giving. These crops usually were given to the priests and Levites—the helpers of the priests—who worked in the tabernacle.

Deuteronomy 14:22,23, NLT

You must set aside a tithe of your crops—one-tenth of all the crops you harvest each year. Bring this tithe to the place the LORD your God chooses for his name to be honored, and eat it there in his presence. This applies to your tithes of grain, new wine, olive oil, and the firstborn males of your flocks and herds. The purpose of tithing is to teach you always to fear the LORD your God.

Here's What I Think

Nicee, age 14

This passage amazed me! God showed Jacob a vision and he acted on it. First Jacob acknowledged that God had spoken to him and promised him the land. Then Jacob trusted God and began to worship him the very first thing the next morning. Then he turned around and pledged to give his tithes on things that he'd later receive. To me, that's awesome!

This helps show me how I need to respond to God. First, I need to listen when God is speaking to me. Then I need to trust what he says to me and act on it. And finally, I need to respond and give back to God what he has given to me. When I follow those steps, I know my faith will become as strong as Jacob's.

Nicee

Listen, trust, act, and give back!
Those are the steps of faith.

»»» JOSEPH AND HIS BROTHERS «««

Introduction

Many years passed after Jacob's dream. During that time Jacob married two sisters, Leah and Rachel, and became the father of 12 sons and one daughter. (Marriage customs were different in Bible times, and men sometimes had more than one wife.) Jacob was even given a new name, Israel, and was forgiven by his brother Esau. Although life seemed great, trouble was far from over. It all started again when Jacob let everyone know that his favorite son was Joseph—the first son born to his favorite wife, Rachel. Joseph's status caused hard feelings in 10 of his brothers. They soon came up with a plan to get rid of Joseph.

Genesis 37:3-13, 18-36, NLT

Now Jacob loved Joseph more than any of his other children because Joseph had been born to him in his old age. So one day he gave Joseph a special gift—a beautiful robe. But his brothers hated Joseph because of their father's partiality. They couldn't say a kind word to him.

One night Joseph had a dream and promptly reported the details to his brothers, causing them to hate him even more. "Listen to this dream," he announced. "We were out in the field tying up bundles of grain. My bundle stood up, and then your bundles all gathered around and bowed low before it!"

"So you are going to be our king, are you?" his brothers taunted. And they hated him all the more for his dream and what he had said.

Then Joseph had another dream and told his brothers about it. "Listen to this dream," he said. "The sun, moon, and eleven stars bowed low before me!"

This time he told his father as well as his brothers, and his father rebuked him. "What do you mean?" his father asked. "Will your mother, your brothers, and I actually come and bow before you?" But while his brothers were jealous of Joseph, his father gave it some thought and wondered what it all meant.

Soon after this, Joseph's brothers went to pasture their father's flocks at

Shechem. When they had been gone for some time, Jacob said to Joseph, "Your brothers are over at Shechem with the flocks. I'm going to send you to them."

Joseph Sold into Slavery, 37:18-36

When Joseph's brothers saw him coming, they recognized him in the distance and made plans to kill him. "Here comes that dreamer!" they exclaimed. "Come on, let's kill him and throw him into a deep pit. We can tell our father that a wild animal has eaten him. Then we'll see what becomes of all his dreams!"

But Reuben came to Joseph's rescue. "Let's not kill him," he said. "Why should we shed his blood? Let's just throw him alive into this pit here. That way he will die without our having to touch him." Reuben was secretly planning to help Joseph escape, and then he would bring him back to his father.

So when Joseph arrived, they pulled off his beautiful robe and threw him into the pit. This pit was normally used to store water, but it was empty at the time. Then, just as they were sitting down to eat, they noticed a caravan of camels in the distance coming toward them. It was a group of Ishmaelite traders taking spices, balm, and myrrh from Gilead to Egypt.

Judah said to the others, "What can we gain by killing our brother? That would just give us a guilty conscience. Let's sell Joseph to those Ishmaelite traders. Let's not be responsible for his death; after all, he is our brother!" And his brothers agreed. So when the traders came by, his brothers pulled Joseph out of the pit and sold him for twenty pieces of silver, and the Ishmaelite traders took him along to Egypt.

Some time later, Reuben returned to get Joseph out of the pit. When he discovered that Joseph was missing, he tore his clothes in anguish and frustration. Then he went back to his brothers and lamented, "The boy is gone! What can I do now?"

Then Joseph's brothers killed a goat and dipped the robe in its blood. They took the beautiful robe to their father and asked him to identify it. "We found this in the field," they told him. "It's Joseph's robe, isn't it?"

Their father recognized it at once. "Yes," he said, "it is my son's robe. A wild animal has attacked and eaten him. Surely Joseph has been torn in pieces!" He mourned deeply for his son for many days. His family all tried to comfort him, but it was no use. "I will die in mourning for my son," he would say, and then begin to weep.

Meanwhile, in Egypt, the traders sold Joseph to Potiphar, an officer of Pharaoh, the king of Egypt. Potiphar was captain of the palace guard.

Do you think that because Jesus was the Son of God, his family life was somehow problem-free? Like Joseph, Jesus had a hard time with his brothers. They didn't believe that he was the promised Savior. But one day, even Jesus' brothers believed in him. One of his brothers, James, wrote the book of James and became an important leader in the early church.

John 7:1-4, NLT

After this, Jesus stayed in Galilee, going from village to village. He wanted to stay out of Judea where the Jewish leaders were plotting his death. But soon it was time for the Festival of Shelters, and Jesus' brothers urged him to go to Judea for the celebration. "Go where your followers can see your miracles!" they scoffed. "You can't become a public figure if you hide like this! If you can do such wonderful things, prove it to the world!" For even his brothers didn't believe in him.

Here's What I Think

Walter, age 13

When my dad bought two expensive tickets to see the Chicago Cubs (one for him and one for my brother), I wasn't exactly thrilled. At the time, it seemed like my dad favored my brother more than me. Even though I'm not a baseball fan, I still felt like I should have gotten some special treatment too. Reading this passage, though, makes me feel differently. I know my thoughts were not right. I was jealous. I was becoming more and more like Joseph's brothers—and that's not a path I want to start going down. Looking back, I realize that I have it pretty good. After all, I'm the one who got a nice camcorder for my birthday!

Walter

Count your blessings—not what others have.

»»» A KING'S DREAM «««

Introduction

Life wasn't easy for Joseph in Egypt. His excellence as a worker earned him the trust of his master, Potiphar. But a false accusation from Potiphar's spiteful wife earned him a stay in prison. Joseph remained in prison for years. There, Joseph met two of Pharaoh's servants: the chief cup-bearer and the chief baker. Both men had dreams, and Joseph was able to tell them what their dreams meant. Everything Joseph told them about their dreams came true. One man was released and one man was put to death. The man who was released promised to remember Joseph. But that promise was not kept for a long time.

Genesis 41:1-17, 25-40, NLT

Two years later, Pharaoh dreamed that he was standing on the bank of the Nile River. In his dream, seven fat, healthy-looking cows suddenly came up out of the river and began grazing along its bank. Then seven other cows came up from the river, but these were very ugly and gaunt. These cows went over and stood beside the fat cows. Then the thin, ugly cows ate the fat ones! At this point in the dream, Pharaoh woke up.

Soon he fell asleep again and had a second dream. This time he saw seven heads of grain on one stalk, with every kernel well formed and plump. Then suddenly, seven more heads appeared on the stalk, but these were shriveled and withered by the east wind. And these thin heads swallowed up the seven plump, well-formed heads! Then Pharaoh woke up again and realized it was a dream.

The next morning, Pharaoh became very concerned as to what the dreams might mean. So he called for all the magicians and wise men of Egypt and told them about his dreams, but not one of them could suggest what they meant. Then the king's cup-bearer spoke up. "Today I have been reminded of my failure," he said. "Some time ago, you were angry with the chief baker and me, and you imprisoned us. One night the chief baker and I each had a dream. We told the dreams to a young Hebrew man who was a servant of the captain of the guard. He told us what each of our dreams meant, and everything happened just as he said it would."

Pharaoh sent for Joseph at once, and he was brought hastily from the dungeon. After a quick shave and change of clothes, he went in and stood in Pharaoh's presence. "I had a dream last night," Pharaoh told him, "and none of these men can tell me what it means. But I have heard that you can interpret dreams, and that is why I have called for you."

"It is beyond my power to do this," Joseph replied. "But God will tell you what it means and will set you at ease."

So Pharaoh told him the dream.

41:25-40

"Both dreams mean the same thing," Joseph told Pharaoh. "God was telling you what he is about to do. The seven fat cows and the seven plump heads of grain both represent seven years of prosperity. The seven thin, ugly cows and the seven withered heads of grain represent seven years of famine. "This will happen just as I have described it, for God has shown you what he is about to do. The next seven years will be a period of great prosperity throughout the land of Egypt. But afterward there will be seven years of famine so great that all the prosperity will be forgotten and wiped out. Famine will destroy the land. This famine will be so terrible that even the memory of the good years will be erased. As for having the dream twice, it means that the matter has been decreed by God and that he will make these events happen soon.

"My suggestion is that you find the wisest man in Egypt and put him in charge of a nationwide program. Let Pharaoh appoint officials over the land, and let them collect one-fifth of all the crops during the seven good years. Have them gather all the food and grain of these good years into the royal storehouses, and store it away so there will be food in the cities. That way there will be enough to eat when the seven years of famine come. Otherwise disaster will surely strike the land, and all the people will die."

Joseph Made Ruler of Egypt

Joseph's suggestions were well received by Pharaoh and his advisers. As they discussed who should be appointed for the job, Pharaoh said, "Who could do it better than Joseph? For he is a man who is obviously filled with the spirit of God." Turning to Joseph, Pharaoh said, "Since God has revealed the meaning of the dreams to you, you are the wisest man in the land! I hereby appoint you to direct this project. You will manage my household and organize all my people. Only I will have a rank higher than yours."

Many times, God gave people warnings through both good and bad dreams. During the time of Jesus, Pilate's wife had a nightmare about Jesus and tried to warn her husband not to condemn Jesus to death. But Pilate chose to ignore the warning. He would forever be known as the person who allowed an innocent man—the Savior of the world—to be crucified.

Matthew 27:15-24, NLT

Now it was the governor's custom to release one prisoner to the crowd each year during the Passover celebration. This year there was a notorious criminal in prison, a man named Barabbas. As the crowds gathered before Pilate's house that morning, he asked them, "Which one do you want me to release to you—Barabbas, or Jesus who is called the Messiah?" (He knew very well that the Jewish leaders had arrested Jesus out of envy.)

Just then, as Pilate was sitting on the judgment seat, his wife sent him this message: "Leave that innocent man alone, because I had a terrible nightmare about him last night."

Meanwhile, the leading priests and other leaders persuaded the crowds to ask for Barabbas to be released and for Jesus to be put to death. So when the governor asked again, "Which of these two do you want me to release to you?" the crowd shouted back their reply: "Barabbas!"

"But if I release Barabbas," Pilate asked them, "what should I do with Jesus who is called the Messiah?" And they all shouted, "Crucify him!"

"Why?" Pilate demanded. "What crime has he committed?" But the crowd only roared the louder, "Crucify him!"

Pilate saw that he wasn't getting anywhere and that a riot was developing. So he sent for a bowl of water and washed his hands before the crowd, saying, "I am innocent of the blood of this man. The responsibility is yours!"

Here's What I Think

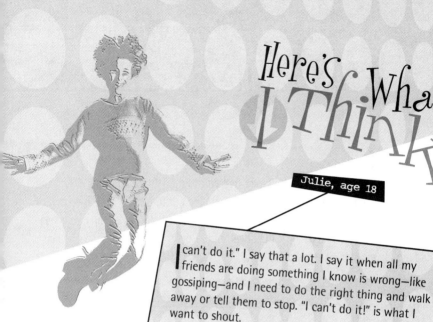

Julie, age 18

I can't do it." I say that a lot. I say it when all my friends are doing something I know is wrong—like gossiping—and I need to do the right thing and walk away or tell them to stop. "I can't do it!" is what I want to shout.

Joseph says it when Pharaoh asks him to interpret his dream. But Joseph says something else as well: "I cannot do it, but *God* will give Pharaoh the answer." In other words, "I can't do it, but *God can.*" Wow! It doesn't matter if I feel unable to do something (like standing up to my friends) because it's actually *God* who will do all the work. Just like God gave Joseph the ability to interpret Pharaoh's dreams, God will give me the strength to overcome any difficult situation I face—even facing my friends and doing the right thing.

Julie

When you can't do it, remember God can.

»»» A FAMILY REUNION «««

ⓘntroduction

Meanwhile, back in Canaan, Jacob's family had run low on food. Only the Egyptians seemed to have grain. Joseph's brothers had no choice but to go to Egypt in search of food. Never in their wildest dreams could they have imagined that they would come face-to-face with Joseph, who had become the governor of Egypt. They hadn't seen him since they sold him as a slave 20 years previously. They were in for a big surprise.

Genesis 42:1-24, NLT

When Jacob heard that there was grain available in Egypt, he said to his sons, "Why are you standing around looking at one another? Go down and buy some for us before we all starve to death." So Joseph's ten older brothers went down to Egypt to buy grain. Jacob wouldn't let Joseph's younger brother, Benjamin, go with them, however, for fear some harm might come to him. So Jacob's sons arrived in Egypt along with others to buy food, for the famine had reached Canaan as well.

Since Joseph was governor of all Egypt and in charge of the sale of the grain, it was to him that his brothers came. They bowed low before him. Joseph recognized them instantly, but he pretended to be a stranger. "Where are you from?" he demanded roughly.

"From the land of Canaan," they replied. "We have come to buy grain."

Joseph's brothers didn't recognize him, but Joseph recognized them. And he remembered the dreams he had had many years before. He said to them, "You are spies! You have come to see how vulnerable our land has become."

"No, my lord!" they exclaimed. "We have come to buy food. We are all brothers and honest men, sir! We are not spies!"

"Yes, you are!" he insisted. "You have come to discover how vulnerable the famine has made us."

"Sir," they said, "there are twelve of us brothers, and our father is in the land of Canaan. Our youngest brother is there with our father, and one of our brothers is no longer with us."

But Joseph insisted, "As I said, you are spies! This is how I will test your story. I swear by the life of Pharaoh that you will not leave Egypt unless your youngest brother comes here. One of you go and get your brother! I'll keep the rest of you here, bound in prison. Then we'll find out whether or not your story is true. If it turns out that you don't have a younger brother, then I'll know you are spies."

So he put them all in prison for three days. On the third day Joseph said to them, "I am a God-fearing man. If you do as I say, you will live. We'll see how honorable you really are. Only one of you will remain in the prison. The rest of you may go on home with grain for your families. But bring your youngest brother back to me. In this way, I will know whether or not you are telling me the truth. If you are, I will spare you." To this they agreed.

Speaking among themselves, they said, "This has all happened because of what we did to Joseph long ago. We saw his terror and anguish and heard his pleadings, but we wouldn't listen. That's why this trouble has come upon us."

"Didn't I tell you not to do it?" Reuben asked. "But you wouldn't listen. And now we are going to die because we murdered him."

Of course, they didn't know that Joseph understood them as he was standing there, for he had been speaking to them through an interpreter. Now he left the room and found a place where he could weep. Returning, he talked some more with them. He then chose Simeon from among them and had him tied up right before their eyes.

Take ANOTHER LOOK

Joseph could have had all of his brothers jailed for life or put to death. But taking revenge against them wasn't an option for Joseph. It's also not an option for any believer. Throughout the Bible, God warns people to avoid taking revenge. No one has the wisdom to deal with it the way that God does. That's why Paul warned Christians to leave revenge to God.

Romans 12:19-21, NLT

Dear friends, never avenge yourselves. Leave that to God. For it is written, "I will take vengeance; I will repay those who deserve it," says the Lord. Instead, do what the Scriptures say: "If your enemies are hungry, feed them. If they are thirsty, give them something to drink, and they will be ashamed of what they have done to you." Don't let evil get the best of you, but conquer evil by doing good.

Here's What I Think

This story is a wonderful picture of how God deals with each one of us. We watch as Joseph has a chance to get even with his brothers, but instead decides to test them. He wanted to see if their hearts were right, if they had turned from evil. From that moment, Joseph begins to forgive his brothers. Though they caused him great hurt and pain, Joseph wants reconciliation between them all—just like God offers to us.

There have been numerous occasions when I have turned away from God thinking he wasn't worth the struggles. Yet whenever I came knocking on his door, he forgave me. A few months ago I turned away completely and wanted nothing to do with him. Soon, he changed my heart and forgave me once I asked. Like Joseph's brothers, I was tested and then reconciled. I am so grateful that even though I hurt him, God still welcomed and wanted me!

Verity

Don't get even—get forgiveness!

»» JOSEPH FORGIVES ««

Ôntroduction

Joseph tested his brothers to see if they were sorry for what they had done to him years ago. He even suggested keeping Benjamin in prison while his brothers returned home to collect their father. But when Judah offered to remain in Egypt in Benjamin's place, Joseph knew that his brothers had changed. Their concern for Benjamin—who was now Jacob's favorite—and for Jacob caused Joseph to reveal his true identity.

Genesis 45:1-20, 24-28, NLT

Joseph could stand it no longer. "Out, all of you!" he cried out to his attendants. He wanted to be alone with his brothers when he told them who he was. Then he broke down and wept aloud. His sobs could be heard throughout the palace, and the news was quickly carried to Pharaoh's palace.

"I am Joseph!" he said to his brothers. "Is my father still alive?" But his brothers were speechless! They were stunned to realize that Joseph was standing there in front of them. "Come over here," he said, So they came closer. And he said again, "I am Joseph, your brother whom you sold into Egypt. But don't be angry with yourselves that you did this to me, for God did it. He sent me here ahead of you to preserve your lives. These two years of famine will grow to seven, during which there will be neither plowing nor harvest. God has sent me here to keep you and your families alive so that you will become a great nation. Yes, it was God who sent me here, not you! And he has made me a counselor to Pharaoh—manager of his entire household and ruler over all Egypt.

"Hurry, return to my father and tell him, 'This is what your son Joseph says: God has made me master over all the land of Egypt. Come down to me right away! You will live in the land of Goshen so you can be near me with all your children and grandchildren, your flocks and herds, and all that you have. I will take care of you there, for there are still five years of famine ahead of us. Otherwise you and your household will come to utter poverty.' "

Then Joseph said, "You can see for yourselves, and so can my brother Benjamin, that I really am Joseph! Tell my father how I am honored here in Egypt. Tell him about everything you have seen, and bring him to me quickly." Weeping with joy, he embraced Benjamin, and Benjamin also began to weep. Then Joseph kissed each of his brothers and wept over them, and then they began talking freely with him.

Pharaoh Invites Jacob to Egypt

The news soon reached Pharaoh: "Joseph's brothers have come!" Pharaoh was very happy to hear this and so were his officials.

Pharaoh said to Joseph, "Tell your brothers to load their pack animals and return quickly to their homes in Canaan. Tell them to bring your father and all of their families, and to come here to Egypt to live. Tell them, 'Pharaoh will assign to you the very best territory in the land of Egypt. You will live off the fat of the land!' And tell your brothers to take wagons from Egypt to carry their wives and little ones and to bring your father here. Don't worry about your belongings, for the best of all the land of Egypt is yours."

45:24-28

So he sent his brothers off, and as they left, he called after them, "Don't quarrel along the way!" And they left Egypt and returned to their father, Jacob, in the land of Canaan.

"Joseph is still alive!" they told him. "And he is ruler over all the land of Egypt!" Jacob was stunned at the news—he couldn't believe it. But when they had given him Joseph's messages, and when he saw the wagons loaded with the food sent by Joseph, his spirit revived.

Then Jacob said, "It must be true! My son Joseph is alive! I will go and see him before I die."

Take ANOTHER LOOK

Joseph realized that, even though his brothers meant him harm, God caused everything to work out. During the first century, Paul came to that same conclusion. He wanted the readers of his letter to be encouraged, even though they faced terrible persecution. Maybe you're feeling troubled right now. Like Paul and Joseph, can you hang on to God's promise to work everything out?

Romans 8:26-28, NLT

And the Holy Spirit helps us in our distress. For we don't even know what we should pray for, nor how we should pray. But the Holy Spirit prays for us with groanings that cannot be expressed in words. And the Father who knows all hearts knows what the Spirit is saying, for the Spirit pleads for us believers in harmony with God's own will. And we know that God causes everything to work together for the good of those who love God and are called according to his purpose for them.

Here's What I Think

Jammeshia, age 17

I'm sure you can think of another person who has mistreated you in some way. There have been times when I have done nothing wrong to a person, but all that person has to say to me are mean and hurtful things. At those times, it's hard to find anything good in a situation like that.

Through this story of Joseph's life, you can totally see, though, how God can take control when something bad happens. A few chapters later, in Genesis 50:20, Joseph says, "As far as I am concerned, God turned into good what you meant for evil." It's so awesome to see that, even though Joseph's brothers meant for bad things to happen, God was still in control. It is so cool to know that, even though you feel like the worst thing has happened to you, God still can make something good out of it.

Jammeshia

God will bring good from the bad in our lives.

A DELIVERER IS BORN

Introduction

Long after Joseph's death, Jacob's family of 70 had grown into a nation of more than two million people. The people of Israel had settled in Egypt, raised families, and had grown in numbers. But Pharaoh, the king of Egypt, feared that these people would one day fight against his own people. So Pharaoh decided to make the people of Israel slaves. When that didn't stop the nation of Israel from growing, Pharaoh ordered his people to kill all of the Israelite male children. But God had his own plan. He would make sure that Moses, the future deliverer of Egypt, would live.

Exodus 1:15–2:10, NLT

Then Pharaoh, the king of Egypt, gave this order to the Hebrew midwives, Shiphrah and Puah: "When you help the Hebrew women give birth, kill all the boys as soon as they are born. Allow only the baby girls to live." But because the midwives feared God, they refused to obey the king and allowed the boys to live, too.

Then the king called for the midwives. "Why have you done this?" he demanded. "Why have you allowed the boys to live?"

"Sir," they told him, "the Hebrew women are very strong. They have their babies so quickly that we cannot get there in time! They are not slow in giving birth like Egyptian women."

So God blessed the midwives, and the Israelites continued to multiply, growing more and more powerful. And because the midwives feared God, he gave them families of their own.

Then Pharaoh gave this order to all his people: "Throw all the newborn Israelite boys into the Nile River. But you may spare the baby girls."

The Birth of Moses

During this time, a man and woman from the tribe of Levi got married. The woman became pregnant and gave birth to a son. She saw what a beautiful baby he was and kept him hidden for three months. But when she could no longer hide him, she got a little basket made of papyrus reeds and waterproofed it with tar and pitch. She put the baby in the basket and laid it among the reeds along the edge of the Nile River. The baby's sister then stood at a distance, watching to see what would happen to him.

Soon after this, one of Pharaoh's daughters came down to bathe in the river, and her servant girls walked along the riverbank. When the princess saw the little basket among the reeds, she told one of her servant girls to get it for her. As the princess opened it, she found the baby boy. His helpless cries touched her heart. "He must be one of the Hebrew children," she said.

Then the baby's sister approached the princess. "Should I go and find one of the Hebrew women to nurse the baby for you?" she asked.

"Yes, do!" the princess replied. So the girl rushed home and called the baby's mother.

"Take this child home and nurse him for me," the princess told her. "I will pay you for your help." So the baby's mother took her baby home and nursed him.

Later, when he was older, the child's mother brought him back to the princess, who adopted him as her son. The princess named him Moses, for she said, "I drew him out of the water."

Take ANOTHER LOOK

During the New Testament times, a man named Stephen was put on trial for being a follower of Jesus. In his defense, Stephen told the history of the people of Israel. That history included the story of Moses. What's below is an extended version of the story you just read. You can see the faith of Moses' mother as she hid her son. You can also see the well-meaning, but misguided steps of Moses, as he attempted to help his fellow Hebrews. Although Moses had the faith to believe that he could help his people, he chose the wrong method to do it.

Acts 7:20-29, NLT

"At that time Moses was born—a beautiful child in God's eyes. His parents cared for him at home for three months. When at last they had to abandon him, Pharaoh's daughter found him and raised him as her own son. Moses was taught all the wisdom of the Egyptians, and he became mighty in both speech and action.

"One day when he was forty years old, he decided to visit his relatives, the people of Israel. During this visit, he saw an Egyptian mistreating a man of Israel. So Moses came to his defense and avenged him, killing the Egyptian. Moses assumed his brothers would realize that God had sent him to rescue them, but they didn't.

"The next day he visited them again and saw two men of Israel fighting. He tried to be a peacemaker. 'Men,' he said, 'you are brothers. Why are you hurting each other?'

"But the man in the wrong pushed Moses aside and told him to mind his own business. 'Who made you a ruler and judge over us?' he asked. 'Are you going to kill me as you killed that Egyptian yesterday?' When Moses heard that, he fled the country and lived as a foreigner in the land of Midian, where his two sons were born."

Here's What I Think

Daniel, age 15

Often I believe that as Christians we forget to take the leap and allow God to do his will through us. I can think of countless times I have missed an opportunity that God brought me to share my faith. I'd see the opportunity and excuse myself from doing anything. I would think that the person will reject me or that the person won't want to hear what I have to say. Or I would make excuses like, *I really don't know that person very well. I should wait till I know him better.*

We need to take the leap and all those risks that God calls us to. Moses' mother sure did. She took the risk of saving her baby son. Because of that one act, God used Moses to later save thousands of Israelites' lives. Moses' mother acted courageously in spite of her fears. Next opportunity God gives you, don't let your fears or excuses stop you. Take the leap!

Daniel

Take a risk—step out in faith.

A DELIVERER
IS CHOSEN

Introduction

Let's recap: After Moses killed an Egyptian, Pharaoh wanted to kill Moses. So Moses had to run away and live in Midian. During his 40 years there, Moses met and married one of the daughters of Jethro. Desert life was much harder than Moses' pampered upbringing as the adopted son of Pharaoh's daughter. But little did Moses know that desert life was the perfect training ground for the deliverer of God's people. Although he had not heard from God, the seemingly silent God was about to act in an amazing way.

Exodus 3:1-14, NLT

One day Moses was tending the flock of his father-in-law, Jethro, and he went deep into the wilderness near Sinai, the mountain of God. Suddenly, the angel of the LORD appeared to him as a blazing fire in a bush. Moses was amazed because the bush was engulfed in flames, but it didn't burn up. "Amazing!" Moses said to himself. "Why isn't that bush burning up? I must go over to see this."

When the LORD saw that he had caught Moses' attention, God called to him from the bush, "Moses! Moses!"

"Here I am!" Moses replied.

"Do not come any closer," God told him. "Take off your sandals, for you are standing on holy ground." Then he said, "I am the God of your ancestors—the God of Abraham, the God of Isaac, and the God of Jacob." When Moses heard this, he hid his face in his hands because he was afraid to look at God.

Then the LORD told him, "You can be sure I have seen the misery of my people in Egypt. I have heard their cries for deliverance from their harsh slave drivers. Yes, I am aware of their suffering. So I have come to rescue them from the Egyptians and lead them out of Egypt into their own good and spacious land. It is a land flowing with milk and honey—the land where the Canaanites, Hittites, Amorites, Perizzites, Hivites, and Jebusites live. The cries of the people of Israel have reached me, and I have seen how the Egyptians have oppressed them with heavy tasks. Now go, for I am sending you to Pharaoh. You will lead my people, the Israelites, out of Egypt."

"But who am I to appear before Pharaoh?" Moses asked God. "How can you expect me to lead the Israelites out of Egypt?"

Then God told him, "I will be with you. And this will serve as proof that I have sent you: When you have brought the Israelites out of Egypt, you will return here to worship God at this very mountain."

But Moses protested, "If I go to the people of Israel and tell them, 'The God of your ancestors has sent me to you,' they won't believe me. They will ask, 'Which god are you talking about? What is his name?' Then what should I tell them?"

God replied, "I AM THE ONE WHO ALWAYS IS. Just tell them, 'I AM has sent me to you.'"

Take ANOTHER LOOK Many centuries later during the New Testament times, Jesus shocked a crowd of people by his words. When he said, "Before Abraham was even born, I Am," he made himself equal to God. Jesus' words were no different from "I AM WHO I AM." That is why the crowd wanted to kill him. As you read the following passage, what's your response to Jesus' words?

John 8:52-59, NLT

The people said, "Now we know you are possessed by a demon. Even Abraham and the prophets died, but you say that those who obey your teaching will never die! Are you greater than our father Abraham, who died? Are you greater than the prophets, who died? Who do you think you are?"

Jesus answered, "If I am merely boasting about myself, it doesn't count. But it is my Father who says these glorious things about me. You say, 'He is our God,' but you do not even know him. I know him. If I said otherwise, I would be as great a liar as you! But it is true—I know him and obey him. Your ancestor Abraham rejoiced as he looked forward to my coming. He saw it and was glad."

The people said, "You aren't even fifty years old. How can you say you have seen Abraham?"

Jesus answered, "The truth is, I existed before Abraham was even born!" At that point they picked up stones to kill him. But Jesus hid himself from them and left the Temple.

Here's What I Think

Janna, age 14

In this passage, when God tells Moses to do something, what does Moses do? He makes excuses! Moses basically says he's just not good enough. A lot of times we give excuses to get out of something we don't want to do.

Last year my teacher signed me up to be in the geography bee. I did not want to be in it at all, and I gave the excuse that I didn't know anything about geography. She still made me be in it, and I ended up being in the final 10. Instead of making excuses I should have obeyed my teacher right away, and Moses should have obeyed God. In verse 12 God says, "I will be with you." That is a great promise for us to remember! It should make us want to do the things God has told us to do.

Janna

With God on our side there are no excuses!

»»» A TIME TO ACT «««

Introduction

Moses' peaceful life in Midian was now over. The time for action had come. God wanted Moses to go to Pharaoh and demand that the people of Israel be released from slavery. Moses' brother Aaron would speak for him. But God knew that Pharaoh would be reluctant to let the people go. In fact, he would make their tasks even harder! So God planned a series of miraculous signs—10 plagues—to force Pharaoh to let the people go. Through these signs, Pharaoh and the people of Egypt would know once and for all that there was only one true God.

Exodus 5:1-23; 7:1-5, NLT

Moses and Aaron went to see Pharaoh. They told him, "This is what the LORD, the God of Israel, says: 'Let my people go, for they must go out into the wilderness to hold a religious festival in my honor.'"

"Is that so?" retorted Pharaoh. "And who is the LORD that I should listen to him and let Israel go? I don't know the LORD, and I will not let Israel go."

But Aaron and Moses persisted. "The God of the Hebrews has met with us," they declared. "Let us take a three-day trip into the wilderness so we can offer sacrifices to the LORD our God. If we don't, we will surely die by disease or the sword."

"Who do you think you are," Pharaoh shouted, "distracting the people from their tasks? Get back to work! Look, there are many people here in Egypt, and you are stopping them from doing their work."

Making Bricks without Straw

That same day Pharaoh sent this order to the slave drivers and foremen he had set over the people of Israel: "Do not supply the people with any more straw for making bricks. Let them get it themselves! But don't reduce their production quotas by a single brick. They obviously don't have enough to do. If they did, they wouldn't be talking about going into the wilderness to offer sacrifices to their God. Load them down with more work. Make them sweat! That will teach them to listen to these liars!"

So the slave drivers and foremen informed the people: "Pharaoh has ordered us not to provide straw for you. Go and get it yourselves. Find it wherever you can. But you must produce just as many bricks as before!" So the people scattered throughout the land in search of straw.

The slave drivers were brutal. "Meet your daily quota of bricks, just as you did before!" they demanded. Then they whipped the Israelite foremen in charge of the work crews. "Why haven't you met your quotas either yesterday or today?" they demanded.

So the Israelite foremen went to Pharaoh and pleaded with him. "Please don't treat us like this," they begged. "We are given no straw, but we are still told to make as many bricks as before. We are beaten for something that isn't our fault! It is the fault of your slave drivers for making such unreasonable demands."

But Pharaoh replied, "You're just lazy! You obviously don't have enough to do. If you did, you wouldn't be saying, 'Let us go, so we can offer sacrifices to the LORD.' Now, get back to work! No straw will be given to you, but you must still deliver the regular quota of bricks."

Since Pharaoh would not let up on his demands, the Israelite foremen could see that they were in serious trouble. As they left Pharaoh's court, they met Moses and Aaron, who were waiting outside for them. The foremen said to them, "May the LORD judge you for getting us into this terrible situation with Pharaoh and his officials. You have given them an excuse to kill us!"

So Moses went back to the LORD and protested, "Why have you mistreated your own people like this, LORD? Why did you send me? Since I gave Pharaoh your message, he has been even more brutal to your people. You have not even begun to rescue them!"

7:1-5

Then the LORD said to Moses, "Pay close attention to this. I will make you seem like God to Pharaoh. Your brother, Aaron, will be your prophet; he will speak for you. Tell Aaron everything I say to you and have him announce it to Pharaoh. He will demand that the people of Israel be allowed to leave Egypt. But I will cause Pharaoh to be stubborn so I can multiply my miraculous signs and wonders in the land of Egypt. Even then Pharaoh will refuse to listen to you. So I will crush Egypt with a series of disasters, after which I will lead the forces of Israel out with great acts of judgment. When I show the Egyptians my power and force them to let the Israelites go, they will realize that I am the LORD."

Ten plagues had to occur before Pharaoh would let the people go. The people of Egypt suffered through water turning into blood; masses of frogs, gnats, and flies; diseased livestock; boils; hail; locusts; and terrible darkness. But the tenth plague would be the worst plague of all.

Exodus 11:4-6, NLT

So Moses announced to Pharaoh, "This is what the LORD says: About midnight I will pass through Egypt. All the firstborn sons will die in every family in Egypt, from the oldest son of Pharaoh, who sits on the throne, to the oldest son of his lowliest slave. Even the firstborn of the animals will die. Then a loud wail will be heard throughout the land of Egypt; there has never been such wailing before, and there never will be again."

Here's What I Think

Faith, age 14

Being around someone who is stubborn isn't fun. One time, my two friends were having this big fight because of some silly disagreement. They didn't understand that not talking to each other didn't accomplish anything. Neither wanted to be the weak one and apologize, so the whole matter got out of control. They also didn't understand that their stubbornness was hurting me too. Finally they sat down, talked things over, and resolved their problems.

Just like my friends, Pharaoh was so determined not to be weak that he brought pain and suffering on his own people. What I learned from my experience with my friends is that, when we ease up on the stubbornness and are open to what God wants us to do, everything works out a lot better.

Faith

Stubborn hearts can hurt others.

>>> # A NEW
CELEBRATION <<<

Introduction

The tenth plague—the death of every firstborn person or animal in Egypt—was about to happen. God gave Moses careful instructions to give to the people of Israel. If they followed all of these instructions, death would "pass over them." The blood of a lamb on a doorway was the sign of obedience. Because they would be saved from death, God wanted his people to establish a new holiday—Passover.

Exodus 12:1-13, 21-30, NLT

Now the LORD gave the following instructions to Moses and Aaron while they were still in the land of Egypt: "From now on, this month will be the first month of the year for you. Announce to the whole community that on the tenth day of this month each family must choose a lamb or a young goat for a sacrifice. If a family is too small to eat an entire lamb, let them share the lamb with another family in the neighborhood. Whether or not they share in this way depends on the size of each family and how much they can eat. This animal must be a one-year-old male, either a sheep or a goat, with no physical defects.

"Take special care of these lambs until the evening of the fourteenth day of this first month. Then each family in the community must slaughter its lamb. They are to take some of the lamb's blood and smear it on the top and sides of the doorframe of the house where the lamb will be eaten. That evening everyone must eat roast lamb with bitter herbs and bread made without yeast. The meat must never be eaten raw or boiled; roast it all, including the head, legs, and internal organs. Do not leave any of it until the next day. Whatever is not eaten that night must be burned before morning.

"Wear your traveling clothes as you eat this meal, as though prepared for a long journey. Wear your sandals, and carry your walking sticks in your hands. Eat the food quickly, for this is the LORD's Passover. On that night I will pass through the land of Egypt and kill all the firstborn sons and firstborn male animals in the land of Egypt. I will execute judgment against all the gods of Egypt, for I am the LORD! The blood you have smeared on your doorposts will serve as a sign. When

I see the blood, I will pass over you. This plague of death will not touch you when I strike the land of Egypt."

12:21-30

Then Moses called for the leaders of Israel and said, "Tell each of your families to slaughter the lamb they have set apart for the Passover. Drain each lamb's blood into a basin. Then take a cluster of hyssop branches and dip it into the lamb's blood. Strike the hyssop against the top and sides of the doorframe, staining it with the blood. And remember, no one is allowed to leave the house until morning. For the LORD will pass through the land and strike down the Egyptians. But when he sees the blood on the top and sides of the doorframe, the LORD will pass over your home. He will not permit the Destroyer to enter and strike down your firstborn.

"Remember, these instructions are permanent and must be observed by you and your descendants forever. When you arrive in the land the LORD has promised to give you, you will continue to celebrate this festival. Then your children will ask, 'What does all this mean? What is this ceremony about?' And you will reply, 'It is the celebration of the LORD's Passover, for he passed over the homes of the Israelites in Egypt. And though he killed the Egyptians, he spared our families and did not destroy us.'" Then all the people bowed their heads and worshiped.

So the people of Israel did just as the LORD had commanded through Moses and Aaron. And at midnight the LORD killed all the firstborn sons in the land of Egypt, from the firstborn son of Pharaoh, who sat on the throne, to the firstborn son of the captive in the dungeon. Even the firstborn of their livestock were killed. Pharaoh and his officials and all the people of Egypt woke up during the night, and loud wailing was heard throughout the land of Egypt. There was not a single house where someone had not died.

Take ANOTHER LOOK Lambs were usually sacrificed for Passover. The lambs had to be perfect—with no flaws or defects. Because Jesus was willing to die for others, he became known as the Lamb of God and also the Passover Lamb. He was perfect, having never done anything wrong. In the book of Revelation, John shares his vision of heaven with an incredible description of Christ as our Lamb, the perfect sacrifice, worthy of our worship and praise.

Revelation 5:6-10, NLT

I looked and I saw a Lamb that had been killed but was now standing between the throne and the four living beings and among the twenty-four elders. He had seven horns and seven eyes, which are the seven spirits of God that are sent out into every part of the earth. He stepped forward and took the scroll from the right hand of the one sitting on the throne. And as he took the scroll, the four living beings and the twenty-four elders fell down before the Lamb. Each one had a harp, and they held gold bowls filled with incense—the prayers of God's people!

And they sang a new song with these words:

"You are worthy to take the scroll and break its seals and open it. For you were killed, and your blood has ransomed people for God from every tribe and language and people and nation. And you have caused them to become God's kingdom and his priests. And they will reign on the earth."

Here's What I Think

Kali, age 18

If I had lived back then, it would have been my life at stake since I'm the oldest of three. The lamb that was killed would have shed its blood for me. The truth is, we are all considered a firstborn child when it comes to Christ's death on the cross. Jesus was the Lamb who shed his blood for each one of us. Jesus' death on the cross was the ultimate sacrifice—made so that we might someday live with him in heaven. I rejoice at the gift that God has so graciously given me and to each one of us. So next time Communion is celebrated at your church, remember the Lamb.

Kali

Celebrate the Lamb—the perfect sacrifice—who died for you.

A SEASIDE MIRACLE

Introduction

After driving the people of Israel out of Egypt, Pharaoh decided that he wanted them back as slaves. He thought that all he had to do was gather his army and go after them. After all, they had nowhere to go but to the Red Sea. And crossing that was impossible! Or was it?

Exodus 14:10-28, NLT

As Pharaoh and his army approached, the people of Israel could see them in the distance, marching toward them. The people began to panic, and they cried out to the LORD for help.

Then they turned against Moses and complained, "Why did you bring us out here to die in the wilderness? Weren't there enough graves for us in Egypt? Why did you make us leave? Didn't we tell you to leave us alone while we were still in Egypt? Our Egyptian slavery was far better than dying out here in the wilderness!"

But Moses told the people, "Don't be afraid. Just stand where you are and watch the Lord rescue you. The Egyptians that you see today will never be seen again. The Lord himself will fight for you. You won't have to lift a finger in your defense!"

Escape through the Red Sea

Then the LORD said to Moses, 'Why are you crying out to me? Tell the people to get moving! Use your shepherd's staff—hold it out over the water, and a path will open up before you through the sea. Then all the people of Israel will walk through on dry ground. Yet I will harden the hearts of the Egyptians, and they will follow the Israelites into the sea. Then I will receive great glory at the expense of Pharaoh and his armies, chariots, and charioteers. When I am finished with Pharaoh and his army, all Egypt will know that I am the LORD!"

Then the angel of God, who had been leading the people of Israel, moved to a position behind them, and the pillar of cloud also moved around behind them. The cloud settled between the Israelite and Egyptian camps. As night came, the pillar of cloud turned into a pillar of fire, lighting the Israelite camp. But the cloud became darkness to the Egyptians, and they couldn't find the Israelites.

Then Moses raised his hand over the sea, and the LORD opened up a path through the water with a strong east wind. The wind blew all that night, turning the seabed into dry land. So the people of Israel walked through the sea on dry ground, with walls of water on each side!

Then the Egyptians—all of Pharaoh's horses, chariots, and charioteers—followed them across the bottom of the sea. But early in the morning, the LORD looked down on the Egyptian army from the pillar of fire and cloud, and he threw them into confusion. Their chariot wheels began to come off, making their chariots impossible to drive. "Let's get out of here!" the Egyptians shouted. "The LORD is fighting for Israel against us!"

When all the Israelites were on the other side, the LORD said to Moses, "Raise your hand over the sea again. Then the waters will rush back over the Egyptian chariots and charioteers." So as the sun began to rise, Moses raised his hand over the sea. The water roared back into its usual place, and the LORD swept the terrified Egyptians into the surging currents. The waters covered all the chariots and charioteers—the entire army of Pharaoh. Of all the Egyptians who had chased the Israelites into the sea, not a single one survived.

Take ANOTHER LOOK

An ocean or a river is usually seen as something powerful and endless. But God is more powerful than the largest ocean on Earth. He demonstrated that power to the people of Israel by rolling back the Red Sea. He also once reminded Job of his power over the sea—and all creation. As you read the following verses, think of the problems in your life that might seem like an endless sea. Do you believe that God can handle them?

Job 38:4-11, NLT

"Where were you when I laid the foundations of the earth? Tell me, if you know so much. Do you know how its dimensions were determined and who did the surveying? What supports its foundations, and who laid its cornerstone as the morning stars sang together and all the angels shouted for joy?

"Who defined the boundaries of the sea as it burst from the womb, and as I clothed it with clouds and thick darkness? For I locked it behind barred gates, limiting its shores. I said, 'Thus far and no farther will you come. Here your proud waves must stop!' "

Here's What I Think

Mike, age 19

There are times when I feel trapped by the situations God has presented me with. I feel as if I am between a rock and a hard place. It seems that no matter what I do there is no way to get out. I imagine the Israelites felt the same sort of dread and fear when they were trapped by the Egyptians, their backs against the Red Sea.

But then God miraculously saved them by parting the sea, giving them a totally unexpected path out of harm's way. God will do the same for us in our lives. At times, there is nothing we can do on our own power to make our situation better. God wants to help us in our time of need. That's when we need to turn to him, and as Moses said, let God fight for us.

Michael

The Lord himself will fight for you.

»»» A HEAVENLY MEAL «««

Introduction

God had rescued the people of Israel from Egypt and defeated the army of Egypt in an amazing way. So the people of Israel had no complaints—until they were hungry, that is. Then they let the complaints fly at Moses and Aaron, their leaders. How quickly they had forgotten the amazing things that God had done for them. Yet God heard their complaints and provided a new food for them with an unusual set of instructions.

Exodus 16:4-31, NLT

Then the LORD said to Moses, "Look, I'm going to rain down food from heaven for you. The people can go out each day and pick up as much food as they need for that day. I will test them in this to see whether they will follow my instructions. Tell them to pick up twice as much as usual on the sixth day of each week."

Then Moses and Aaron called a meeting of all the people of Israel and told them, "In the evening you will realize that it was the LORD who brought you out of the land of Egypt. In the morning you will see the glorious presence of the LORD. He has heard your complaints, which are against the LORD and not against us. The LORD will give you meat to eat in the evening and bread in the morning, for he has heard all your complaints against him. Yes, your complaints are against the LORD, not against us."

Then Moses said to Aaron, "Say this to the entire community of Israel: 'Come into the LORD's presence, and hear his reply to your complaints.'" And as Aaron spoke to the people, they looked out toward the desert. Within the guiding cloud, they could see the awesome glory of the LORD.

And the LORD said to Moses, "I have heard the people's complaints. Now tell them, 'In the evening you will have meat to eat, and in the morning you will be filled with bread. Then you will know that I am the Lord your God.'"

That evening vast numbers of quail arrived and covered the camp. The next morning the desert all around the camp was wet with dew. When the dew disappeared later in the morning, thin flakes, white like frost, covered the ground.

The Israelites were puzzled when they saw it. "What is it?" they asked.

And Moses told them, "It is the food the LORD has given you. The LORD says that each household should gather as much as it needs. Pick up two quarts for each person."

So the people of Israel went out and gathered this food—some getting more, and some getting less. By gathering two quarts for each person, everyone had just enough. Those who gathered a lot had nothing left over, and those who gathered only a little had enough. Each family had just what it needed.

Then Moses told them, "Do not keep any of it overnight." But, of course, some of them didn't listen and kept some of it until morning. By then it was full of maggots and had a terrible smell. And Moses was very angry with them.

The people gathered the food morning by morning, each family according to its need. And as the sun became hot, the food they had not picked up melted and disappeared. On the sixth day, there was twice as much as usual on the ground— four quarts for each person instead of two. The leaders of the people came and asked Moses why this had happened. He replied, "The LORD has appointed tomorrow as a day of rest, a holy Sabbath to the LORD. On this day we will rest from our normal daily tasks. So bake or boil as much as you want today, and set aside what is left for tomorrow."

The next morning the leftover food was wholesome and good, without maggots or odor. Moses said, "This is your food for today, for today is a Sabbath to the LORD. There will be no food on the ground today. Gather the food for six days, but the seventh day is a Sabbath. There will be no food on the ground for you on that day."

Some of the people went out anyway to gather food, even though it was the Sabbath day. But there was none to be found. "How long will these people refuse to obey my commands and instructions?" the LORD asked Moses. "Do they not realize that I have given them the seventh day, the Sabbath, as a day of rest? That is why I give you twice as much food on the sixth day, so there will be enough for two days. On the Sabbath day you must stay in your places. Do not pick up food from the ground on that day." So the people rested on the seventh day.

In time, the food became known as manna. It was white like coriander seed, and it tasted like honey cakes.

Forty years later, as the people of Israel got ready to enter the promised land, Moses reminded them about the manna. Following God's instructions about the manna was a way for God to teach them obedience. So the manna wasn't just food—it was also a daily pop quiz. As you read the following passage, think about the daily pop quizzes God places in your life.

Deuteronomy 8:2,3, NLT

Remember how the LORD your God led you through the wilderness for forty years, humbling you and testing you to prove your character, and to find out whether or not you would really obey his commands. Yes, he humbled you by letting you go hungry and then feeding you with manna, a food previously unknown to you and your ancestors. He did it to teach you that people need more than bread for their life; real life comes by feeding on every word of the LORD.

Here's What I Think

Nicee, age 14

As children of God we should never worry about anything. What will we eat? What will we wear? If we will see tomorrow. God instructs us to cast all our cares on him no matter what the circumstances may be. Here God took a hot, dry desert and turned it into an all-you-can-eat buffet. He proved to his people that he was in control and would supply their every need.

This story simply explains why I should trust God and not worry about the situations that I face. This story gives me hope. It allows me to see that I serve a God who is all-powerful and holy. I serve the creator of the world! And since he's my Father, he gives me equal access to every resource known to man. All I have to do is be obedient and trust him to provide.

Nicee

Give your worries to the one who's in control.

»»»» A GOLDEN PROBLEM ««««

()ntroduction

After Moses led the people of Israel to Mt. Sinai, he went up on the mountain to talk with God for 40 days. There God gave Moses the Ten Commandments and other rules for living. But the people grew bored waiting for Moses to return. They got into trouble when they decided that they needed a god they could see. They weren't satisfied until Aaron, Moses' brother, had produced a gold calf. God was not pleased.

Exodus 32:1-16, NLT

When Moses failed to come back down the mountain right away, the people went to Aaron. "Look," they said, "make us some gods who can lead us. This man Moses, who brought us here from Egypt, has disappeared. We don't know what has happened to him."

So Aaron said, "Tell your wives and sons and daughters to take off their gold earrings, and then bring them to me."

All the people obeyed Aaron and brought him their gold earrings. Then Aaron took the gold, melted it down, and molded and tooled it into the shape of a calf. The people exclaimed, "O Israel, these are the gods who brought you out of Egypt!"

When Aaron saw how excited the people were about it, he built an altar in front of the calf and announced, "Tomorrow there will be a festival to the LORD!"

So the people got up early the next morning to sacrifice burnt offerings and peace offerings. After this, they celebrated with feasting and drinking, and indulged themselves in pagan revelry.

Then the LORD told Moses, "Quick! Go down the mountain! The people you brought from Egypt have defiled themselves. They have already turned from the way I commanded them to live. They have made an idol shaped like a calf, and they have worshiped and sacrificed to it. They are saying, 'These are your gods, O Israel, who brought you out of Egypt.'"

Then the LORD said, "I have seen how stubborn and rebellious these people are. Now leave me alone so my anger can blaze against them and destroy them all. Then I will make you, Moses, into a great nation instead of them."

But Moses pleaded with the LORD his God not to do it. "O LORD!" he exclaimed. "Why are you so angry with your own people whom you brought from the land of Egypt with such great power and mighty acts? The Egyptians will say, 'God tricked them into coming to the mountains so he could kill them and wipe them from the face of the earth.' Turn away from your fierce anger. Change your mind about this terrible disaster you are planning against your people! Remember your covenant with your servants—Abraham, Isaac, and Jacob. You swore by your own self, 'I will make your descendants as numerous as the stars of heaven. Yes, I will give them all of this land that I have promised to your descendants, and they will possess it forever.'"

So the LORD withdrew his threat and didn't bring against his people the disaster he had threatened.

Then Moses turned and went down the mountain. He held in his hands the two stone tablets inscribed with the terms of the covenant. They were inscribed on both sides, front and back. These stone tablets were God's work; the words on them were written by God himself.

Take ANOTHER LOOK

God wanted his people to worship him only. That's why the second of the Ten Commandments spoke against making idols—statues that represented false gods. This wasn't just a suggestion; it was an order. Check out the passage below. Consider the fact that idols today aren't just statues of gold. An idol can be anything you worship more than God. What, if anything, is your "gold calf"?

Exodus 20:2-5, NLT

"I am the LORD your God, who rescued you from slavery in Egypt. Do not worship any other gods besides me. Do not make idols of any kind, whether in the shape of birds or animals or fish. You must never worship or bow down to them, for I, the LORD your God, am a jealous God who will not share your affection with any other god! I do not leave unpunished the sins of those who hate me, but I punish the children for the sins of their parents to the third and fourth generations."

Here's What I Think

Walter, age 13

I used to watch TV, play video games, and get on the computer whenever I got the chance. And when I wasn't doing that, I was goofing off with my friends. To tell you the truth, I still fight the temptations of those idols. Just like the Israelites. But one thing has changed.

I never used to spend time with God. I mean *never*. It was really bad. But now that I'm in the youth group at our church, I've started developing a more intimate relationship with God. Worship is what really motivates me to think about God more. When I put God at the center of my life through worship, I find that all those other things—TV, video games, etc.—are less important.

Walter

Guard against the idols in your life.

THE TWELVE SPIES

Introduction

Centuries ago, God had promised Abraham that he would give the land of Canaan to the people in Abraham's family line. He also reminded Moses of this promise before sending Moses to talk to Pharaoh. God planned to keep his word. But the negative report of 10 spies concerning the land and the people who lived there made the people of Israel forget all about God's promise and his power.

Numbers 13:25–14:30, NLT

After exploring the land for forty days, the men returned to Moses, Aaron, and the people of Israel at Kadesh in the wilderness of Paran. They reported to the whole community what they had seen and showed them the fruit they had taken from the land. This was their report to Moses: "We arrived in the land you sent us to see, and it is indeed a magnificent country—a land flowing with milk and honey. Here is some of its fruit as proof. But the people living there are powerful, and their cities and towns are fortified and very large. We also saw the descendants of Anak who are living there! The Amalekites live in the Negev, and the Hittites, Jebusites, and Amorites live in the hill country. The Canaanites live along the coast of the Mediterranean Sea and along the Jordan Valley."

But Caleb tried to encourage the people as they stood before Moses. "Let's go at once to take the land," he said. "We can certainly conquer it!"

But the other men who had explored the land with him answered, "We can't go up against them! They are stronger than we are!" So they spread discouraging reports about the land among the Israelites: "The land we explored will swallow up any who go to live there. All the people we saw were huge. We even saw giants there, the descendants of Anak. We felt like grasshoppers next to them, and that's what we looked like to them!"

The People Rebel

Then all the people began weeping aloud, and they cried all night. Their voices rose in a great chorus of complaint against Moses and Aaron. "We wish we had died in Egypt, or even here in the wilderness!" they wailed. "Why is the LORD taking us to this country only to have us die in battle? Our wives and little ones will be carried off as slaves! Let's get out of here and return to Egypt!" Then they plotted among themselves, "Let's choose a leader and go back to Egypt!"

Then Moses and Aaron fell face down on the ground before the people of Israel. Two of the men who had explored the land, Joshua son of Nun and Caleb son of Jephunneh, tore their clothing. They said to the community of Israel, "The land we explored is a wonderful land! And if the LORD is pleased with us, he will bring us safely into that land and give it to us. It is a rich land flowing with milk and honey, and he will give it to us! Do not rebel against the LORD, and don't be afraid of the people of the land. They are only helpless prey to us! They have no protection, but the LORD is with us! Don't be afraid of them!"

But the whole community began to talk about stoning Joshua and Caleb. Then the glorious presence of the LORD appeared to all the Israelites from above the Tabernacle. And the LORD said to Moses, "How long will these people reject me? Will they never believe me, even after all the miraculous signs I have done among them? I will disown them and destroy them with a plague. Then I will make you into a nation far greater and mightier than they are!"

Moses Intercedes for the People

"But what will the Egyptians think when they hear about it?" Moses pleaded with the LORD. "They know full well the power you displayed in rescuing these people from Egypt. They will tell this to the inhabitants of this land, who are well aware that you are with this people. They know, LORD, that you have appeared in full view of your people in the pillar of cloud that hovers over them. They know that you go before them in the pillar of cloud by day and the pillar of fire by night. Now if you slaughter all these people, the nations that have heard of your fame will say, 'The LORD was not able to bring them into the land he swore to give them, so he killed them in the wilderness.'

"Please, Lord, prove that your power is as great as you have claimed it to be. For you said, 'The LORD is slow to anger and rich in unfailing love, forgiving every kind of sin and rebellion. Even so he does not leave sin unpunished, but he punishes the children for the sins of their parents to the third and fourth generations.' Please pardon the sins of this people because of your magnificent, unfailing love, just as you have forgiven them ever since they left Egypt."

Then the LORD said, "I will pardon them as you have requested. But as surely as I live, and as surely as the earth is filled with the LORD's glory, not one of these people will ever enter that land. They have seen my glorious presence and the miraculous signs I performed both in Egypt and in the wilderness, but again and again they tested me by refusing to listen. They will never even see the land

I swore to give their ancestors. None of those who have treated me with contempt will enter it. But my servant Caleb is different from the others. He has remained loyal to me, and I will bring him into the land he explored. His descendants will receive their full share of that land. Now turn around and don't go on toward the land where the Amalekites and Canaanites live. Tomorrow you must set out for the wilderness in the direction of the Red Sea."

The Lord Punishes the Israelites

Then the LORD said to Moses and Aaron, "How long will this wicked nation complain about me? I have heard everything the Israelites have been saying. Now tell them this: 'As surely as I live, I will do to you the very things I heard you say. I, the LORD, have spoken! You will all die here in this wilderness! Because you complained against me, none of you who are twenty years old or older and were counted in the census will enter the land I swore to give you. The only exceptions will be Caleb son of Jephunneh and Joshua son of Nun.' "

Take ANOTHER LOOK As you can see by the story of the 12 spies, doubting God can sometimes lead to bad consequences. Because of doubt, most of the people of Israel didn't enter the promised land. Doubt also kept an Old Testament king from fully conquering his enemies. God wants his people to stop doubting and believe.

2 Kings 13:14-19, NLT

When Elisha was in his last illness, King Jehoash of Israel visited him and wept over him. "My father! My father! The chariots and charioteers of Israel!" he cried.

Elisha told him, "Get a bow and some arrows." And the king did as he was told. Then Elisha told the king of Israel to put his hand on the bow, and Elisha laid his own hands on the king's hands.

Then he commanded, "Open that eastern window," and he opened it. Then he said, "Shoot!" So he did. Then Elisha proclaimed, "This is the LORD's arrow, full of victory over Aram, for you will completely conquer the Arameans at Aphek.

"Now pick up the other arrows and strike them against the ground." So the king picked them up and struck the ground three times. But the man of God was angry with him. "You should have struck the ground five or six times!" he exclaimed. "Then you would have beaten Aram until they were entirely destroyed. Now you will be victorious only three times."

Here's What I Think

Julie, age 18

Have you ever felt like the 12 spies—both excited and frightened about doing something? Last summer, I decided to be a Christian camp counselor. At the beginning, I felt just like that—*excited*, because camp is fun and God does amazing things there—and *scared*, because I didn't know if my campers would like me or if I'd be a good teacher to them (and because it's hard to live without electricity for six weeks!).

I went to camp despite my nervousness about how hard it would be. And guess what—God took care of everything I had worried about! I learned something important that summer: Even if a situation scares us (like going into Canaan or going to camp), God will help us to do his will. Next time you feel afraid of doing something God wants you to do, just remember Caleb and Joshua. They knew God would help conquer the Canaanites—and he can help you too!

Julie

God can help you conquer new experiences.

»»» BALAAM'S DONKEY «««

Introduction

During the Israelites' years of wandering in the wilderness, a strange episode occurred. Balaam was a prophet working for himself, instead of for God. But God knew all about him and the terrible thing he was asked to do. To get Balaam's attention, God did something so out of the ordinary that Balaam could hardly doubt that God had spoken. He had to choose between obeying God and obeying Balak, the king of Moab.

Numbers 22:7-38, NLT

Balak's messengers, officials of both Moab and Midian, set out and took money with them to pay Balaam to curse Israel. They went to Balaam and urgently explained to him what Balak wanted. "Stay here overnight," Balaam said. "In the morning I will tell you whatever the LORD directs me to say." So the officials from Moab stayed there with Balaam.

That night God came to Balaam and asked him, "Who are these men with you?"

So Balaam said to God, "Balak son of Zippor, king of Moab, has sent me this message: 'A vast horde of people has come from Egypt and has spread out over the whole land. Come at once to curse them. Perhaps then I will be able to conquer them and drive them from the land.'"

"Do not go with them," God told Balaam. "You are not to curse these people, for I have blessed them!"

The next morning Balaam got up and told Balak's officials, "Go on home! The LORD will not let me go with you."

So the Moabite officials returned to King Balak and reported, "Balaam refused to come with us." Then Balak tried again. This time he sent a larger number of even more distinguished officials than those he had sent the first time. They went to Balaam and gave him this message:

"This is what Balak son of Zippor says: Please don't let anything stop you from coming. I will pay you well and do anything you ask of me. Just come and curse these people for me!"

But Balaam answered them, "Even if Balak were to give me a palace filled with silver and gold, I would be powerless to do anything against the will of the LORD my God. But stay here one more night to see if the LORD has anything else to say to me."

That night God came to Balaam and told him, "Since these men have come for you, get up and go with them. But be sure to do only what I tell you to do.

Balaam and His Donkey

So the next morning Balaam saddled his donkey and started off with the Moabite officials. But God was furious that Balaam was going, so he sent the angel of the LORD to stand in the road to block his way. As Balaam and two servants were riding along, Balaam's donkey suddenly saw the angel of the LORD standing in the road with a drawn sword in his hand. The donkey bolted off the road into a field, but Balaam beat it and turned it back onto the road. Then the angel of the LORD stood at a place where the road narrowed between two vineyard walls. When the donkey saw the angel of the LORD standing there, it tried to squeeze by and crushed Balaam's foot against the wall. So Balaam beat the donkey again. Then the angel of the LORD moved farther down the road and stood in a place so narrow that the donkey could not get by at all. This time when the donkey saw the angel, it lay down under Balaam. In a fit of rage Balaam beat it again with his staff.

Then the LORD caused the donkey to speak. "What have I done to you that deserves your beating me these three times?" it asked Balaam.

"Because you have made me look like a fool!" Balaam shouted. "If I had a sword with me, I would kill you!"

"But I am the same donkey you always ride on," the donkey answered. "Have I ever done anything like this before?"

"No," he admitted.

Then the LORD opened Balaam's eyes, and he saw the angel of the LORD standing in the roadway with a drawn sword in his hand. Balaam fell face down on the ground before him.

"Why did you beat your donkey those three times?" the angel of the LORD demanded. "I have come to block your way because you are stubbornly resisting me. Three times the donkey saw me and shied away; otherwise, I would certainly have killed you by now and spared the donkey."

Then Balaam confessed to the angel of the LORD, "I have sinned. I did not realize you were standing in the road to block my way. I will go back home if you are against my going."

But the angel of the LORD told him, "Go with these men, but you may say only what I tell you to say." So Balaam went on with Balak's officials. When King Balak heard that Balaam was on the way, he went out to meet him at a Moabite town on the Arnon River at the border of his land.

"Did I not send you an urgent invitation? Why didn't you come right away?" Balak asked Balaam. "Didn't you believe me when I said I would reward you richly?"

Balaam replied, "I have come, but I have no power to say just anything. I will speak only the messages that God gives me."

TAKE ANOTHER LOOK

Peter, one of Jesus' followers, warned Christians against false teachers in his second letter to believers in the early church. These teachers were like Balaam—on the wrong path. They didn't really believe in God and had the wrong influence over people. Peter wanted the Christians to guard against false teaching.

2 Peter 2:12-16, NLT

These false teachers are like unthinking animals, creatures of instinct, who are born to be caught and killed. They laugh at the terrifying powers they know so little about, and they will be destroyed along with them. Their destruction is their reward for the harm they have done. They love to indulge in evil pleasures in broad daylight. They are a disgrace and a stain among you. They revel in deceitfulness while they feast with you. They commit adultery with their eyes, and their lust is never satisfied. They make a game of luring unstable people into sin. They train themselves to be greedy; they are doomed and cursed. They have wandered off the right road and followed the way of Balaam son of Beor, who loved to earn money by doing wrong. But Balaam was stopped from his mad course when his donkey rebuked him with a human voice.

Here's What I Think

Verity, age 13

Donkeys were dependable animals. So when Baalam's donkey started acting funny and refused to move, Baalam beat it. Though he beat the donkey, it still saved Baalam's life three times. Sometimes we act just like Baalam, lashing out at others because we are embarrassed or our pride is damaged, or because we really don't understand what's going on. The donkey was trying to save Baalam's life, but it made Baalam look silly in the process.

Once when my friend mentioned something personal about me to someone else, I lashed out at my friend. I was embarrassed, angry, and distressed by what was said—and not ready to forgive. Like Baalam, I did not see the whole picture. It turned out that my friend was really trying to protect me. Rather than lashing out as a first response, take time to see what's really going on. It might just save you—and others—some hurt and embarrassment.

Verity

Check it out first; then react.

»» JOSHUA'S NEW JOB ««

Introduction

Forty years passed after the first spy mission into Canaan. Out of all of the adults who left Egypt under Moses' leadership, only Joshua and Caleb were still alive. They were the only two spies who had agreed that God could help them take over the promised land. Now Joshua, who had been Moses' assistant, was the leader of Israel. He took over one of the toughest jobs ever. Joshua would be responsible for leading Israel's army into many battles in order to take over the promised land. So he was understandably afraid. That's why God gave Joshua a pep talk. Joshua used God's encouraging words to pump up the rest of the team.

Joshua 1:1-18, NLT

After the death of Moses the LORD's servant, the LORD spoke to Joshua son of Nun, Moses' assistant. He said, "Now that my servant Moses is dead, you must lead my people across the Jordan River into the land I am giving them. I promise you what I promised Moses: 'Everywhere you go, you will be on land I have given you—from the Negev Desert in the south to the Lebanon mountains in the north, from the Euphrates River on the east to the Mediterranean Sea on the west, and all the land of the Hittites.' No one will be able to stand their ground against you as long as you live. For I will be with you as I was with Moses. I will not fail you or abandon you.

"Be strong and courageous, for you will lead my people to possess all the land I swore to give their ancestors. Be strong and very courageous. Obey all the laws Moses gave you. Do not turn away from them, and you will be successful in everything you do. Study this Book of the Law continually. Meditate on it day and night so you may be sure to obey all that is written in it. Only then will you succeed. I command you—be strong and courageous! Do not be afraid or discouraged. For the LORD your God is with you wherever you go."

Joshua then commanded the leaders of Israel, "Go through the camp and tell the people to get their provisions ready. In three days you will cross the Jordan River and take possession of the land the LORD your God has given you."

Then Joshua called together the tribes of Reuben, Gad, and the half-tribe of Manasseh. He told them, "Remember what Moses, the servant of the LORD, commanded you: 'The LORD your God is giving you rest and has given you this land.' Your wives, children, and cattle may remain here on the east side of the Jordan River, but your warriors, fully armed, must lead the other tribes across the Jordan to help them conquer their territory. Stay with them until the LORD gives rest to them as he has given rest to you, and until they, too, possess the land the LORD your God is giving them. Only then may you settle here on the east side of the Jordan River in the land that Moses, the servant of the LORD, gave you."

They answered Joshua, "We will do whatever you command us, and we will go wherever you send us. We will obey you just as we obeyed Moses. And may the LORD your God be with you as he was with Moses. Anyone who rebels against your word and does not obey your every command will be put to death. So be strong and courageous!"

Take ANOTHER LOOK

Like Joshua, have you ever been afraid of a new task or responsibility? Usually, whenever God had a job for someone to do, he started by encouraging that person not to be afraid. Instead he or she could depend on God for help, whether it was overcoming a fear or getting the job done. Here are some encouraging words found in the psalms.

Psalm 27:1-3, NLT

The Lord is my light and my salvation—
    so why should I be afraid?
The Lord protects me from danger—
    so why should I tremble?
When evil people come to destroy me,
    when my enemies and foes attack me,
    they will stumble and fall.

Though a mighty army surrounds me,
    my heart will know no fear.
Even if they attack me,
    I remain confident.

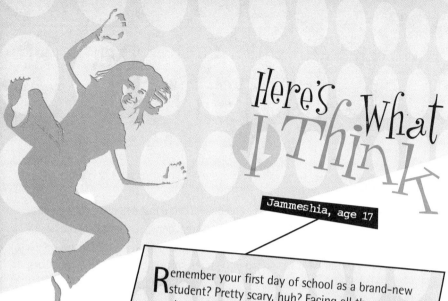

Here's What I Think

Jammeshia, age 17

Remember your first day of school as a brand-new student? Pretty scary, huh? Facing all those new people and having a whole new set of rules? That's how I felt when I entered a new school. I thought, *I am not going to be able to get through this.*

Then I remembered that I probably was a lot like Joshua. I am sure he was scared when he became the new leader. He was leading over two million people! God told Joshua that as long as he obeyed God's commands, he would succeed.

It's really cool that God knows everything about us—what we're scared of, what we're going through every moment of the day. I know sometimes our situation can be frightening, but I am happy to know that the same promise he gave to Joshua, he gives to us—"Do not be afraid or discouraged. For the Lord your God is with you wherever you go!" (Joshua 1:9).

Jammeshia

Be confident that God is with you.

RAHAB AND THE SPIES

Introduction

Jericho was the first city in Canaan to be conquered. Before that battle could take place, more spies were chosen to check out the land. This time, only two were sent. They knew just where to go—Rahab's house. Rahab's house was built into the wall of Jericho, which helped her to see and hear what was going on. But the spies' visit placed all of their lives in danger. A daring escape was needed—one that only God could pull off.

Joshua 2:1-21, NLT

Then Joshua secretly sent out two spies from the Israelite camp at Acacia. He instructed them, "Spy out the land on the other side of the Jordan River, especially around Jericho." So the two men set out and came to the house of a prostitute named Rahab and stayed there that night.

But someone told the king of Jericho, "Some Israelites have come here tonight to spy out the land." So the king of Jericho sent orders to Rahab: "Bring out the men who have come into your house. They are spies sent here to discover the best way to attack us."

Rahab, who had hidden the two men, replied, "The men were here earlier, but I didn't know where they were from. They left the city at dusk, as the city gates were about to close, and I don't know where they went. If you hurry, you can probably catch up with them." (But she had taken them up to the roof and hidden them beneath piles of flax.) So the king's men went looking for the spies along the road leading to the shallow crossing places of the Jordan River. And as soon as the king's men had left, the city gate was shut.

Before the spies went to sleep that night, Rahab went up on the roof to talk with them. "I know the LORD has given you this land," she told them. "We are all afraid of you. Everyone is living in terror. For we have heard how the LORD made a dry path for you through the Red Sea when you left Egypt. And we know what you did to Sihon and Og, the two Amorite kings east of the Jordan River, whose people you completely destroyed. No wonder our hearts have melted in fear! No one has the courage to fight after hearing such things. For the LORD your God is the supreme God of the heavens above and the earth below. Now swear to me by the LORD that you will be kind to me and my family since I have helped you. Give me some guarantee that when Jericho is conquered, you will let me live, along with my father and mother, my brothers and sisters, and all their families."

"We offer our own lives as a guarantee for your safety," the men agreed. "If you don't betray us, we will keep our promise when the LORD gives us the land."

Then, since Rahab's house was built into the city wall, she let them down by a rope through the window. "Escape to the hill country," she told them. "Hide there for three days until the men who are searching for you have returned; then go on your way."

Before they left, the men told her, "We can guarantee your safety only if you leave this scarlet rope hanging from the window. And all your family members— your father, mother, brothers, and all your relatives—must be here inside the house. If they go out into the street, they will be killed, and we cannot be held to our oath. But we swear that no one inside this house will be killed—not a hand will be laid on any of them. If you betray us, however, we are not bound by this oath in any way."

"I accept your terms," she replied. And she sent them on their way, leaving the scarlet rope hanging from the window.

Take ANOTHER LOOK

Rahab's faithfulness to the two spies was remembered for many generations. God blessed her with a family. In fact, she was the great-grandmother of David. Jesus was later born through this family line. Rahab was honored not just for having faith, but for acting on that faith. As James points out, faith that doesn't show itself is dead. Read about it.

James 2:21-25, NLT

Don't you remember that our ancestor Abraham was declared right with God because of what he did when he offered his son Isaac on the altar? You see, he was trusting God so much that he was willing to do whatever God told him to do. His faith was made complete by what he did—by his actions. And so it happened just as the Scriptures say: "Abraham believed God, so God declared him to be righteous." He was even called "the friend of God." So you see, we are made right with God by what we do, not by faith alone.

Rahab the prostitute is another example of this. She was made right with God by her actions—when she hid those messengers and sent them safely away by a different road.

Don't think that because you sin God can't or won't use you to accomplish his plans. Rahab is a prime example. I mean she was a prostitute. Yeah, umm, not exactly what I call sinless. Yet by making herself available and acting in faith, God was able to use her in a great way.

Often I sin and then I'll beat myself up about it, saying to myself, *You're not good enough for God. God hates sin.* The fact is when I think that way, I'm sinning! I'm saying, *God, you're not powerful enough to work past my blemishes.* The Devil is the one who gives me that shame— not the Holy Spirit. That kind of thinking is like tying an anchor around your waist to go swimming. In the end it will only drag you down. We need to focus not on what we can't do but, rather, on what God will *do* through us if we make ourselves available.

Daniel

Believe in what God can do—
not what you can't do.

THE FALL
OF JERICHO

Introduction

The time for battle had now come. The people of Israel had already crossed the Jordan River and were ready to go to war. Yet the city of Jericho looked impossible to defeat with its thick walls and fierce people. But God had already assured Joshua that he was with Israel. He had a plan that seemed almost foolish: march around the city and blow on horns. Why such a foolish-sounding plan? God wanted everyone to know that only he could win the battle.

Joshua 6:1-20, NLT

Now the gates of Jericho were tightly shut because the people were afraid of the Israelites. No one was allowed to go in or out. But the LORD said to Joshua, "I have given you Jericho, its king, and all its mighty warriors. Your entire army is to march around the city once a day for six days. Seven priests will walk ahead of the Ark, each carrying a ram's horn. On the seventh day you are to march around the city seven times, with the priests blowing the horns. When you hear the priests give one long blast on the horns, have all the people give a mighty shout. Then the walls of the city will collapse, and the people can charge straight into the city."

So Joshua called together the priests and said, "Take up the Ark of the Covenant, and assign seven priests to walk in front of it, each carrying a ram's horn." Then he gave orders to the people: "March around the city, and the armed men will lead the way in front of the Ark of the LORD."

After Joshua spoke to the people, the seven priests with the rams' horns started marching in the presence of the LORD, blowing the horns as they marched. And the priests carrying the Ark of the LORD's covenant followed behind them. Armed guards marched both in front of the priests and behind the Ark, with the priests continually blowing the horns. "Do not shout; do not even talk," Joshua commanded. "Not a single word from any of you until I tell you to shout. Then shout!" So the Ark of the LORD was carried around the city once that day, and then everyone returned to spend the night in the camp.

Joshua got up early the next morning, and the priests again carried the Ark of the LORD. The seven priests with the rams' horns marched in front of the Ark of the LORD, blowing their horns. Armed guards marched both in front of the priests with the horns and behind the Ark of the LORD. All this time the priests were sounding their horns. On the second day they marched around the city once and returned to the camp. They followed this pattern for six days.

On the seventh day the Israelites got up at dawn and marched around the city as they had done before. But this time they went around the city seven times. The seventh time around, as the priests sounded the long blast on their horns, Joshua commanded the people, "Shout! For the LORD has given you the city! The city and everything in it must be completely destroyed as an offering to the LORD. Only Rahab the prostitute and the others in her house will be spared, for she protected our spies. "Do not take any of the things set apart for destruction, or you yourselves will be completely destroyed, and you will bring trouble on all Israel. Everything made from silver, gold, bronze, or iron is sacred to the LORD and must be brought into his treasury."

When the people heard the sound of the horns, they shouted as loud as they could. Suddenly, the walls of Jericho collapsed, and the Israelites charged straight into the city from every side and captured it.

Take ANOTHER LOOK

There are many stories in the Bible in which God's help was just as obvious as the falling walls of Jericho. Only he could make the impossible possible. But God's people also played a part in these stories. Their role was to have faith in God. That's why these stories are faith builders. They remind you of what God can do and how you can trust him with any problem. Like the time Joshua and the people of Israel needed more time to fight a battle. God gave them extra "sun" time. If God can do that, is there anything he can't do?

Hebrews 11:1, 2, 30-31, NLT

What is faith? It is the confident assurance that what we hope for is going to happen. It is the evidence of things we cannot yet see. God gave his approval to people in days of old because of their faith. . . . It was by faith that the people of Israel marched around Jericho seven days, and the walls came crashing down. It was by faith that Rahab the prostitute did not die with all the others in her city who refused to obey God. For she had given a friendly welcome to the spies.

Joshua 10:12,13, NLT

On the day the LORD gave the Israelites victory over the Amorites, Joshua prayed to the Lord in front of all the people of Israel. He said, "Let the sun stand still over Gibeon, and the moon over the valley of Aijalon."

So the sun and moon stood still until the Israelites had defeated their enemies. Is this event not recorded in *The Book of Jashar*? The sun stopped in the middle of the sky, and it did not set as on a normal day.

Here's What I Think

Janna, age 14

I really like this story. Marching around Jericho probably seemed kind of silly to some of them—maybe even all of them! I'm sure it got discouraging doing it for seven days, not knowing what exactly was going to happen. But they kept pressing on—they knew they had God on their side.

I play volleyball, and I cannot get an overhand serve. I don't have enough upper body strength, and it is discouraging to me. That's when I need to remember the Israelites marching around the walls of Jericho. I have to remember that God is with me just like he was with the Israelites. One of my favorite verses, Psalm 46:1, says, "God is our refuge and strength, always ready to help in times of trouble." Whenever you get discouraged, do what I do: repeat this verse to yourself—and keep going! God knows what we're going through, and he's ready and willing to help.

Janna

You can keep going with God's help.

»»» ACHAN FORSAKEN «««

Introduction

Before the wall around Jericho was destroyed, God told the people of Israel to grab the gold, silver, bronze, and iron treasures for his Tabernacle. Everything else was to be destroyed. Notice the word "everything." Anyone who took treasures for himself would be put to death. That was a strong warning. But one Israelite didn't listen. Maybe he thought that God wouldn't notice if he took a few souvenirs. But God did notice. And because of one man's wrongdoing, the entire army of Israel was defeated during a battle with the people of Ai. Something drastic had to be done.

Joshua 7:2-12, 16-23, NLT

Joshua sent some of his men from Jericho to spy out the city of Ai, east of Bethel, near Beth-aven. When they returned, they told Joshua, "It's a small town, and it won't take more than two or three thousand of us to destroy it. There's no need for all of us to go there."

So approximately three thousand warriors were sent, but they were soundly defeated. The men of Ai chased the Israelites from the city gate as far as the quarries, and they killed about thirty-six who were retreating down the slope. The Israelites were paralyzed with fear at this turn of events, and their courage melted away.

Joshua and the leaders of Israel tore their clothing in dismay, threw dust on their heads, and bowed down facing the Ark of the LORD until evening. Then Joshua cried out, "Sovereign LORD, why did you bring us across the Jordan River if you are going to let the Amorites kill us? If only we had been content to stay on the other side! Lord, what am I to say, now that Israel has fled from its enemies? For when the Canaanites and all the other people living in the land hear about it, they will surround us and wipe us off the face of the earth. And then what will happen to the honor of your great name?"

But the LORD said to Joshua, "Get up! Why are you lying on your face like this? Israel has sinned and broken my covenant! They have stolen the things that I commanded to be set apart for me. And they have not only stolen them; they have also lied about it and hidden the things among their belongings. That is why the Israelites are running from their enemies in defeat. For now Israel has been set apart for destruction. I will not remain with you any longer unless you destroy the things among you that were set apart for destruction."

Achan's Sin, 7:16-23

Early the next morning Joshua brought the tribes of Israel before the LORD, and the tribe of Judah was singled out. Then the clans of Judah came forward, and the clan of Zerah was singled out. Then the families of Zerah came before the LORD, and the family of Zimri was singled out. Every member of Zimri's family was brought forward person by person, and Achan was singled out.

Then Joshua said to Achan, "My son, give glory to the LORD, the God of Israel, by telling the truth. Make your confession and tell me what you have done. Don't hide it from me."

Achan replied, "I have sinned against the LORD, the God of Israel. For I saw a beautiful robe imported from Babylon, two hundred silver coins, and a bar of gold weighing more than a pound. I wanted them so much that I took them. They are hidden in the ground beneath my tent, with the silver buried deeper than the rest."

So Joshua sent some men to make a search. They ran to the tent and found the stolen goods hidden there, just as Achan had said, with the silver buried beneath the rest. They took the things from the tent and brought them to Joshua and all the Israelites. Then they laid them on the ground in the presence of the LORD.

Take ANOTHER LOOK

Achan and his family weren't the only ones who paid with their lives for a wrongdoing. In New Testament times, a couple lied about a donation they made to the church. But, as Peter told them in the story below, the Holy Spirit knew that they lied. This chilling story is a sad reminder of why disobeying God is always a mistake.

Acts 5:1-10, NLT

There was also a man named Ananias who, with his wife, Sapphira, sold some property. He brought part of the money to the apostles, but he claimed it was the full amount. His wife had agreed to this deception.

Then Peter said, "Ananias, why has Satan filled your heart? You lied to the Holy Spirit, and you kept some of the money for yourself. The property was yours to sell or not sell, as you wished. And after selling it, the money was yours to give away. How could you do a thing like this? You weren't lying to us but to God."

As soon as Ananias heard these words, he fell to the floor and died. Everyone who heard about it was terrified. Then some young men wrapped him in a sheet and took him out and buried him.

About three hours later his wife came in, not knowing what had happened. Peter asked her, "Was this the price you and your husband received for your land?"

"Yes," she replied, "that was the price."

And Peter said, "How could the two of you even think of doing a thing like this—conspiring together to test the Spirit of the Lord? Just outside that door are the young men who buried your husband, and they will carry you out, too."

Instantly, she fell to the floor and died.

Here's What I Think

Faith, age 14

Maybe Achan thought it wasn't such a big deal to take a few things from Jericho. Maybe he thought that God wouldn't notice. But it was a big deal, and God did notice. Sometimes we act the same way as Achan. We think that it's OK to tell a little lie or download a song from the Internet or skip giving money to the church because we want something else.

Like the time my favorite band came out with a new CD that I just had to have. I had barely enough money to get it, but then I remembered that I always put some of my money into the offering plate at church. I had to decide whether to buy my CD or sacrifice some of my money to God and wait to get the CD. It was such a small thing, really. Would God really care if I didn't put the usual amount in the offering plate or if I skipped a week? In the end, I went with my conscience and gave the money to the church. And you know what happened? The very next day, my friend came over and handed me the CD. She said, "Hey, you want to borrow this for a while?" I was so excited because even if I couldn't own the CD right now, I could listen to it. God does notice the small things!

Faith

Be faithful in the small things.

»» WONDER WOMEN ««

introduction

This next story takes place about 150 years after Joshua's death. As you know, Israel didn't have a king. To help rule his people, God gave Israel leaders called judges who would lead them in the fight against their enemies. Two of these judges were Ehud and Shamgar. But after them came Deborah. Among the list of Israel's leaders, a woman's name was rare. After all, the women of Israel never fought in wars. But as Deborah predicted, the war would be won by God, and he would use an unlikely person—another woman.

Judges 4:1-24, NLT

After Ehud's death, the Israelites again did what was evil in the LORD's sight. So the LORD handed them over to King Jabin of Hazor, a Canaanite king. The commander of his army was Sisera, who lived in Harosheth-haggoyim. Sisera, who had nine hundred iron chariots, ruthlessly oppressed the Israelites for twenty years. Then the Israelites cried out to the LORD for help.

Deborah, the wife of Lappidoth, was a prophet who had become a judge in Israel. She would hold court under the Palm of Deborah, which stood between Ramah and Bethel in the hill country of Ephraim, and the Israelites came to her to settle their disputes. One day she sent for Barak son of Abinoam, who lived in Kedesh in the land of Naphtali. She said to him, "This is what the LORD, the God of Israel, commands you: Assemble ten thousand warriors from the tribes of Naphtali and Zebulun at Mount Tabor. I will lure Sisera, commander of Jabin's army, along with his chariots and warriors, to the Kishon River. There I will give you victory over him."

Barak told her, "I will go, but only if you go with me!"

"Very well," she replied, "I will go with you. But since you have made this choice, you will receive no honor. For the LORD's victory over Sisera will be at the hands of a woman." So Deborah went with Barak to Kedesh. At Kedesh, Barak called together the tribes of Zebulun and Naphtali, and ten thousand warriors marched up with him. Deborah also marched with them.

Now Heber the Kenite, a descendant of Moses' brother-in-law Hobab, had moved away from the other members of his tribe and pitched his tent by the Oak of Zaanannim, near Kedesh.

When Sisera was told that Barak son of Abinoam had gone up to Mount Tabor, he called for all nine hundred of his iron chariots and all of his warriors, and they marched from Harosheth-haggoyim to the Kishon River.

Then Deborah said to Barak, "Get ready! Today the LORD will give you victory over Sisera, for the LORD is marching ahead of you." So Barak led his ten thousand warriors down the slopes of Mount Tabor into battle. When Barak attacked, the LORD threw Sisera and all his charioteers and warriors into a panic. Then Sisera leaped down from his chariot and escaped on foot. Barak chased the enemy and their chariots all the way to Harosheth-haggoyim, killing all of Sisera's warriors. Not a single one was left alive.

Meanwhile, Sisera ran to the tent of Jael, the wife of Heber the Kenite, because Heber's family was on friendly terms with King Jabin of Hazor. Jael went out to meet Sisera and said to him, "Come into my tent, sir. Come in. Don't be afraid." So he went into her tent, and she covered him with a blanket.

"Please give me some water," he said. "I'm thirsty." So she gave him some milk to drink and covered him again.

"Stand at the door of the tent," he told her. "If anybody comes and asks you if there is anyone here, say no."

But when Sisera fell asleep from exhaustion, Jael quietly crept up to him with a hammer and tent peg. Then she drove the tent peg through his temple and into the ground, and so he died.

When Barak came looking for Sisera, Jael went out to meet him. She said, "Come, and I will show you the man you are looking for." So he followed her into the tent and found Sisera lying there dead, with the tent peg through his temple.

So on that day Israel saw God subdue Jabin, the Canaanite king. And from that time on Israel became stronger and stronger against King Jabin, until they finally destroyed him.

Take ANOTHER LOOK

Whenever Israel won a victory, the leaders or other individuals often sang a song to thank God. Moses and Miriam led the people in a song after Israel crossed the Red Sea. Now Deborah and Barak wanted to celebrate by singing. Here is a portion of their song.

Judges 5:1-5, NLT

On that day Deborah and Barak son of Abinoam sang this song:
   "When Israel's leaders take charge,

and the people gladly follow — bless the Lord!
"Listen, you kings!
Pay attention, you mighty rulers!
For I will sing to the Lord.
I will lift up my song to the Lord, the God of Israel.

"Lord, when you set out from Seir
and marched across the fields of Edom,
the earth trembled
and the cloudy skies poured down rain.
The mountains quaked at the coming of the Lord.
Even Mount Sinai shook in the presence of the Lord, the God of Israel.

Here's What I Think

Kali, age 18

I can't even count the times when I have been in situations where I've thought, *God can't use me*. But God has proved me wrong every time. The truth is God uses ordinary people in extraordinary ways, just like he did with the people of the Bible. Consider today's story. Deborah was an exceptional prophetess and a judge of Israel, chosen by God to lead his people with wisdom and courage. Jael, a housewife, was the one who received the honor for defeating Sisera because she didn't back down when given an opportunity to kill him. If God can use these people, why can't he use me? Or you? If we are willing to let God use us, he will do amazing things. We just need to make ourselves available and be willing to step up when given the opportunity—just like Deborah and Jael. Are you ready and willing to allow God to use you today? I know I am. *Kali*

Make yourself available to God's leading.

»» OUTNUMBERED!

Introduction

The people of Israel had 40 years of peace after Deborah and Barak led the people into battle against Sisera and his army. But even though God had won the battle for Israel, the people soon turned away from him again. So he allowed another enemy nation—the Midianites—to torment them for seven years. The Midianites constantly stole their animals and destroyed their crops. So the people of Israel finally turned to God for help. God chose Gideon, an unlikely leader, to lead them into battle against the army of Midian. Gideon wasn't a professional soldier. He was an ordinary, scared man. But that was all part of God's plan—a plan that took another unusual turn.

Judges 7:1-22, NLT

So Jerubbaal (that is, Gideon) and his army got up early and went as far as the spring of Harod. The armies of Midian were camped north of them in the valley near the hill of Moreh. The LORD said to Gideon, "You have too many warriors with you. If I let all of you fight the Midianites, the Israelites will boast to me that they saved themselves by their own strength. Therefore, tell the people, 'Whoever is timid or afraid may leave and go home.'" Twenty-two thousand of them went home, leaving only ten thousand who were willing to fight.

But the LORD told Gideon, "There are still too many! Bring them down to the spring, and I will sort out who will go with you and who will not." When Gideon took his warriors down to the water, the LORD told him, "Divide the men into two groups. In one group put all those who cup water in their hands and lap it up with their tongues like dogs. In the other group put all those who kneel down and drink with their mouths in the stream." Only three hundred of the men drank from their hands. All the others got down on their knees and drank with their mouths in the stream. The LORD told Gideon, "With these three hundred men I will rescue you and give you victory over the Midianites. Send all the others home." So Gideon collected the provisions and rams' horns of the other warriors and sent them home. But he kept the three hundred men with him.

Now the Midianite camp was in the valley just below Gideon. During the night, the LORD said, "Get up! Go down into the Midianite camp, for I have given you victory over them! But if you are afraid to attack, go down to the camp with your servant Purah. Listen to what the Midianites are saying, and you will be greatly encouraged. Then you will be eager to attack."

So Gideon took Purah and went down to the outposts of the enemy camp. The armies of Midian, Amalek, and the people of the east had settled in the valley like a swarm of locusts. Their camels were like grains of sand on the seashore—too many to count! Gideon crept up just as a man was telling his friend about a dream. The man said, "I had this dream, and in my dream a loaf of barley bread came tumbling down into the Midianite camp. It hit a tent, turned it over, and knocked it flat!"

His friend said, "Your dream can mean only one thing—God has given Gideon son of Joash, the Israelite, victory over all the armies united with Midian!"

When Gideon heard the dream and its interpretation, he thanked God. Then he returned to the Israelite camp and shouted, "Get up! For the LORD has given you victory over the Midianites!" He divided the three hundred men into three groups and gave each man a ram's horn and a clay jar with a torch in it. Then he said to them, "Keep your eyes on me. When I come to the edge of the camp, do just as I do. As soon as my group blows the rams' horns, those of you on the other sides of the camp blow your horns and shout, 'For the LORD and for Gideon!'"

It was just after midnight, after the changing of the guard, when Gideon and the one hundred men with him reached the outer edge of the Midianite camp. Suddenly, they blew the horns and broke their clay jars. Then all three groups blew their horns and broke their jars. They held the blazing torches in their left hands and the horns in their right hands and shouted, "A sword for the LORD and for Gideon!" Each man stood at his position around the camp and watched as all the Midianites rushed around in a panic, shouting as they ran. When the three hundred Israelites blew their horns, the LORD caused the warriors in the camp to fight against each other with their swords. Those who were not killed fled to places as far away as Beth-shittah near Zererah and to the border of Abel-meholah near Tabbath.

Hundreds of years later, after the nation of Israel divided (see page 140), another person faced a tough army. He was King Hezekiah of Judah. There was no way that Hezekiah's army could win against the Assyrians, who were one of the toughest enemies of Judah. The Assyrian army surrounded the cities of Judah and kept threatening the people with war. They wouldn't allow anyone in or out of the city. The king of that nation hoped to starve the people of Judah into surrendering. But once again, God proved that he could conquer any army at any time.

2 Chronicles 32:10-21, NLT

"This is what King Sennacherib of Assyria says: What are you trusting in that makes you think you can survive my siege of Jerusalem? Hezekiah has said, 'The Lord our God will rescue us from the king of Assyria.' Surely Hezekiah is misleading you, sentencing you to death by famine and thirst! Surely you must realize that Hezekiah is the very person who destroyed all the Lord's shrines and altars. He commanded Judah and Jerusalem to worship at only the one altar at the Temple and to make sacrifices on it alone.

"Surely you must realize what I and the other kings of Assyria before me have done to all the people of the earth! Were any of the gods of those nations able to rescue their people from my power? Name just one time when any god, anywhere, was able to rescue his people from me! What makes you think your God can do any better? Don't let Hezekiah fool you! Don't let him deceive you like this! I say it again—no god of any nation has ever yet been able to rescue his people from me or my ancestors. How much less will your God rescue you from my power!"

And Sennacherib's officials further mocked the LORD God and his servant Hezekiah, heaping insult upon insult. The king also sent letters scorning the LORD, the God of Israel. He wrote, "Just as the gods of all the other nations failed to rescue their people from my power, so the God of Hezekiah will also fail." The Assyrian officials who brought the letters shouted this in the Hebrew language to the people gathered on the walls of the city, trying to terrify them so it would be easier to capture the city. These officials talked about the God of Jerusalem as though he were one of the pagan gods, made by human hands.

Then King Hezekiah and the prophet Isaiah son of Amoz cried out in prayer to God in heaven. And the Lord sent an angel who destroyed the Assyrian army with all its commanders and officers. So Sennacherib returned home in disgrace to his own land. And when he entered the temple of his god, some of his own sons killed him there with a sword.

Here's What I Think

Mike, age 18

If I know something big is about to happen in my life, I usually try to overcompensate so I can handle it easily on my own. Gideon did the same thing. He had amassed a huge army to crush the Midianites. Gideon had planned for a large battle, but in doing so, he had left God out of the picture.

But God didn't want to win this battle with the might of Israel's army. He wanted victory in battle to bring glory to *him*. God destroyed the avenging army using only a fraction of the manpower Gideon had intended to use. In my own life I find that, if I simply place my trust in God to take care of the big things as well as the small things, I do not have to worry about how things are going to turn out. God is able to overcome anything that I might face.

Michel

You are never outnumbered
if God's on your side.

A LOYAL FRIEND

Introduction

The story of Ruth takes place during the time of the judges. In this story, names mean a lot. Mahlon, Ruth's husband, and Kilion, the man whom her sister-in-law, Orpah, married, had names that mean "weakling" and "failing." Neither man lived long. Naomi, Ruth's mother-in-law, got involved in the name game by changing her name to one that means "bitterness" because of her sad circumstances. But something happened to turn this tragic story into a triumph. You see, Ruth's name means "friendship." She chose to live up to her name by being loyal to her mother-in-law. For Ruth loyalty meant leaving her land as Abraham had done centuries before and going to a place she had never been before. It also meant following the laws of a new God—the one true God of Israel.

Ruth 1:1-19; 2:1-12, 17-23, NLT

In the days when the judges ruled in Israel, a man from Bethlehem in Judah left the country because of a severe famine. He took his wife and two sons and went to live in the country of Moab. The man's name was Elimelech, and his wife was Naomi. Their two sons were Mahlon and Kilion. They were Ephrathites from Bethlehem in the land of Judah. During their stay in Moab, Elimelech died and Naomi was left with her two sons. The two sons married Moabite women. One married a woman named Orpah, and the other a woman named Ruth. But about ten years later, both Mahlon and Kilion died. This left Naomi alone, without her husband or sons.

Naomi and Ruth Return

Then Naomi heard in Moab that the LORD had blessed his people in Judah by giving them good crops again. So Naomi and her daughters-in-law got ready to leave Moab to return to her homeland. With her two daughters-in-law she set out from the place where she had been living, and they took the road that would lead them back to Judah.

But on the way, Naomi said to her two daughters-in-law, "Go back to your mothers' homes instead of coming with me. And may the LORD reward you for your kindness to your husbands and to me. May the LORD bless you with the security of another marriage." Then she kissed them good-bye, and they all broke down and wept.

"No," they said. "We want to go with you to your people."

But Naomi replied, "Why should you go on with me? Can I still give birth to other sons who could grow up to be your husbands? No, my daughters, return to your parents' homes, for I am too old to marry again. And even if it were possible, and I were to get married tonight and bear sons, then what? Would you wait for them to grow up and refuse to marry someone else? No, of course not, my daughters! Things are far more bitter for me than for you, because the LORD himself has caused me to suffer."

And again they wept together, and Orpah kissed her mother-in-law good-bye. But Ruth insisted on staying with Naomi. "See," Naomi said to her, "your sister-in-law has gone back to her people and to her gods. You should do the same."

But Ruth replied, "Don't ask me to leave you and turn back. I will go wherever you go and live wherever you live. Your people will be my people, and your God will be my God. I will die where you die and will be buried there. May the LORD punish me severely if I allow anything but death to separate us!" So when Naomi saw that Ruth had made up her mind to go with her, she stopped urging her.

So the two of them continued on their journey. When they came to Bethlehem, the entire town was stirred by their arrival. "Is it really Naomi?" the women asked.

Ruth Works in Boaz's Field, 2:1-12

Now there was a wealthy and influential man in Bethlehem named Boaz, who was a relative of Naomi's husband, Elimelech.

One day Ruth said to Naomi, "Let me go out into the fields to gather leftover grain behind anyone who will let me do it."

And Naomi said, "All right, my daughter, go ahead." So Ruth went out to gather grain behind the harvesters. And as it happened, she found herself working in a field that belonged to Boaz, the relative of her father-in-law, Elimelech.

While she was there, Boaz arrived from Bethlehem and greeted the harvesters. "The LORD be with you!" he said.

"The LORD bless you!" the harvesters replied.

Then Boaz asked his foreman, "Who is that girl over there?"

And the foreman replied, "She is the young woman from Moab who came back with Naomi. She asked me this morning if she could gather grain behind the harvesters. She has been hard at work ever since, except for a few minutes' rest over there in the shelter."

Boaz went over and said to Ruth, "Listen, my daughter. Stay right here with us when you gather grain; don't go to any other fields. Stay right behind the women working in my field. See which part of the field they are harvesting, and then follow them. I have warned the young men not to bother you. And when you are thirsty, help yourself to the water they have drawn from the well."

Ruth fell at his feet and thanked him warmly. "Why are you being so kind to me?" she asked. "I am only a foreigner."

"Yes, I know," Boaz replied. "But I also know about the love and kindness you have shown your mother-in-law since the death of your husband. I have heard how you left your father and mother and your own land to live here among complete strangers. May the LORD, the God of Israel, under whose wings you have come to take refuge, reward you fully."

2:17-23

So Ruth gathered barley there all day, and when she beat out the grain that evening, it came to about half a bushel. She carried it back into town and showed it to her mother-in-law. Ruth also gave her the food that was left over from her lunch.

"So much!" Naomi exclaimed. "Where did you gather all this grain today? Where did you work? May the LORD bless the one who helped you!"

So Ruth told her mother-in-law about the man in whose field she had worked. And she said, "The man I worked with today is named Boaz."

"May the LORD bless him!" Naomi told her daughter-in-law. "He is showing his kindness to us as well as to your dead husband. That man is one of our closest relatives, one of our family redeemers."

Then Ruth said, "What's more, Boaz even told me to come back and stay with his harvesters until the entire harvest is completed."

"This is wonderful!" Naomi exclaimed. "Do as he said. Stay with his workers right through the whole harvest. You will be safe there, unlike in other fields."

So Ruth worked alongside the women in Boaz's fields and gathered grain with them until the end of the barley harvest. Then she worked with them through the wheat harvest, too. But all the while she lived with her mother-in-law.

4:9,10

Then Boaz said to the leaders and to the crowd standing around, "You are witnesses that today I have bought from Naomi all the property of Elimelech, Kilion, and Mahlon. And with the land I have acquired Ruth, the Moabite widow of Mahlon, to be my wife. This way she can have a son to carry on the family name of her dead husband and to inherit the family property here in his hometown. You are all witnesses today."

Like Rahab, Ruth was a Gentile—a person who is not Jewish. She also had something else in common with Rahab: loyalty. Because of Ruth's loyalty to Naomi, God rewarded her with a family. Her great-grandson was David, Israel's greatest king. Through this family line came Jesus, the King of Kings. Ruth is one of the few women mentioned in Jesus' family line.

Matthew 1:5, NLT

Salmon was the father of Boaz (his mother was Rahab).
Boaz was the father of Obed (his mother was Ruth).
Obed was the father of Jesse.

Here's What I Think

Walter, age 13

It was tough for me when I had to start over at a new school. I was sure that my world was about to end. It was a big leap of faith. Why? It was a pretty big academic jump. And I hardly knew any of the kids in my class. I felt like a freak. Looking back I've realized that I was in the same boat as Ruth. She was a new girl, in a new place, trusting God to get her through each day. I trusted God the same way, and he brought new friends into my life just as he brought Boaz into Ruth's life. I bet Boaz made things a lot easier for Ruth. My new friends did for me. God really does help us when we need him!

Walter

New kid in town? Look to God for help.

A CUTTING BETRAYAL

Introduction

About 30 years after Gideon, Samson became the twelfth judge of Israel. This time, the Philistines were the enemy. Although Samson is the last judge mentioned in the book of Judges, he wasn't the last judge. But he was the judge most remembered because of an unusual gift that God gave him: super strength. Samson was an Old Testament super-hero—an army of one. But unlike some of the superheroes we read about in comic books, Samson had a weakness.

Judges 16:4-30, NLT

Later, Samson fell in love with a woman named Delilah, who lived in the valley of Sorek. The leaders of the Philistines went to her and said, "Find out from Samson what makes him so strong and how he can be over-powered and tied up securely. Then each of us will give you eleven hundred pieces of silver."

So Delilah said to Samson, "Please tell me what makes you so strong and what it would take to tie you up securely."

Samson replied, "If I am tied up with seven new bowstrings that have not yet been dried, I will be as weak as anyone else."

So the Philistine leaders brought Delilah seven new bowstrings, and she tied Samson up with them. She had hidden some men in one of the rooms of her house, and she cried out, "Samson! The Philistines have come to capture you!" But Samson snapped the bowstrings as if they were string that had been burned in a fire. So the secret of his strength was not discovered.

Afterward Delilah said to him, "You made fun of me and told me a lie! Now please tell me how you can be tied up securely."

Samson replied, "If I am tied up with brand-new ropes that have never been used, I will be as weak as anyone else."

So Delilah took new ropes and tied him up with them. The men were hiding in the room as before, and again Delilah cried out, "Samson! The Philistines have come to capture you!" But Samson snapped the ropes from his arms as if they were thread.

Then Delilah said, "You have been making fun of me and telling me lies! Won't you please tell me how you can be tied up securely?"

Samson replied, "If you weave the seven braids of my hair into the fabric on your loom and tighten it with the loom shuttle, I will be as weak as anyone else."

So while he slept, Delilah wove the seven braids of his hair into the fabric and tightened it with the loom shuttle. Again she cried out, "Samson! The Philistines have come to capture you!" But Samson woke up, pulled back the loom shuttle, and yanked his hair away from the loom and the fabric.

Then Delilah pouted, "How can you say you love me when you don't confide in me? You've made fun of me three times now, and you still haven't told me what makes you so strong!" So day after day she nagged him until he couldn't stand it any longer.

Finally, Samson told her his secret. "My hair has never been cut," he confessed, "for I was dedicated to God as a Nazirite from birth. If my head were shaved, my strength would leave me, and I would become as weak as anyone else."

Delilah realized he had finally told her the truth, so she sent for the Philistine leaders. "Come back one more time," she said, "for he has told me everything." So the Philistine leaders returned and brought the money with them. Delilah lulled Samson to sleep with his head in her lap, and she called in a man to shave off his hair, making his capture certain. And his strength left him. Then she cried out, "Samson! The Philistines have come to capture you!"

When he woke up, he thought, "I will do as before and shake myself free." But he didn't realize the LORD had left him.

So the Philistines captured him and gouged out his eyes. They took him to Gaza, where he was bound with bronze chains and made to grind grain in the prison. But before long his hair began to grow back.

Samson's Final Victory

The Philistine leaders held a great festival, offering sacrifices and praising their god, Dagon. They said, "Our god has given us victory over our enemy Samson!"

When the people saw him, they praised their god, saying, "Our god has delivered our enemy to us! The one who killed so many of us is now in our power!"

Half drunk by now, the people demanded, "Bring out Samson so he can perform for us!" So he was brought from the prison and made to stand at the center of the temple, between the two pillars supporting the roof.

Samson said to the servant who was leading him by the hand, "Place my hands against the two pillars. I want to rest against them." The temple was completely filled with people. All the Philistine leaders were there, and there were about three thousand on the roof who were watching Samson and making fun of him.

Then Samson prayed to the LORD, "Sovereign LORD, remember me again.

O God, please strengthen me one more time so that I may pay back the Philistines for the loss of my eyes." Then Samson put his hands on the center pillars of the temple and pushed against them with all his might. "Let me die with the Philistines," he prayed. And the temple crashed down on the Philistine leaders and all the people. So he killed more people when he died than he had during his entire lifetime.

Take ANOTHER LOOK

Samson's defeat of the Philistines was only the beginning. They weren't completely defeated until the time of David almost 100 years later. But even David and his trained army couldn't defeat the Philistines without God's help. As you read the story below, consider what David did about his problem. When you are struggling with problems, are you willing to seek God's help like David did?

2 Samuel 5:17-21, NLT

When the Philistines heard that David had been anointed king of Israel, they mobilized all their forces to capture him. But David was told they were coming and went into the stronghold. The Philistines arrived and spread out across the valley of Rephaim. So David asked the LORD, "Should I go out to fight the Philistines? Will you hand them over to me?"

The LORD replied, "Yes, go ahead. I will certainly give you the victory."

So David went to Baal-perazim and defeated the Philistines there. "The LORD has done it!" David exclaimed. "He burst through my enemies like a raging flood!" So David named that place Baal-perazim (which means "the Lord who bursts through"). The Philistines had abandoned their idols there, so David and his troops confiscated them.

Here's What I Think

This particular passage taught me to be attentive to whom I choose as friends. I need to guard against being so caught up in friendships that I forget the gifts God has given me. I find that there are many people around me who dislike what God wants me to do. And as a result, they try to use me or convince me to doing something wrong.

Some people only want to see me fail, just as Delilah did with Samson. I believe that Samson was so relaxed in his new *love* that he let down his guard, and as a result, she took advantage of him and betrayed him. Had he been more attentive, he would have seen through her flattery and deceit. It's a hard lesson to learn, but we can ask God to help us determine who is a true friend and who is trying to deceive us.

Nicee

Guard against false friends.

»»» A VOICE IN THE NIGHT «««

Introduction

Ever been last? Maybe you were the last kid born in your family or you sit in the last seat of the classroom, thanks to your last name. Samuel was the last of the judges of Israel. He was the first child of Hannah, a woman who could not have children for many years. When she asked God to give her a son, Hannah promised to give the child back to God. So Samuel had been taken to the Tabernacle to live and work with Eli, the priest. God had plans for Samuel. But Samuel didn't yet know God. That would soon change.

1 Samuel 3:1-18, NLT

Meanwhile, the boy Samuel was serving the LORD by assisting Eli. Now in those days messages from the LORD were very rare, and visions were quite uncommon.

One night Eli, who was almost blind by now, had just gone to bed. The lamp of God had not yet gone out, and Samuel was sleeping in the Tabernacle near the Ark of God. Suddenly, the LORD called out, "Samuel! Samuel!"

"Yes?" Samuel replied. "What is it?" He jumped up and ran to Eli. "Here I am. What do you need?"

"I didn't call you," Eli replied. "Go on back to bed." So he did.

Then the LORD called out again, "Samuel!"

Again Samuel jumped up and ran to Eli. "Here I am," he said. "What do you need?"

"I didn't call you, my son," Eli said. "Go on back to bed."

Samuel did not yet know the LORD because he had never had a message from the LORD before. So now the LORD called a third time, and once more Samuel jumped up and ran to Eli. "Here I am," he said. "What do you need?"

Then Eli realized it was the LORD who was calling the boy. So he said to Samuel, "Go and lie down again, and if someone calls again, say, 'Yes, LORD, your servant is listening.'" So Samuel went back to bed.

And the LORD came and called as before, "Samuel! Samuel!"

And Samuel replied, "Yes, your servant is listening."

Then the LORD said to Samuel, "I am about to do a shocking thing in Israel. I am going to carry out all my threats against Eli and his family. I have warned him continually that judgment is coming for his family, because his sons are blaspheming God and he hasn't disciplined them. So I have vowed that the sins of Eli and his sons will never be forgiven by sacrifices or offerings."

Samuel Speaks for the LORD

Samuel stayed in bed until morning, then got up and opened the doors of the Tabernacle as usual. He was afraid to tell Eli what the LORD had said to him. But Eli called out to him, "Samuel, my son."

"Here I am," Samuel replied.

"What did the LORD say to you? Tell me everything. And may God punish you if you hide anything from me!" So Samuel told Eli everything; he didn't hold anything back. "It is the LORD's will," Eli replied. "Let him do what he thinks best."

Take ANOTHER LOOK

Ezekiel was another prophet who also heard from God unexpectedly. Like Samuel, he had a hard message to deliver. The people of Israel had rebelled against God, just as Eli's sons had done. God wanted to warn them that he knew about their wrongdoings. Even though this message was a tough one to deliver, and even if no one listened, God wanted Ezekiel to say it anyway.

Ezekiel 2:1-7, NLT

"Stand up, son of man," said the voice. "I want to speak with you." The Spirit came into me as he spoke and set me on my feet. I listened carefully to his words. "Son of man," he said, "I am sending you to the nation of Israel, a nation that is rebelling against me. Their ancestors have rebelled against me from the beginning, and they are still in revolt to this very day. They are a hard-hearted and stubborn people. But I am sending you to say to them, 'This is what the Sovereign LORD says!' And whether they listen or not—for remember, they are rebels—at least they will know they have had a prophet among them.

"Son of man, do not fear them. Don't be afraid even though their threats are sharp as thorns and barbed like briers, and they sting like scorpions. Do not be dismayed by their dark scowls. For remember, they are rebels! You must give them my messages whether they listen or not. But they won't listen, for they are completely rebellious!"

Here's What I Think

Julie, age 18

To whom does God speak? It's easy to imagine God communicating with certain people—priests like Eli, your minister, missionaries, maybe even other adults in the church. But *kids*? God speaking to young people like *me* . . . or *you*? It almost seems crazy, but . . .

He does. God wants to talk to YOU! I know he talks to me—maybe not through a voice in the night, but God teaches me about himself in other ways. When I see a terrifying thunderstorm, I know he is powerful. When I'm kept safe on a trip or something good happens unexpectedly, I know he is watching over me. And, most importantly, when I read the Bible, it's like reading a love letter from God!

How about you? God's speaking to you too. You just have to be listening for him—in the world around you, in what others say, and in his Word!

Julie

God's talking to you. Are you listening?

»» WE WANT A KING! «««

Ⓘntroduction

Sometimes, people don't learn from the mistakes of others. Samuel grew up and stayed obedient to God. But like Eli, Samuel had two sons who did evil things. So the people of Israel decided that enough was enough. They wanted to be like other nations and have a king to rule over them. But God knew that they weren't rejecting Samuel's sons or Samuel. They were really rejecting God himself. Samuel knew that a king wouldn't solve their problems. Actually, having a king would end up creating brand-new ones.

1 Samuel 8:1-22, NLT

As Samuel grew old, he appointed his sons to be judges over Israel. Joel and Abijah, his oldest sons, held court in Beersheba. But they were not like their father, for they were greedy for money. They accepted bribes and perverted justice.

Finally, the leaders of Israel met at Ramah to discuss the matter with Samuel. "Look," they told him, "you are now old, and your sons are not like you. Give us a king like all the other nations have."

Samuel was very upset with their request and went to the LORD for advice. "Do as they say," the LORD replied, "for it is me they are rejecting, not you. They don't want me to be their king any longer. Ever since I brought them from Egypt they have continually forsaken me and followed other gods. And now they are giving you the same treatment. Do as they ask, but solemnly warn them about how a king will treat them."

Samuel Warns against a Kingdom

So Samuel passed on the LORD's warning to the people. "This is how a king will treat you," Samuel said. "The king will draft your sons into his army and make them run before his chariots. Some will be commanders of his troops, while others will be slave laborers. Some will be forced to plow in his fields and harvest his crops, while others will make his weapons and chariot equipment. The king will take your daughters from you and force them to cook and bake and make perfumes for him. He will take away the best of your fields and vineyards and olive groves and give them to his own servants. He will take a tenth of your harvest and distribute it among his officers and attendants. He will want your male and female slaves and demand the finest of your cattle and donkeys for his own use. He will demand a tenth of your flocks, and you will be his slaves. When that day comes, you will beg for relief from this king you are demanding, but the LORD will not help you."

But the people refused to listen to Samuel's warning. "Even so, we still want a king," they said. "We want to be like the nations around us. Our king will govern us and lead us into battle." So Samuel told the LORD what the people had said, and the LORD replied, "Do as they say, and give them a king." Then Samuel agreed and sent the people home.

Take ANOTHER LOOK Samuel's words about a king came true, as you'll see in the next story. Another king who ruled Israel long after Saul also gathered a huge force of horses and people. That king was Solomon. He had the authority to call men and animals into service. The people had to obey. This is an example of how one decision can affect life for years to come. As you read the following, think about the last thing you insisted on having. Are you willing to pay the price for it, no matter what?

1 Kings 9:20-23, NLT

There were still some people living in the land who were not Israelites. . . . These were descendants of the nations that Israel had not completely destroyed. So Solomon conscripted them for his labor force, and they serve in the labor force to this day. But Solomon did not conscript any of the Israelites for forced labor. Instead, he assigned them to serve as fighting men, government officials, officers in his army, commanders of his chariots, and charioteers. He also appointed 550 of them to supervise the various projects.

1 Kings 10:26, NLT

Solomon built up a huge force of chariots and horses. He had fourteen hundred chariots and twelve thousand horses. He stationed many of them in the chariot cities, and some near him in Jerusalem.

Here's What I Think

Verity, age 13

The Israelites wanted a king to rule over them, a leader to settle their problems. They were so persistent, so God told them he would give them what they wanted. But God also gave them a warning—a king would be a terrible burden on them. In their request, God knew that the Israelites were actually refusing to acknowledge him as king.

We still have that same problem in accepting that God is in control and that he is the ruler of everything. We often demand what we want instead of what God wants for us, which is what's best.

Here's one example. I like to watch scary movies. Each time before I pop that movie into the VCR, I'm always hesitant because I know the effect of watching it. But instead of choosing not to watch it, I play it anyway. Then after the movie ends, I am so scared that it's hard to sleep! God knows that if I hadn't watched the movie, I wouldn't be so scared! Speaking through my conscience, he warns me not to watch it; yet, like the Israelites, I disregard what God is saying to me and choose my way. That's when I remember—God always has our best in mind, if we only listen!

Verity

God wants the best for you.

»»» SAUL DISOBEYS ««««

Introduction

The people of Israel thought they had it made with their new king. He was handsome and tall and . . . well . . . kingly looking. And he started his reign off well by winning a battle. But he messed up big time, as this story describes. Although a king had great authority, there were certain things that he couldn't do. Saul did the one thing that only priests were allowed to do: offer a sacrifice to God. Although this action might not have seemed like a big deal, it was to God. He knew that one person's disobedience, especially that of a king, would mess up things for everyone. (Remember Achan? See page 84.) But God had a way of dealing with disobedience.

1 Samuel 13:1-14, NLT

Saul was thirty years old when he became king, and he reigned for forty-two years.

Saul selected three thousand special troops from the army of Israel and sent the rest of the men home. He took two thousand of the chosen men with him to Micmash and the hill country of Bethel. The other thousand went with Saul's son Jonathan to Gibeah in the land of Benjamin.

Soon after this, Jonathan attacked and defeated the garrison of Philistines at Geba. The news spread quickly among the Philistines that Israel was in revolt, so Saul sounded the call to arms throughout Israel. He announced that the Philistine garrison at Geba had been destroyed, and he warned the people that the Philistines now hated the Israelites more than ever. So the entire Israelite army mobilized again and met Saul at Gilgal.

The Philistines mustered a mighty army of three thousand chariots, six thousand horsemen, and as many warriors as the grains of sand along the seashore! When the men of Israel saw the vast number of enemy troops, they lost their nerve entirely and tried to hide in caves, holes, rocks, tombs, and cisterns. Some of them crossed the Jordan River and escaped into the land of Gad and Gilead.

Saul's Disobedience and Samuel's Rebuke

Meanwhile, Saul stayed at Gilgal, and his men were trembling with fear. Saul waited there seven days for Samuel, as Samuel had instructed him earlier, but Samuel still didn't come. Saul realized that his troops were rapidly slipping away. So he demanded, "Bring me the burnt offering and the peace offerings!" And Saul sacrificed the burnt offering himself. Just as Saul was finishing with the burnt offering, Samuel arrived. Saul went out to meet and welcome him, but Samuel said, "What is this you have done?"

Saul replied, "I saw my men scattering from me, and you didn't arrive when you said you would, and the Philistines are at Micmash ready for battle. So I said, 'The Philistines are ready to march against us, and I haven't even asked for the LORD's help!' So I felt obliged to offer the burnt offering myself before you came."

"How foolish!" Samuel exclaimed. "You have disobeyed the command of the LORD your God. Had you obeyed, the LORD would have established your kingdom over Israel forever. But now your dynasty must end, for the LORD has sought out a man after his own heart. The LORD has already chosen him to be king over his people, for you have not obeyed the LORD's command."

Take ANOTHER LOOK

Soon Saul failed to do yet another thing that God told him to do and that was the last straw. Saul definitely had to be removed as king. But Samuel wanted Saul to understand that his actions were wrong. God didn't want or need Saul to offer a sacrifice. What he wanted was Saul's obedience. What do you think God would rather have from you: a big donation of time and money or your obedience?

1 Samuel 15:22,23, NLT

But Samuel replied, "What is more pleasing to the LORD: your burnt offerings and sacrifices or your obedience to his voice? Obedience is far better than sacrifice. Listening to him is much better than offering the fat of rams. Rebellion is as bad as the sin of witchcraft, and stubbornness is as bad as worshiping idols. So because you have rejected the word of the LORD, he has rejected you from being king."

Here's What I Think

Jammeshia, age 17

I *can handle it!* Have you heard those words before? I know I've said those words a lot. Many times right before a test I seem to always think, *Should I pray and ask God for help or not?* Then I say, "I can handle it. After all, it's only a test." I was a lot like Saul.

Saul knew that he needed God's help, but he figured that he could handle it so he made a sacrifice himself. From this story we can see that in order for life to go right we need to ask God for his help. Isn't that a good thing? I mean who would want to make all their decisions by themselves? That would be crazy!

Jammeshia

Seek God's help first—not last.

THE SHEPHERD KING

Introduction

Have you ever been tempted to judge someone by how he or she looks on the outside? Saul had the right look for a king, but he didn't have the right heart. So God sent Samuel to anoint a replacement—a man "after his own heart." God had given Israel the tallest and handsomest man in the country as their king—someone they would have chosen. This time, however, he chose a man who loved him and wanted to obey him. But this king-to-be wasn't at all what Samuel expected.

1 Samuel 16:1-13, NLT

Finally, the LORD said to Samuel, "You have mourned long enough for Saul. I have rejected him as king of Israel. Now fill your horn with olive oil and go to Bethlehem. Find a man named Jesse who lives there, for I have selected one of his sons to be my new king."

But Samuel asked, "How can I do that? If Saul hears about it, he will kill me."

"Take a heifer with you," the LORD replied, "and say that you have come to make a sacrifice to the LORD. Invite Jesse to the sacrifice, and I will show you which of his sons to anoint for me."

So Samuel did as the LORD instructed him. When he arrived at Bethlehem, the leaders of the town became afraid. "What's wrong?" they asked. "Do you come in peace?"

"Yes," Samuel replied. "I have come to sacrifice to the LORD. Purify yourselves and come with me to the sacrifice." Then Samuel performed the purification rite for Jesse and his sons and invited them, too.

When they arrived, Samuel took one look at Eliab and thought, "Surely this is the LORD's anointed!"

But the LORD said to Samuel, "Don't judge by his appearance or height, for I have rejected him. The LORD doesn't make decisions the way you do! People judge by outward appearance, but the LORD looks at a person's thoughts and intentions."

Then Jesse told his son Abinadab to step forward and walk in front of Samuel. But Samuel said, "This is not the one the LORD has chosen." Next Jesse summoned Shammah, but Samuel said, "Neither is this the one the LORD has chosen." In the same way all seven of Jesse's sons were presented to Samuel. But Samuel said to Jesse, "The LORD has not chosen any of these." Then Samuel asked, "Are these all the sons you have?"

"There is still the youngest," Jesse replied. "But he's out in the fields watching the sheep."

"Send for him at once," Samuel said. "We will not sit down to eat until he arrives." So Jesse sent for him. He was ruddy and handsome, with pleasant eyes.

And the LORD said, "This is the one; anoint him."

So as David stood there among his brothers, Samuel took the olive oil he had brought and poured it on David's head. And the Spirit of the LORD came mightily upon him from that day on. Then Samuel returned to Ramah.

Take ANOTHER LOOK

As a shepherd, David knew a lot about sheep. Maybe that's why, years later, he wrote a psalm that showed how God is a shepherd to all of us. That familiar psalm is below.

Psalm 23, NLT

The Lord is my shepherd;
  I have everything I need.
He lets me rest in green meadows;
  he leads me beside peaceful streams.
  He renews my strength.
He guides me along right paths,
  bringing honor to his name.

Even when I walk
  through the dark valley of death,
I will not be afraid,
  for you are close beside me.
Your rod and your staff
  protect and comfort me.

You prepare a feast for me
  in the presence of my enemies.
You welcome me as a guest,
  anointing my head with oil.
  My cup overflows with blessings.
Surely your goodness and unfailing love will pursue me
  all the days of my life,
and I will live in the house of the Lord
  forever.

Here's What I Think

Daniel, age 15

Have you ever eaten out of a box of assorted chocolates? When I was younger my mom offered me a chocolate out of one such box. Of course I looked for the biggest, tastiest chocolate. I found it! A beautiful something—of what, I wasn't sure yet. So I took the plunge, threw the whole thing in my mouth and started chewing.

Only then did I realize that it had some nasty almond center. I judged that candy by its outward appearance, not by looking to the heart of the candy.

I'm really fortunate that God doesn't do that. "The LORD looks at a person's thoughts and intentions" (1 Samuel 16:7). God doesn't see the big tasty exterior but that nasty almond center. Since God looks at our hearts, our thoughts, and our intentions, we had better make sure we are keeping our hearts pure.

Daniel

Look beyond what's on the outside to the inner heart.

DAVID AND GOLIATH

Introduction

Remember the Philistines—the people Samson battled? They're baaaack. This time, they had a champion with them. Sometimes, two armies would send out one fighter each, instead of everyone going into battle. That person was usually their best fighter. Goliath was the champion of the Philistines. The soldiers of Israel were terrified of him. So nobody wanted to be Israel's champion . . . except David. But David was just a teen. In size he seemed like a toddler in comparison with a professional basketball player. But David had a secret weapon, one that Goliath didn't have. He had God.

1 Samuel 17:32-51, NLT

"Don't worry about a thing," David told Saul. "I'll go fight this Philistine!"

"Don't be ridiculous!" Saul replied. "There is no way you can go against this Philistine. You are only a boy, and he has been in the army since he was a boy!"

But David persisted. "I have been taking care of my father's sheep," he said. "When a lion or a bear comes to steal a lamb from the flock, I go after it with a club and take the lamb from its mouth. If the animal turns on me, I catch it by the jaw and club it to death. I have done this to both lions and bears, and I'll do it to this pagan Philistine, too, for he has defied the armies of the living God! The LORD who saved me from the claws of the lion and the bear will save me from this Philistine!"

Saul finally consented. "All right, go ahead," he said. "And may the LORD be with you!"

Then Saul gave David his own armor—a bronze helmet and a coat of mail. David put it on, strapped the sword over it, and took a step or two to see what it was like, for he had never worn such things before. "I can't go in these," he protested. "I'm not used to them." So he took them off again. He picked up five smooth stones from a stream and put them in his shepherd's bag. Then, armed only with his shepherd's staff and sling, he started across to fight Goliath.

Goliath walked out toward David with his shield bearer ahead of him, sneering in contempt at this ruddy-faced boy. "Am I a dog," he roared at David, "that you come at me with a stick?" And he cursed David by the names of his gods. "Come over here, and I'll give your flesh to the birds and wild animals!" Goliath yelled.

David shouted in reply, "You come to me with sword, spear, and javelin, but I come to you in the name of the LORD Almighty—the God of the armies of Israel, whom you have defied. Today the LORD will conquer you, and I will kill you and cut off your head. And then I will give the dead bodies of your men to the birds and wild animals, and the whole world will know that there is a God in Israel! And everyone will know that the LORD does not need weapons to rescue his people. It is his battle, not ours. The LORD will give you to us!"

As Goliath moved closer to attack, David quickly ran out to meet him. Reaching into his shepherd's bag and taking out a stone, he hurled it from his sling and hit the Philistine in the forehead. The stone sank in, and Goliath stumbled and fell face downward to the ground. So David triumphed over the Philistine giant with only a stone and sling. And since he had no sword, he ran over and pulled Goliath's sword from its sheath. David used it to kill the giant and cut off his head.

Take ANOTHER LOOK

Like David, we might face some "giant" problems. But our secret weapon is God. During the New Testament times, the apostle Paul wrote a letter to Christians in Rome who were being mistreated because of their faith. He wanted them to know that, through God, we can be victorious like David.

Romans 8:35-37, NLT

Can anything ever separate us from Christ's love? Does it mean he no longer loves us if we have trouble or calamity, or are persecuted, or are hungry or cold or in danger or threatened with death? (Even the Scriptures say, "For your sake we are killed every day; we are being slaughtered like sheep.") No, despite all these things, overwhelming victory is ours through Christ, who loved us.

Here's What I Think

Janna, age 14

David was a young guy. He was only a teenager! (Think of a friend of yours going to fight a giant!) Yet he still was man enough to trust God and fight Goliath. David knew that he was fighting for the Lord—and more importantly, that God was fighting for him.

In our lives we have many giants. They may not look like Goliath, but those giants are every bit as scary and frightening. Even if we think they aren't important, we still need to conquer them. And we can only do that with the help of God. Something I struggle with is telling others about my faith. Though at times it doesn't seem like a big deal, I still get afraid when I need to tell people about Jesus and what he is doing in my life. That's a giant in my life that I need God to help me overcome. And the awesome thing is, I know all I have to do is ask!

Janna

God will help you defeat
the giants in your life.

»»» A FRIEND IN NEED—
A FRIEND INDEED «««

Introduction

Jonathan had it all: success as a soldier and a father who was king of Israel. But one of the most important things to him was his friendship with David. In a time when rivals to the throne were usually put to death, the friendship of David and Jonathan was rare. David's popularity as a result of defeating Goliath was not unknown to Jonathan. It certainly made a bad impression on Saul. Yet Jonathan chose not to be jealous. Instead, he risked his life to befriend a man his father hated. This man would someday become something that Jonathan would never be—king of Israel.

1 Samuel 20:1-17, NLT

David now fled from Naioth in Ramah and found Jonathan. "What have I done?" he exclaimed. "What is my crime? How have I offended your father that he is so determined to kill me?"

"That's not true!" Jonathan protested. "I'm sure he's not planning any such thing, for he always tells me everything he's going to do, even the little things. I know he wouldn't hide something like this from me. It just isn't so!"

Then David took an oath before Jonathan and said, "Your father knows perfectly well about our friendship, so he has said to himself, 'I won't tell Jonathan—why should I hurt him?' But I swear to you that I am only a step away from death! I swear it by the LORD and by your own soul!"

"Tell me what I can do!" Jonathan exclaimed.

David replied, "Tomorrow we celebrate the new moon festival. I've always eaten with your father on this occasion, but tomorrow I'll hide in the field and stay there until the evening of the third day. If your father asks where I am, tell him I asked permission to go home to Bethlehem for an annual family sacrifice. If he says, 'Fine!' then you will know all is well. But if he is angry and loses his temper, then you will know he was planning to kill me. Show me this kindness as my sworn friend—for we made a covenant together before the

LORD—or kill me yourself if I have sinned against your father. But please don't betray me to him!"

"Never!" Jonathan exclaimed. "You know that if I had the slightest notion my father was planning to kill you, I would tell you at once."

Then David asked, "How will I know whether or not your father is angry?"

"Come out to the field with me," Jonathan replied. And they went out there together. Then Jonathan told David, "I promise by the LORD, the God of Israel, that by this time tomorrow, or the next day at the latest, I will talk to my father and let you know at once how he feels about you. If he speaks favorably about you, I will let you know. But if he is angry and wants you killed, may the LORD kill me if I don't warn you so you can escape and live. May the LORD be with you as he used to be with my father. And may you treat me with the faithful love of the LORD as long as I live. But if I die, treat my family with this faithful love, even when the LORD destroys all your enemies."

So Jonathan made a covenant with David, saying, "May the LORD destroy all your enemies!" And Jonathan made David reaffirm his vow of friendship again, for Jonathan loved David as much as he loved himself.

Take ANOTHER LOOK

Wonder what happened next? David and Jonathan worked out a plan to signal whether it was safe for David to return to the king's service or whether he should leave immediately. Then Jonathan went to the celebration to check on his father's reaction to David's absence. What Jonathan observed and heard left no doubt as to what Saul's intentions were toward David. Read on.

1 Samuel 20:24-34, NLT

So David hid himself in the field, and when the new moon festival began, the king sat down to eat. He sat at his usual place against the wall, with Jonathan sitting opposite him and Abner beside him. But David's place was empty. Saul didn't say anything about it that day, for he said to himself, "Something must have made David ceremonially unclean. Yes, that must be why he's not here." But when David's place was empty again the next day, Saul asked Jonathan, "Why hasn't the son of Jesse been here for dinner either yesterday or today?"

Jonathan replied, "David earnestly asked me if he could go to Bethlehem. He wanted to take part in a family sacrifice. His brother demanded that he be there, so I told him he could go. That's why he isn't here."

Saul boiled with rage at Jonathan. "You stupid son of a whore!" he swore at him. "Do you think I don't know that you want David to be king in your place, shaming yourself and your mother? As long as that son of Jesse is alive, you'll never be king. Now go and get him so I can kill him!"

"But what has he done?" Jonathan demanded. "Why should he be put to death?" Then Saul hurled his spear at Jonathan, intending to kill him. So at last Jonathan realized that his father was really determined to kill David. Jonathan left the table in fierce anger and refused to eat all that day, for he was crushed by his father's shameful behavior toward David.

Here's What I Think

Faith, age 14

Friends are so cool! Even if we have some little disagreements, I know that they love and support me. There's nothing like going through life with a friend who would give his life for you—like David and Jonathan's friendship.

I don't know if I'd be able to give my life for someone else, but I do know that I can be there for my friends when life's storms are hitting them hard. Whether it's dealing with their parents' divorce, health problems, the stresses of school, or just life in general, I try to be the best friend I can. Sometimes they need a shoulder to cry on more than they need someone to make them smile. As it says in Ecclesiastes 3:4, there's "a time to cry and a time to laugh." A real friend knows the difference. What kind of friend are you?

Faith

Friends are one of God's special gifts.

»»» DAVID SPARES SAUL'S LIFE «««

Óntroduction

Saul's actions showed a man who had lost control. He tried numerous times to kill David and anyone else who offered David protection. Saul's persistence kept David on the run for many years. But one day, God allowed Saul to fall into David's hands. If an enemy were at your mercy, what would you do?

1 Samuel 24:1-22, NLT

After Saul returned from fighting the Philistines, he was told that David had gone into the wilderness of Engedi. So Saul chose three thousand special troops from throughout Israel and went to search for David and his men near the rocks of the wild goats. At the place where the road passes some sheepfolds, Saul went into a cave to relieve himself. But as it happened, David and his men were hiding in that very cave!

"Now's your opportunity!" David's men whispered to him. "Today is the day the LORD was talking about when he said, 'I will certainly put Saul into your power, to do with as you wish.'" Then David crept forward and cut off a piece of Saul's robe.

But then David's conscience began bothering him because he had cut Saul's robe. "The LORD knows I shouldn't have done it," he said to his men. "It is a serious thing to attack the LORD's anointed one, for the LORD himself has chosen him." So David sharply rebuked his men and did not let them kill Saul.

After Saul had left the cave and gone on his way, David came out and shouted after him, "My lord the king!" And when Saul looked around, David bowed low before him.

Then he shouted to Saul, "Why do you listen to the people who say I am trying to harm you? This very day you can see with your own eyes it isn't true. For the LORD placed you at my mercy back there in the cave, and some of my men told me to kill you, but I spared you. For I said, 'I will never harm him—he is the LORD's anointed one.' Look, my father, at what I have in my hand. It is a piece of your robe! I cut it off, but I didn't kill you. This proves that I am not trying to harm you and that I have not sinned against you, even though you have been hunting for me to kill me. "The LORD will decide between us. Perhaps the LORD will punish you for what you are trying to do to me, but I will never harm you. As that old proverb says, 'From evil people come evil deeds.' So you can be sure I will never harm you. Who is the king of Israel trying to catch anyway? Should he spend his time chasing one who is as worthless as a dead dog or a flea? May the LORD judge which of us is right and punish the guilty one. He is my advocate, and he will rescue me from your power!"

Saul called back, "Is that really you, my son David?" Then he began to cry. And he said to David, "You are a better man than I am, for you have repaid me good for evil. Yes, you have been wonderfully kind to me today, for when the LORD put me in a place where you could have killed me, you didn't do it. Who else would let his enemy get away when he had him in his power? May the LORD reward you well for the kindness you have shown me today. And now I realize that you are surely going to be king, and Israel will flourish under your rule. Now, swear to me by the LORD that when that happens you will not kill my family and destroy my line of descendants!"

So David promised, and Saul went home. But David and his men went back to their stronghold.

Take ANOTHER LOOK God kept David from taking revenge another time too. After guarding the flocks of a man named Nabal, David asked him for food for himself and for his men. But Nabal said no! So David went to take revenge on Nabal, but was stopped by Nabal's wife.

1 Samuel 25:23-33, NLT

When Abigail saw David, she quickly got off her donkey and bowed low before him. She fell at his feet and said, "I accept all blame in this matter, my lord. Please listen to what I have to say. I know Nabal is a wicked and ill-tempered man; please don't pay any attention to him. He is a fool, just as his name suggests. But I never even saw the messengers you sent.

"Now, my lord, as surely as the LORD lives and you yourself live, since the LORD has kept you from murdering and taking vengeance into your own hands, let all your enemies be as cursed as Nabal is. And here is a present I have brought to you and your young men. Please forgive me if I have offended in any way. The LORD will surely reward you with a lasting dynasty, for you are fighting the LORD's battles. And you have not done wrong throughout your entire life.

"Even when you are chased by those who seek your life, you are safe in the care of the LORD your God, secure in his treasure pouch! But the lives of your enemies will disappear like stones shot from a sling! When the LORD has done all he promised and has made you leader of Israel, don't let this be a blemish on your record. Then you won't have to carry on your conscience the staggering burden of needless bloodshed and vengeance. And when the LORD has done these great things for you, please remember me!"

David replied to Abigail, "Praise the LORD, the God of Israel, who has sent you to meet me today! Thank God for your good sense! Bless you for keeping me from murdering the man and carrying out vengeance with my own hands."

Here's What I Think

Kali, age 18

Whenever I am in a situation where I'm being picked on or made fun of, I always want to get back at those people. Whether I beat them in a game, fight back, or think up a smart comeback to a mean joke, I like to give them a taste of their own medicine. But I've learned over the years that my immediate reaction is not always the best solution. James 1:2-4 talks about dealing with hard situations and turning them into opportunities for joy so that our faith, endurance, and strength of character can grow.

Consider David's situation. He was in hiding, knowing that Saul was out to kill him. And when Saul was on a break in the very cave where David was hiding, David *spared* Saul's life. The easier route would seem to have been killing Saul, but in sparing his enemy's life, David was able to build his faith and character. So before we are tempted to drop that nasty comeback, throw that punch, or play that practical joke, remember David and the grace he showed Saul. Then we can try giving the "Sauls" in our lives a little grace as well.

Kali

Treat your enemies with love, not hate.

KING
AT LAST

Introduction

Samuel anointed David as the next king of Israel. But David spent several years running for his life. During that time, the Philistines killed Saul's sons, including David's good friend Jonathan. Sadly, Saul took his own life. But still, David didn't rush to take over the kingdom. First, he talked to God. After that, he became king of Judah—one tribe out of 12. Seven years later he was ready for the whole kingdom. In the end, David waited about 20 years to be king over all of Israel. Now that he was king, David wanted to build God a temple. Read what God told the prophet Nathan to say.

2 Samuel 7:5-16, NLT

"Go and tell my servant David, 'This is what the LORD says: Are you the one to build me a temple to live in? I have never lived in a temple, from the day I brought the Israelites out of Egypt until now. My home has always been a tent, moving from one place to another. And I have never once complained to Israel's leaders, the shepherds of my people Israel. I have never asked them, "Why haven't you built me a beautiful cedar temple?"'

"Now go and say to my servant David, 'This is what the LORD Almighty says: I chose you to lead my people Israel when you were just a shepherd boy, tending your sheep out in the pasture. I have been with you wherever you have gone, and I have destroyed all your enemies. Now I will make your name famous throughout the earth! And I have provided a permanent homeland for my people Israel, a secure place where they will never be disturbed. It will be their own land where wicked nations won't oppress them as they did in the past, from the time I appointed judges to rule my people. And I will keep you safe from all your enemies.

" 'And now the LORD declares that he will build a house for you—a dynasty of kings! For when you die, I will raise up one of your descendants, and I will make his kingdom strong. He is the one who will build a house—a temple—for my name. And I will establish the throne of his kingdom forever. I will be his father, and he will be my son. If he sins, I will use other nations to punish him. But my unfailing love will not be taken from him as I took it from Saul, whom I removed before you. Your dynasty and your kingdom will continue for all time before me, and your throne will be secure forever.'"

Take ANOTHER LOOK

God's promise to David was fulfilled over 1000 years later. Jesus was the one whose throne God promised to secure forever. He was born into David's family line, as the angel Gabriel told his mother Mary.

Luke 1:30-33, NLT

"Don't be frightened, Mary," the angel told her, "for God has decided to bless you! You will become pregnant and have a son, and you are to name him Jesus. He will be very great and will be called the Son of the Most High. And the Lord God will give him the throne of his ancestor David. And he will reign over Israel forever; his Kingdom will never end!"

Here's What I Think

Mike, age 19

A lot of times I worry about my future. What will I be when I get older? What skills do I need to learn now so that I will be ready for life when that time comes? But then I think of David. Chances are he was not attending King of Israel School when he was younger. But out of David's obedient heart God produced greatness. If he could take a young shepherd boy and make him a king, then the only thing I need to be worried about is how I can serve God the best way possible. That means preparing myself the best way I can—just like David did—so that at the right time, I'll be ready to serve.

Mike

When it comes to your future, put God in charge.

»» A PROMISE KEPT ««

Introduction

Remember (see page 117) how David and Jonathan promised to be friends forever? They also promised to look out for each other's families. Even though Jonathan was dead, David wanted to keep his promise by being kind to Jonathan's son. Usually, one of the first things that a new king did was to wipe out the family members of past kings. They did this to make sure that no one would challenge their right to rule. Not David! He depended on God to make his kingdom secure. David also depended on God to help him show love to the grandson of an enemy.

2 Samuel 9:1-13, NLT

One day David began wondering if anyone in Saul's family was still alive, for he had promised Jonathan that he would show kindness to them. He summoned a man named Ziba, who had been one of Saul's servants. "Are you Ziba?" the king asked.

"Yes sir, I am," Ziba replied.

The king then asked him, "Is anyone still alive from Saul's family? If so, I want to show God's kindness to them in any way I can."

Ziba replied, "Yes, one of Jonathan's sons is still alive, but he is crippled."

"Where is he?" the king asked.

"In Lo-debar," Ziba told him, "at the home of Makir son of Ammiel." So David sent for him and brought him from Makir's home. His name was Mephibosheth; he was Jonathan's son and Saul's grandson. When he came to David, he bowed low in great fear and said, "I am your servant."

But David said, "Don't be afraid! I've asked you to come so that I can be kind to you because of my vow to your father, Jonathan. I will give you all the land that once belonged to your grandfather Saul, and you may live here with me at the palace!"

Mephibosheth fell to the ground before the king. "Should the king show such kindness to a dead dog like me?" he exclaimed.

Then the king summoned Saul's servant Ziba and said, "I have given your master's grandson everything that belonged to Saul and his family. You and your sons and servants are to farm the land for him to produce food for his family. But Mephibosheth will live here at the palace with me."

Ziba, who had fifteen sons and twenty servants, replied, "Yes, my lord; I will do all that you have commanded." And from that time on, Mephibosheth ate regularly with David, as though he were one of his own sons. Mephibosheth had a young son named Mica. And from then on, all the members of Ziba's household were Mephibosheth's servants. And Mephibosheth, who was crippled in both feet, moved to Jerusalem to live at the palace.

Take ANOTHER LOOK

When he preached the Sermon on the Mount Jesus gave advice on showing love to an enemy. It was hard advice for the people to hear because the Jewish people despised the Romans who were cruel and oppressive. But Jesus wasn't talking about having affection for our enemies. Rather, he was talking about acting in the best interest of our enemies. Check it out.

Luke 6:27-36, NLT

"But if you are willing to listen, I say, love your enemies. Do good to those who hate you. Pray for the happiness of those who curse you. Pray for those who hurt you. If someone slaps you on one cheek, turn the other cheek. If someone demands your coat, offer your shirt also. Give what you have to anyone who asks you for it; and when things are taken away from you, don't try to get them back. Do for others as you would like them to do for you.

"Do you think you deserve credit merely for loving those who love you? Even the sinners do that! And if you do good only to those who do good to you, is that so wonderful? Even sinners do that much! And if you lend money only to those who can repay you, what good is that? Even sinners will lend to their own kind for a full return.

"Love your enemies! Do good to them! Lend to them! And don't be concerned that they might not repay. Then your reward from heaven will be very great, and you will truly be acting as children of the Most High, for he is kind to the unthankful and to those who are wicked. You must be compassionate, just as your Father is compassionate."

Here's What I Think

Nicee, age 14

Low self-esteem can be a huge problem for many people. Just like Mephibosheth considered himself a "dead dog" until David befriended him, there may be people in our own lives who don't feel very good about themselves. I once knew a girl who had very low self-esteem due to the negative things her friends constantly said to her. Over time we became good friends, and we talked about everything.

She asked me for advice, and I'd always tell her what I felt was right, based on what my parents taught me. As a result of our close relationship, she began to think differently about a lot of things. One day, out of the blue, her mother thanked me for being such a good friend, role model, and positive influence in her daughter's life. I was honored that day because God was changing lives through me without my even knowing. For her mother to acknowledge and appreciate it was a mind-blowing experience for me. Who can you be a "David" to in your life?

Nicee

Being a friend can make a
big difference in someone's life.

CRIME AND PUNISHMENT

Introduction

Even a man after God's own heart can mess up. And David did in a major way. The problem started with downtime. The king was at home, bored, while his army went out to battle. Big mistake. He even came up with a plan to cover his tracks. But Mess-up + Cover-up still = Busted. God knew everything. The consequences of David's actions were more damaging than he could have imagined.

2 Samuel 11:1-5, 14-22; 12:1-12, NLT

The following spring, the time of year when kings go to war, David sent Joab and the Israelite army to destroy the Ammonites. In the process they laid siege to the city of Rabbah. But David stayed behind in Jerusalem.

Late one afternoon David got out of bed after taking a nap and went for a stroll on the roof of the palace. As he looked out over the city, he noticed a woman of unusual beauty taking a bath. He sent someone to find out who she was, and he was told, "She is Bathsheba, the daughter of Eliam and the wife of Uriah the Hittite." Then David sent for her; and when she came to the palace, he slept with her. (She had just completed the purification rites after having her menstrual period.) Then she returned home. Later, when Bathsheba discovered that she was pregnant, she sent a message to inform David.

David Arranges for Uriah's Death, 11:14-22

So the next morning David wrote a letter to Joab and gave it to Uriah to deliver. The letter instructed Joab, "Station Uriah on the front lines where the battle is fiercest. Then pull back so that he will be killed." So Joab assigned Uriah to a spot close to the city wall where he knew the enemy's strongest men were fighting. And Uriah was killed along with several other Israelite soldiers.

Then Joab sent a battle report to David. He told his messenger, "Report all the news of the battle to the king. But he might get angry and ask, 'Why did the troops go so close to the city? Didn't they know there would be shooting from the walls? Wasn't Gideon's son Abimelech killed at Thebez by a woman who threw a millstone down on him?' Then tell him, 'Uriah the Hittite was killed, too.' "

So the messenger went to Jerusalem and gave a complete report to David.

Nathan Rebukes David, 12:1-12

So the LORD sent Nathan the prophet to tell David this story: "There were two men in a certain town. One was rich, and one was poor. The rich man owned many sheep and cattle. The poor man owned nothing but a little lamb he had worked hard to buy. He raised that little lamb, and it grew up with his children. It ate from the man's own plate and drank from his cup. He cuddled it in his arms like a baby daughter. One day a guest arrived at the home of the rich man. But instead of killing a lamb from his own flocks for food, he took the poor man's lamb and killed it and served it to his guest."

David was furious. "As surely as the LORD lives," he vowed, "any man who would do such a thing deserves to die! He must repay four lambs to the poor man for the one he stole and for having no pity."

Then Nathan said to David, "You are that man! The LORD, the God of Israel, says, 'I anointed you king of Israel and saved you from the power of Saul. I gave you his house and his wives and the kingdoms of Israel and Judah. And if that had not been enough, I would have given you much, much more. Why, then, have you despised the word of the LORD and done this horrible deed? For you have murdered Uriah and stolen his wife. From this time on, the sword will be a constant threat to your family, because you have despised me by taking Uriah's wife to be your own.

" 'Because of what you have done, I, the LORD, will cause your own household to rebel against you. I will give your wives to another man, and he will go to bed with them in public view. You did it secretly, but I will do this to you openly in the sight of all Israel.' "

Take ANOTHER LOOK

David wrote Psalm 51 as a way of telling God, "I'm sorry." In this psalm, David doesn't blame others or try to make excuses. He accepted the responsibility for what he did and admitted that he had hurt God. Best of all, he wanted to be right with God. His actions showed one reason why he was a man after God's own heart.

Psalm 51:1-2, NLT

Have mercy on me, O God,
   because of your unfailing love.
Because of your great compassion,
   blot out the stain of my sins.
Wash me clean from my guilt.
   Purify me from my sin.

Here's What I Think

Jammeshia, age 17

We usually don't like to think about our sins. But sin is the one big thing that keeps us separated from God. A lot of times when we do something wrong, we try to cover it up—thinking that will make things better. Trust me. It won't! I remember a time when I lied to cover up something that I had done, but it didn't stop there. Soon I had to lie again to cover up for the first lie I told. Like David, I did not want to admit to my sin. But it only led to more trouble. In this passage you can see that David (like all of us) had messed up. And he made his situation worse by not coming to God for help. God only wants what is best for us, but we first have to recognize our sin, confess it, and then turn from it before we can be really happy!

Jammeshia

Confess your sin—don't cover it up.

A SON REBELS

Introduction

Remember God's promise to David? "Because of what you have done, I . . . will cause your own household to rebel against you." Well, that's what happened. After killing his half brother because of another family matter, David's son Absalom ran away. Although David allowed him to return to the kingdom, David ignored his son for two years. But after making up with his father, Absalom began to think that he would make a better king than David. So Absalom led a rebellion against his father. Read to see what happened.

2 Samuel 18:1-18, NLT

David now appointed generals and captains to lead his troops. One-third were placed under Joab, one-third under Joab's brother Abishai son of Zeruiah, and one-third under Ittai the Gittite. The king told his troops, "I am going out with you."

But his men objected strongly. "You must not go," they urged. "If we have to turn and run—and even if half of us die—it will make no difference to Absalom's troops; they will be looking only for you. You are worth ten thousand of us, and it is better that you stay here in the city and send us help if we need it."

"If you think that's the best plan, I'll do it," the king finally agreed. So he stood at the gate of the city as all the divisions of troops passed by. And the king gave this command to Joab, Abishai, and Ittai: "For my sake, deal gently with young Absalom." And all the troops heard the king give this order to his commanders.

So the battle began in the forest of Ephraim, and the Israelite troops were beaten back by David's men. There was a great slaughter, and twenty thousand men laid down their lives that day. The battle raged all across the countryside, and more men died because of the forest than were killed by the sword.

During the battle, Absalom came unexpectedly upon some of David's men. He tried to escape on his mule, but as he rode beneath the thick branches of a great oak, his head got caught. His mule kept going and left him dangling in the air. One of David's men saw what had happened and told Joab, "I saw Absalom dangling in a tree."

"What?" Joab demanded. "You saw him there and didn't kill him? I would have rewarded you with ten pieces of silver and a hero's belt!"

"I wouldn't do it for a thousand pieces of silver," the man replied. "We all heard the king say to you and Abishai and Ittai, 'For my sake, please don't harm young Absalom.' And if I had betrayed the king by killing his son—and the king would certainly find out who did it—you yourself would be the first to abandon me."

"Enough of this nonsense," Joab said. Then he took three daggers and plunged them into Absalom's heart as he dangled from the oak still alive. Ten of Joab's young armor bearers then surrounded Absalom and killed him. Then Joab blew the trumpet, and his men returned from chasing the army of Israel. They threw Absalom's body into a deep pit in the forest and piled a great heap of stones over it. And the army of Israel fled to their homes.

During his lifetime, Absalom had built a monument to himself in the King's Valley, for he had said, "I have no son to carry on my name." He named the monument after himself, and it is known as Absalom's Monument to this day.

Take ANOTHER LOOK

David still loved his son, even though Absalom had rebelled against him. He wrote Psalm 3 while on the run from Absalom. How sad David must have felt, knowing that his own son wanted to hurt him. Yet he trusted God to help him.

Psalm 3:1-6, NLT

O Lord, I have so many enemies;
    so many are against me.
So many are saying,
    "God will never rescue him!"

But you, O Lord, are a shield around me,
    my glory, and the one who lifts my head high.
I cried out to the Lord,
    and he answered me from his holy mountain.

I lay down and slept.
    I woke up in safety,
    for the Lord was watching over me.
I am not afraid of ten thousand enemies
    who surround me on every side.

Here's What I Think

Julie, age 18

Sometimes rebellion feels like a good idea. No, you probably don't want to lead an army in battle like Absalom did . . . but when you feel like going against authority, breaking the rules, or arguing with your parents' decisions, you're being tempted to rebel.

Just like it did for Absalom, rebellion usually means trouble. A friend of mine rebelled by piercing her ears when her parents told her *not* to do so. Because she didn't have her parents' permission, my friend decided to pierce them by herself . . . and because she didn't have the right equipment, her ears became very infected. In the end, my friend's rebellion only brought her trouble—not the fun and fashion she'd expected!

When you feel like going against your parents or breaking a rule, remember Absalom's story. Rebellion will only lead to trouble!

Julie

Rebellion is a one-way ticket to trouble.

A WISE CHOICE

Introduction

David ruled Israel for **40 years** (seven years as king over Judah; 33 years as king of the rest of Israel). Before he died, one of his sons tried to take over the throne. But David promised Bathsheba that their son Solomon would be king. And that's what happened. Now, running a kingdom was a huge responsibility—one that Solomon took seriously. He wanted to rule the people wisely. So when God offered to give Solomon whatever he wanted, he knew just what to ask for.

1 Kings 3:3-28, NLT

Solomon loved the LORD and followed all the instructions of his father, David, except that Solomon, too, offered sacrifices and burned incense at the local altars. The most important of these altars was at Gibeon, so the king went there and sacrificed one thousand burnt offerings. That night the LORD appeared to Solomon in a dream, and God said, "hat do you want? Ask, and I will give it to you!"

Solomon replied, "You were wonderfully kind to my father, David, because he was honest and true and faithful to you. And you have continued this great kindness to him today by giving him a son to succeed him. O LORD my God, now you have made me king instead of my father, David, but I am like a little child who doesn't know his way around. And here I am among your own chosen people, a nation so great they are too numerous to count! Give me an understanding mind so that I can govern your people well and know the difference between right and wrong. For who by himself is able to govern this great nation of yours?"

The Lord was pleased with Solomon's reply and was glad that he had asked for wisdom. So God replied, "Because you have asked for wisdom in governing my people and have not asked for a long life or riches for yourself or the death of your enemies—I will give you what you asked for! I will give you a wise and understanding mind such as no one else has ever had or ever will have! And I will also give you what you did not ask for—riches and honor! No other king in all the world will be compared to you for the rest of your life! And if you follow me and obey my commands as your father, David, did, I will give you a long life."

Then Solomon woke up and realized it had been a dream. He returned to Jerusalem and stood before the Ark of the Lord's covenant, where he sacrificed burnt offerings and peace offerings. Then he invited all his officials to a great banquet.

Solomon Judges Wisely

Some time later, two prostitutes came to the king to have an argument settled. "Please, my lord," one of them began, "this woman and I live in the same house. I gave birth to a baby while she was with me in the house. Three days later, she also had a baby. We were alone; there were only two of us in the house. But her baby died during the night when she rolled over on it. Then she got up in the night and took my son from beside me while I was asleep. She laid her dead child in my arms and took mine to sleep beside her. And in the morning when I tried to nurse my son, he was dead! But when I looked more closely in the morning light, I saw that it wasn't my son at all."

Then the other woman interrupted, "It certainly was your son, and the living child is mine."

"No," the first woman said, "the dead one is yours, and the living one is mine." And so they argued back and forth before the king.

Then the king said, "Let's get the facts straight. Both of you claim the living child is yours, and each says that the dead child belongs to the other. All right, bring me a sword." So a sword was brought to the king. Then he said, "Cut the living child in two and give half to each of these women!"

Then the woman who really was the mother of the living child, and who loved him very much, cried out, "Oh no, my lord! Give her the child—please do not kill him!"

But the other woman said, "All right, he will be neither yours nor mine; divide him between us!"

Then the king said, "Do not kill him, but give the baby to the woman who wants him to live, for she is his mother!"

Word of the king's decision spread quickly throughout all Israel, and the people were awed as they realized the great wisdom God had given him to render decisions with justice.

Take ANOTHER LOOK

Solomon used his wisdom to write some of the wise sayings found in the book of Proverbs. The whole point of the book was to help people grow in wisdom. According to Solomon, a good place to start is by respecting God.

Proverbs 1:2-4,7, NLT

The purpose of these proverbs is to teach people wisdom and discipline, and to help them understand wise sayings. Through these proverbs, people will receive instruction in discipline, good conduct, and doing what is right, just, and fair. These proverbs will make the simpleminded clever. They will give knowledge and purpose to young people.

Fear of the LORD is the beginning of knowledge. Only fools despise wisdom and discipline.

Here's What I Think

Verity, age 13

Imagine getting to ask God for whatever you wanted! What would you ask for? Think about what we typically ask God for in our prayers—a good grade on a test, to be more popular, to win the game. We don't usually ask God to make us more wise or more faithful or loving. When Solomon asked God for wisdom, God was pleased because Solomon wanted good judgment instead of earthly desires. So God gave him not just wisdom, but also riches, and a long life too. I know that I ask for such selfish desires. Thankfully, God knows better than to give them to me. He knows that it would make me only more selfish and make me want even more earthly things. We can learn a good lesson from Solomon—ask God for characteristics that count and that please him, not ourselves.

Verity

Ask God for what counts—not what can be counted.

»» A HOUSE FOR GOD ««

Introduction

For centuries the people of Israel worshiped at the Tabernacle. They had moved it from place to place in the wilderness for 40 years. During David's time, a tabernacle had been placed in Jerusalem. But David wanted to build a more permanent home for God—a temple. But God told him no. (See page 123.) A warrior could not build the Temple for God. But a man of peace could. Israel was now in a time of peace, so the task of building the Temple fell on Solomon's shoulders. From start to finish, it took 13 years.

1 Kings 6:1-13; 8:1-11, NLT

It was in midspring, during the fourth year of Solomon's reign, that he began the construction of the Temple of the LORD. This was 480 years after the people of Israel were delivered from their slavery in the land of Egypt.

The Temple that King Solomon built for the LORD was 90 feet long, 30 feet wide, and 45 feet high. The foyer at the front of the Temple was 30 feet wide, running across the entire width of the Temple. It projected outward 15 feet from the front of the Temple. Solomon also made narrow, recessed windows throughout the Temple.

A complex of rooms was built against the outer walls of the Temple, all the way around the sides and rear of the building. The complex was three stories high, the bottom floor being 7 1/2 feet wide, the second floor 9 feet wide, and the top floor 10 1/2 feet wide. The rooms were connected to the walls of the Temple by beams resting on ledges built out from the wall. So the beams were not inserted into the walls themselves.

The stones used in the construction of the Temple were prefinished at the quarry, so the entire structure was built without the sound of hammer, ax, or any other iron tool at the building site.

The entrance to the bottom floor was on the south side of the Temple. There were winding stairs going up to the second floor, and another flight of stairs between the second and third floors. After completing the Temple structure, Solomon put in a ceiling made of beams and planks of cedar. As already stated, there was a complex of rooms on three sides of the building, attached to the Temple walls by cedar timbers. Each story of the complex was 7 1/2 feet high.

Then the LORD gave this message to Solomon: "Concerning this Temple you are building, if you keep all my laws and regulations and obey all my commands, I will fulfill through you the promise I made to your father, David. I will live among the people of Israel and never forsake my people."

The Ark Brought to the Temple, 8:1-11

Solomon then summoned the leaders of all the tribes and families of Israel to assemble in Jerusalem. They were to bring the Ark of the LORD's covenant from its location in the City of David, also known as Zion, to its new place in the Temple. They all assembled before the king at the annual Festival of Shelters in early autumn. When all the leaders of Israel arrived, the priests picked up the Ark. Then the priests and Levites took the Ark of the LORD, along with the Tabernacle and all its sacred utensils, and carried them up to the Temple. King Solomon and the entire community of Israel sacrificed sheep and oxen before the Ark in such numbers that no one could keep count!

Then the priests carried the Ark of the LORD's covenant into the inner sanctuary of the Temple—the Most Holy Place—and placed it beneath the wings of the cherubim. The cherubim spread their wings over the Ark, forming a canopy over the Ark and its carrying poles. These poles were so long that their ends could be seen from the front entrance of the Temple's main room—the Holy Place—but not from outside it. They are still there to this day. Nothing was in the Ark except the two stone tablets that Moses had placed there at Mount Sinai, where the LORD made a covenant with the people of Israel as they were leaving the land of Egypt.

As the priests came out of the inner sanctuary, a cloud filled the Temple of the LORD. The priests could not continue their work because the glorious presence of the LORD filled the Temple.

Take ANOTHER LOOK

Do you ever wonder why we don't worship in a temple today? Paul provided some insight into that question when he explained that, as believers in Christ, the Holy Spirit now lives in us so we together are the temple of God.

1 Corinthians 3:16,17, NLT

Don't you realize that all of you together are the temple of God and that the Spirit of God lives in you? God will bring ruin upon anyone who ruins this temple. For God's temple is holy, and you Christians are that temple.

1 Corinthians 6:19,20, NLT

Or don't you know that your body is the temple of the Holy Spirit, who lives in you and was given to you by God? You do not belong to yourself, for God bought you with a high price. So you must honor God with your body.

Here's What I Think

Jammeshia, age 17

Silence! Can you imagine silently building God's temple? No sound of a hammer or any tool. Just think of all the workers working hand in hand, but being silent out of respect for God. From this passage you can see how much these people cared about and loved God. They respected and honored him so much that they were willing to go the extra mile to keep his temple holy. That makes me stop and think how I should regard God's sanctuary today. Do I come into his presence with a bad attitude or totally focused on all the stuff I need to do after church? This passage helps me understand that the next time I enter into his building, I will enter with respect and honor for the God who created me!

Jammeshia

Enter God's presence with honor and respect.

A KINGDOM
DIVIDES

Introduction

Even though he was the wisest man around, Solomon didn't always make wise decisions. One unwise decision that he made was to marry hundreds of women from other nations. Many kings married princesses from other nations to gain political allies. That was Solomon's plan. But his plan broke one of God's rules. What was worse, some of these women influenced him to worship idols—statues that represented false gods. Because Solomon's heart turned away from him, God promised to take most of the kingdom away from him. He would leave Solomon's family line only one tribe.

1 Kings

12:1-20, NLT

Rehoboam went to Shechem, where all Israel had gathered to make him king. When Jeroboam son of Nebat heard of Solomon's death, he returned from Egypt, for he had fled to Egypt to escape from King Solomon. The leaders of Israel sent for Jeroboam, and the whole assembly of Israel went to speak with Rehoboam. "Your father was a hard master," they said. "Lighten the harsh labor demands and heavy taxes that your father imposed on us. Then we will be your loyal subjects."

Rehoboam replied, "Give me three days to think this over. Then come back for my answer." So the people went away.

Then King Rehoboam went to discuss the matter with the older men who had counseled his father, Solomon. "What is your advice?" he asked. "How should I answer these people?"

The older counselors replied, "If you are willing to serve the people today and give them a favorable answer, they will always be your loyal subjects."

But Rehoboam rejected the advice of the elders and instead asked the opinion of the young men who had grown up with him and who were now his advisers. "What is your advice?" he asked them. "How should I answer these people who want me to lighten the burdens imposed by my father?"

The young men replied, "This is what you should tell those complainers: 'My little finger is thicker than my father's waist—if you think he was hard on you, just wait and see what I'll be like! Yes, my father was harsh on you, but I'll be even harsher! My father used whips on you, but I'll use scorpions!'"

Three days later, Jeroboam and all the people returned to hear Rehoboam's decision, just as the king had requested. But Rehoboam spoke harshly to them, for he rejected the advice of the older counselors and followed the counsel of his younger advisers. He told the people, "My father was harsh on you, but I'll be even harsher! My father used whips on you, but I'll use scorpions!" So the king paid no attention to the people's demands. This turn of events was the will of the LORD, for it fulfilled the LORD's message to Jeroboam son of Nebat through the prophet Ahijah from Shiloh.

When all Israel realized that the king had rejected their request, they shouted, "Down with David and his dynasty! We have no share in Jesse's son! Let's go home, Israel! Look out for your own house, O David!" So the people of Israel returned home. But Rehoboam continued to rule over the Israelites who lived in the towns of Judah.

King Rehoboam sent Adoniram, who was in charge of the labor force, to restore order, but all Israel stoned him to death. When this news reached King Rehoboam, he quickly jumped into his chariot and fled to Jerusalem. The northern tribes of Israel have refused to be ruled by a descendant of David to this day.

When the people of Israel learned of Jeroboam's return from Egypt, they called an assembly and made him king over all Israel. So only the tribe of Judah remained loyal to the family of David.

Take ANOTHER LOOK

Many, many years later, one man's death would reunite the divided nation in a way that no one thought possible. Who was that man? Jesus, the Son of God. As the Jewish religious leaders plotted Jesus' death, the high priest made a surprising announcement. God led him to prophesy about Jesus, even though he didn't understand what he was saying. This event took place right after Jesus had raised Lazarus from the dead.

John 11:45-52, NLT

Many of the people who were with Mary believed in Jesus when they saw this happen. But some went to the Pharisees and told them what Jesus had done. Then the leading priests and Pharisees called the high council together to discuss the situation. "What are we going to do?" they asked each other. "This man certainly performs many miraculous signs. If we leave him alone, the whole nation will follow him, and then the Roman army will come and destroy both our Temple and our nation."

And one of them, Caiaphas, who was high priest that year, said, "How can you be so stupid? Why should the whole nation be destroyed? Let this one man die for the people."

This prophecy that Jesus should die for the entire nation came from Caiaphas in his position as high priest. He didn't think of it himself; he was inspired to say it. It was a prediction that Jesus' death would be not for Israel only, but for the gathering together of all the children of God scattered around the world.

Here's What I Think

Daniel, age 15

Have you ever said something so vile, so mean-spirited and painful that you would give anything just for a chance to make it right? Well, I have, and words are so powerful that you can never really fix what you say. Once it's out, it's out there, never to be taken back. You can apologize, but every time that person remembers what you've said, those words will play again in his head driving him into a deeper funk. I bet you can think of something someone said to you that you can't forget.

If you don't believe words have the power to change worlds then reread 1 Kings 12:1-20. Rehoboam destroyed his whole empire and the nation of Israel for generations to come with his hurtful words. Proverbs tells us that "the tongue can kill or nourish life" (18:21). Since words are so powerful, we need to think before we speak, asking, "Is what I'm going to say pleasing God and spreading his love, or will my words hurt others?"

Daniel

Think before you speak.

»»» PUT WINGS ON THAT ORDER! ««

Introduction

Israel was now two kingdoms: a northern kingdom (Israel) and a southern kingdom (Judah). From time to time, God instructed special speakers—prophets—to deliver his messages to the people of the divided nation of Israel. Over 60 years after Solomon's death, Elijah was selected to be a prophet. His territory was the northern kingdom—the kingdom of Ahab. Elijah's job was a tough and thankless one, because Ahab was the most evil king in Israel's history. The fact that Ahab was married to Jezebel, a woman from another nation, made Elijah's job even harder. Jezebel worshiped a false god named Baal, who was considered to be the god of rain and harvest. She encouraged her husband to worship this false god. Many of the people of Israel began to worship Baal too. Because Ahab led the people to stop worshiping the one true God, Elijah had a hard message for the king.

1 Kings 16:29–17:7, NLT

Ahab son of Omri began to rule over Israel in the thirty-eighth year of King Asa's reign in Judah. He reigned in Samaria twenty-two years. But Ahab did what was evil in the LORD's sight, even more than any of the kings before him. And as though it were not enough to live like Jeroboam, he married Jezebel, the daughter of King Ethbaal of the Sidonians, and he began to worship Baal. First he built a temple and an altar for Baal in Samaria. Then he set up an Asherah pole. He did more to arouse the anger of the LORD, the God of Israel, than any of the other kings of Israel before him.

It was during his reign that Hiel, a man from Bethel, rebuilt Jericho. When he laid the foundations, his oldest son, Abiram, died. And when he finally completed it by setting up the gates, his youngest son, Segub, died. This all happened according to the message from the LORD concerning Jericho spoken by Joshua son of Nun.

Elijah Fed by Ravens

Now Elijah, who was from Tishbe in Gilead, told King Ahab, "As surely as the LORD, the God of Israel, lives—the God whom I worship and serve—there will be no dew or rain during the next few years unless I give the word!"

Then the LORD said to Elijah, "Go to the east and hide by Kerith Brook at a place east of where it enters the Jordan River. Drink from the brook and eat what the ravens bring you, for I have commanded them to bring you food."

So Elijah did as the LORD had told him and camped beside Kerith Brook. The ravens brought him bread and meat each morning and evening, and he drank from the brook. But after a while the brook dried up, for there was no rainfall anywhere in the land.

Take ANOTHER LOOK

God used the ravens in other stories to teach important spiritual lessons. He taught Job about his care of the ravens. Later, during the first century, Jesus taught his disciples not to worry by reminding them of the way that God cares for the ravens. Next time you see a raven, maybe you'll remember that God cares for you too.

Job 38:41, NLT

Who provides food for the ravens when their young cry out to God as they wander about in hunger?

Luke 12:22-25, NLT

Then turning to his disciples, Jesus said, "So I tell you, don't worry about everyday life—whether you have enough food to eat or clothes to wear. For life consists of far more than food and clothing. Look at the ravens. They don't need to plant or harvest or put food in barns because God feeds them. And you are far more valuable to him than any birds! Can all your worries add a single moment to your life? Of course not!"

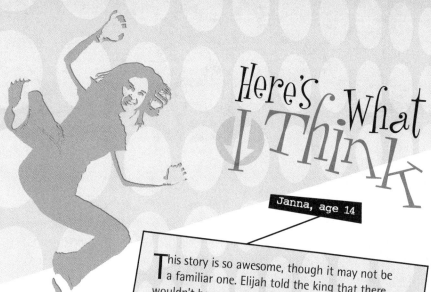

Here's What I Think

Janna, age 14

This story is so awesome, though it may not be a familiar one. Elijah told the king that there wouldn't be any rain unless God said so. That meant no water. Can you imagine not having water to drink? It's something so common that we often take it for granted. But God provided for his servant Elijah. He gave Elijah water from a brook and sent ravens to feed him.

About six months ago my mom got laid off from her job. She was making a lot of the income for our family. Yet God still provided. He may not send food via birds. But we have never gone without food or without water. God met all our needs. When we read a story like the one about Elijah, or when we see God at work in our own lives, we can know that our God can be trusted to provide—any time, any place, any way!

Janna

God will provide for you!

A WIDOW'S FAITH

Introduction

When rain doesn't fall, crops can't grow. That makes sense, right? As Elijah had predicted, God would allow no rain to fall on the land until he gave the word. Many people in and around Israel suffered during the drought. But God showed his concern for Elijah and for another family in an unusual way. He sent Elijah to an unlikely source for food—a poor widow in a foreign land. But providing food for Elijah, her son, and herself required that the widow have faith in Elijah's God.

1 Kings 17:8-24, NLT

Then the LORD said to Elijah, "Go and live in the village of Zarephath, near the city of Sidon. There is a widow there who will feed you. I have given her my instructions."

So he went to Zarephath. As he arrived at the gates of the village, he saw a widow gathering sticks, and he asked her, "Would you please bring me a cup of water?" As she was going to get it, he called to her, "Bring me a bite of bread, too."

But she said, "I swear by the LORD your God that I don't have a single piece of bread in the house. And I have only a handful of flour left in the jar and a little cooking oil in the bottom of the jug. I was just gathering a few sticks to cook this last meal, and then my son and I will die."

But Elijah said to her, "Don't be afraid! Go ahead and cook that 'last meal,' but bake me a little loaf of bread first. Afterward there will still be enough food for you and your son. For this is what the LORD, the God of Israel, says: There will always be plenty of flour and oil left in your containers until the time when the LORD sends rain and the crops grow again!"

So she did as Elijah said, and she and Elijah and her son continued to eat from her supply of flour and oil for many days. For no matter how much they used, there was always enough left in the containers, just as the LORD had promised through Elijah.

Some time later, the woman's son became sick. He grew worse and worse, and finally he died. She then said to Elijah, "O man of God, what have you done to me? Have you come here to punish my sins by killing my son?"

But Elijah replied, "Give me your son." And he took the boy's body from her, carried him up to the upper room, where he lived, and laid the body on his bed. Then Elijah cried out to the LORD, "O LORD my God, why have you brought tragedy on this widow who has opened her home to me, causing her son to die?"

And he stretched himself out over the child three times and cried out to the LORD, "O LORD my God, please let this child's life return to him." The LORD heard Elijah's prayer, and the life of the child returned, and he came back to life! Then Elijah brought him down from the upper room and gave him to his mother. "Look, your son is alive!" he said.

Then the woman told Elijah, "Now I know for sure that you are a man of God, and that the LORD truly speaks through you."

Take ANOTHER LOOK

In this story of Elijah and the widow, faith in God was the key ingredient. That's what Jesus wanted the people of his home-town to understand. They didn't believe that he could possibly be the promised Savior, because they had seen him grow up. They thought that Jesus was just the son of a carpenter. But Jesus wanted them to have faith in him. He used the example of the widow of Zarephath to remind the people that God always responds to faith.

Luke 4:16-26, NLT

When he came to the village of Nazareth, his boyhood home, he went as usual to the synagogue on the Sabbath and stood up to read the Scriptures. The scroll containing the messages of Isaiah the prophet was handed to him, and he unrolled the scroll to the place where it says:

"The Spirit of the Lord is upon me,
   for he has appointed me to preach Good News to the poor.
He has sent me to proclaim
   that captives will be released,
   that the blind will see,
   that the downtrodden will be freed from their oppressors,
   and that the time of the Lord's favor has come."

He rolled up the scroll, handed it back to the attendant, and sat down. Everyone in the synagogue stared at him intently. Then he said, "This Scripture has come true today before your very eyes!"

All who were there spoke well of him and were amazed by the gracious words that fell from his lips. "How can this be?" they asked. "Isn't this Joseph's son?"

Then he said, "Probably you will quote me that proverb, 'Physician, heal yourself"—meaning, 'Why don't you do miracles here in your hometown like those you did in Capernaum?' But the truth is, no prophet is accepted in his own hometown.

"Certainly there were many widows in Israel who needed help in Elijah's time, when there was no rain for three and a half years and hunger stalked the land. Yet Elijah was not sent to any of them. He was sent instead to a widow of Zarephath—a foreigner in the land of Sidon."

Here's What I Think

Faith, age 14

God provides us with so many things. He not only provides us with food, clothing, and shelter, but also with strength in hard situations, love for those who don't love us, and the opportunity to learn about him.

If you think about it, our lives are a lot like the widow's flour and oil jars. You could say we have a jar full of joy, love, courage, patience, etc. Every time we lose all patience with something (or someone), we can just ask God for a refill, and he gives us just what we need for that particular situation. And the best part is we will never run out—God keeps giving us more and more as we turn to him and ask him. It helps me get through so many difficult situations and problems, knowing that God is there, waiting to fill up my jars!

Faith

**God will fill you with what you need.
Just ask!**

»»» SHOWDOWN AT MOUNT CARMEL «««

Introduction

For years the people of Israel had been indecisive about whom they wanted to worship. Some wanted to worship Baal. Others wanted to worship God. But they wouldn't stick with either one for very long. Elijah wanted the people to decide once and for all who the real God was. So he sent Obadiah, one of the palace officials, with a challenge for Ahab. On Mount Carmel there would be a showdown between God's prophet, Elijah, and the prophets of Baal and Asherah, a false goddess. Although the odds were 850 to 1, Elijah didn't stand alone. God was with him.

1 Kings 18:16-40, NLT

So Obadiah went to tell Ahab that Elijah had come, and Ahab went out to meet him. "So it's you, is it—Israel's troublemaker?" Ahab asked when he saw him.

"I have made no trouble for Israel," Elijah replied. "You and your family are the troublemakers, for you have refused to obey the commands of the LORD and have worshiped the images of Baal instead. Now bring all the people of Israel to Mount Carmel, with all 450 prophets of Baal and the 400 prophets of Asherah, who are supported by Jezebel."

So Ahab summoned all the people and the prophets to Mount Carmel. Then Elijah stood in front of them and said, "How long are you going to waver between two opinions? If the LORD is God, follow him! But if Baal is God, then follow him!" But the people were completely silent.

Then Elijah said to them, "I am the only prophet of the LORD who is left, but Baal has 450 prophets. Now bring two bulls. The prophets of Baal may choose whichever one they wish and cut it into pieces and lay it on the wood of their altar, but without setting fire to it. I will prepare the other bull and lay it on the wood on the altar, but not set fire to it. Then call on the name of your god, and I will call on the name of the LORD. The god who answers by setting fire to the wood is the true God!" And all the people agreed.

Then Elijah said to the prophets of Baal, "You go first, for there are many of you. Choose one of the bulls and prepare it and call on the name of your god. But do not set fire to the wood."

So they prepared one of the bulls and placed it on the altar. Then they called on the name of Baal all morning, shouting, "O Baal, answer us!" But there was no reply of any kind. Then they danced wildly around the altar they had made.

About noontime Elijah began mocking them. "You'll have to shout louder," he scoffed, "for surely he is a god! Perhaps he is deep in thought, or he is relieving himself. Or maybe he is away on a trip, or he is asleep and needs to be wakened!"

So they shouted louder, and following their normal custom, they cut themselves with knives and swords until the blood gushed out. They raved all afternoon until the time of the evening sacrifice, but still there was no reply, no voice, no answer.

Then Elijah called to the people, "Come over here!" They all crowded around him as he repaired the altar of the LORD that had been torn down. He took twelve stones, one to represent each of the tribes of Israel, and he used the stones to rebuild the LORD's altar. Then he dug a trench around the altar large enough to hold about three gallons. He piled wood on the altar, cut the bull into pieces, and laid the pieces on the wood. Then he said, "Fill four large jars with water, and pour the water over the offering and the wood." After they had done this, he said, "Do the same thing again!" And when they were finished, he said, "Now do it a third time!" So they did as he said, and the water ran around the altar and even overflowed the trench.

At the customary time for offering the evening sacrifice, Elijah the prophet walked up to the altar and prayed, "O LORD, God of Abraham, Isaac, and Jacob, prove today that you are God in Israel and that I am your servant. O LORD, answer me! Answer me so these people will know that you, O LORD, are God and that you have brought them back to yourself."

Immediately the fire of the LORD flashed down from heaven and burned up the young bull, the wood, the stones, and the dust. It even licked up all the water in the ditch! And when the people saw it, they fell on their faces and cried out, "The LORD is God! The LORD is God!"

Then Elijah commanded, "Seize all the prophets of Baal. Don't let a single one escape!" So the people seized them all, and Elijah took them down to the Kishon Valley and killed them there.

The Old Testament prophet Malachi told the people of Israel that a second "Elijah" would one day be born in Israel. This man would come to announce the arrival of the Messiah—the promised Savior. Hundreds of years later, John the Baptist fulfilled this prophecy.

Malachi 4:5,6, NLT

"Look, I am sending you the prophet Elijah before the great and dreadful day of the LORD arrives. His preaching will turn the hearts of parents to their children, and the hearts of children to their parents. Otherwise I will come and strike the land with a curse."

Here's What I Think

Kali, age 18

Isn't it amazing? So many times God had saved the people of Israel. He rescued them from Egypt, provided them daily with food for 40 years, defeated their enemies, and never broke a promise. And here we find the Israelites in this story doubting again! So Elijah again must prove God's power through another miracle to help sway the people back to worshiping God. Elijah called out, "O Lord, answer me so these people will know that you, O Lord, are God."

Today, we don't see altars bursting into flame or a sea parting, but God works in more hidden ways to prove that he indeed is God. Our faith is based on the promise of Jesus' blood on the cross when he died for our sins. That's all the proof I need. How about you?

Kali

Need proof that God is God? Look to Jesus.

>>>>> ELISHA GETS THE CALL <<<

Introduction

After the showdown with Ahab and the prophets of Baal and Asherah, you can imagine how angry Ahab and Jezebel were. In fact, Jezebel threatened to kill Elijah! But God wouldn't let anything happen to his prophet. So, during a time when Elijah felt depressed, God revealed to him that a new prophet would soon take his place. Elijah had been a prophet for about five years. But now his task was almost over. He would definitely be a tough act to follow. But God knew just the man to replace Elijah.

2 Kings 2:1-15, NLT

When the LORD was about to take Elijah up to heaven in a whirlwind, Elijah and Elisha were traveling from Gilgal. And Elijah said to Elisha, "Stay here, for the LORD has told me to go to Bethel."

But Elisha replied, "As surely as the LORD lives and you yourself live, I will never leave you!" So they went on together to Bethel.

The group of prophets from Bethel came to Elisha and asked him, "Did you know that the LORD is going to take your master away from you today?"

"Quiet!" Elisha answered. "Of course I know it."

Then Elijah said to Elisha, "Stay here, for the LORD has told me to go to Jericho."

But Elisha replied again, "As surely as the LORD lives and you yourself live, I will never leave you." So they went on together to Jericho.

Then the group of prophets from Jericho came to Elisha and asked him, "Did you know that the LORD is going to take your master away from you today?"

"Quiet!" he answered again. "Of course I know it."

Then Elijah said to Elisha, "Stay here, for the LORD has told me to go to the Jordan River."

But again Elisha replied, "As surely as the LORD lives and you yourself live, I will never leave you." So they went on together.

Fifty men from the group of prophets also went and watched from a distance as Elijah and Elisha stopped beside the Jordan River. Then Elijah folded his cloak together and struck the water with it. The river divided, and the two of them went across on dry ground!

When they came to the other side, Elijah said to Elisha, "What can I do for you before I am taken away?"

And Elisha replied, "Please let me become your rightful successor."

"You have asked a difficult thing," Elijah replied. "If you see me when I am taken from you, then you will get your request. But if not, then you won't."

As they were walking along and talking, suddenly a chariot of fire appeared, drawn by horses of fire. It drove between them, separating them, and Elijah was carried by a whirlwind into heaven. Elisha saw it and cried out, "My father! My father! The chariots and charioteers of Israel!" And as they disappeared from sight, Elisha tore his robe in two.

Then Elisha picked up Elijah's cloak and returned to the bank of the Jordan River. He struck the water with the cloak and cried out, "Where is the LORD, the God of Elijah?" Then the river divided, and Elisha went across.

When the group of prophets from Jericho saw what happened, they exclaimed, "Elisha has become Elijah's successor!" And they went to meet him and bowed down before him.

Take Another Look

Elijah wasn't the only man on Earth who didn't die. Early in the history of people, we find a man named Enoch. He was the great-great-great-great grandson of Adam, the first man on Earth! Enoch had such a great relationship with God that God just took Enoch up to heaven to be with him. As you read the passage below, think about your relationship with God. Is it a "close fellowship" like Enoch's?

Genesis 5:21-24, NLT

When Enoch was 65 years old, his son Methuselah was born. After the birth of Methuselah, Enoch lived another 300 years in close fellowship with God, and he had other sons and daughters. Enoch lived 365 years in all. He enjoyed a close relationship with God throughout his life. Then suddenly, he disappeared because God took him.

Here's What I Think

Mike, age 19

I remember being anxious at the end of the year during the first few years in my youth group, watching the seniors graduate and leave. What would it be like without the influence of the seniors who had such an impact on the group during their last year? But every year someone new stepped up and emerged as the leader.

Until finally it was my turn. At that point I realized the pressure Elisha must have felt. He had been under Elijah's mentoring for a long time but now it was his turn. He was so upset that he wouldn't talk to anyone about it. But then after Elijah left, Elisha picked up Elijah's cloak and took over as Israel's prophet. It is a scary idea to think that we may one day be called to be some sort of spiritual leader among other Christians. But with God's help, we can be ready to graduate into that role, just like Elisha.

Mike

When the time comes, step up for God.

»» HELP FOR A WIDOW «««

①ntroduction

Elisha quickly earned a reputation as a man of God. Like Elijah, Elisha also came in contact with a widow. Widows were usually the poorest of the poor. Some of the poor had little choice but to sell themselves or other family members as slaves to pay off debts. There was even a rule concerning this in the law of Moses. But the life of a slave was hard. And a widow whose sons were sold as slaves had no one to provide for her. Well, no one except God.

2 Kings 4:1-7, NLT

One day the widow of one of Elisha's fellow prophets came to Elisha and cried out to him, "My husband who served you is dead, and you know how he feared the LORD. But now a creditor has come, threatening to take my two sons as slaves."

"What can I do to help you?" Elisha asked. "Tell me, what do you have in the house?"

"Nothing at all, except a flask of olive oil," she replied.

And Elisha said, "Borrow as many empty jars as you can from your friends and neighbors. Then go into your house with your sons and shut the door behind you. Pour olive oil from your flask into the jars, setting the jars aside as they are filled."

So she did as she was told. Her sons brought many jars to her, and she filled one after another. Soon every container was full to the brim! "Bring me another jar," she said to one of her sons.

"There aren't any more!" he told her. And then the olive oil stopped flowing. When she told the man of God what had happened, he said to her, "Now sell the olive oil and pay your debts, and there will be enough money left over to support you and your sons."

Elisha did many other things to show God's care for his people. But sometimes people wanted to help him too, just as Elijah was helped by the widow of Zarephath. When a woman and her husband offered Elisha a place to stay in their home, Elisha found a way to repay their kindness.

2 Kings 4:8-17, NLT

One day Elisha went to the town of Shunem. A wealthy woman lived there, and she invited him to eat some food. From then on, whenever he passed that way, he would stop there to eat.

She said to her husband, "I am sure this man who stops in from time to time is a holy man of God. Let's make a little room for him on the roof and furnish it with a bed, a table, a chair, and a lamp. Then he will have a place to stay whenever he comes by."

One day Elisha returned to Shunem, and he went up to his room to rest. He said to his servant Gehazi, "Tell the woman I want to speak to her." When she arrived, Elisha said to Gehazi, "Tell her that we appreciate the kind concern she has shown us. Now ask her what we can do for her. Does she want me to put in a good word for her to the king or to the commander of the army?"

"No," she replied, "my family takes good care of me."

Later Elisha asked Gehazi, "What do you think we can do for her?"

He suggested, "She doesn't have a son, and her husband is an old man."

"Call her back again," Elisha told him. When the woman returned, Elisha said to her as she stood in the doorway, "Next year at about this time you will be holding a son in your arms!"

"No, my lord!" she protested. "Please don't lie to me like that, O man of God."

But sure enough, the woman soon became pregnant. And at that time the following year she had a son, just as Elisha had said.

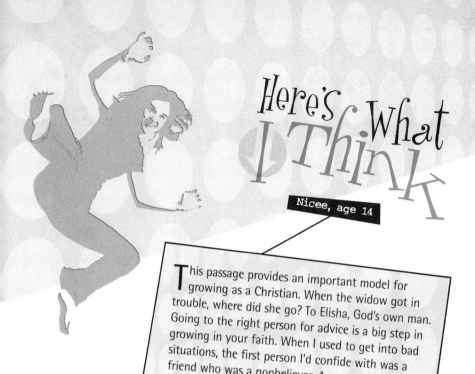

Here's What I Think

Nicee, age 14

This passage provides an important model for growing as a Christian. When the widow got in trouble, where did she go? To Elisha, God's own man. Going to the right person for advice is a big step in growing in your faith. When I used to get into bad situations, the first person I'd confide with was a friend who was a nonbeliever. As a result, the situation would only get worse.

Now, whenever I find myself in a tight situation, I go to the adults in my family and my youth minister. These people give me good insight filled with wisdom. They are people I can trust and know that they have my best interest in mind. I confide in these adults because they've been where I am today and can show me a variety of ways through a problem. Youth my age can simply give me youthful advice, and not the good ol' been-there-done-that advice from adults.

Nicee

Consider the source when asking for advice.

»» A CURE FOR NAAMAN ««

Introduction

Over the years, the divided nation of Israel gained many enemies. One of their enemies was the nation of Aram (Syria). Although Naaman was the commander of the army of Aram, God had given him many victories. He seemed to have it made, except for one thing—Naaman had leprosy. This skin disease had no cure. But a young Israelite slave knew of one man who could help—Elisha. Elisha had performed many amazing miracles through the power of God. But would Elisha offer help to an enemy?

2 Kings 5:1-16, NLT

The king of Aram had high admiration for Naaman, the commander of his army, because through him the LORD had given Aram great victories. But though Naaman was a mighty warrior, he suffered from leprosy.

Now groups of Aramean raiders had invaded the land of Israel, and among their captives was a young girl who had been given to Naaman's wife as a maid. One day the girl said to her mistress, "I wish my master would go to see the prophet in Samaria. He would heal him of his leprosy."

So Naaman told the king what the young girl from Israel had said. "Go and visit the prophet," the king told him. "I will send a letter of introduction for you to carry to the king of Israel." So Naaman started out, taking as gifts 750 pounds of silver, 150 pounds of gold, and ten sets of clothing. The letter to the king of Israel said: "With this letter I present my servant Naaman. I want you to heal him of his leprosy."

When the king of Israel read it, he tore his clothes in dismay and said, "This man sends me a leper to heal! Am I God, that I can kill and give life? He is only trying to find an excuse to invade us again."

But when Elisha, the man of God, heard about the king's reaction, he sent this message to him: "Why are you so upset? Send Naaman to me, and he will learn that there is a true prophet here in Israel."

So Naaman went with his horses and chariots and waited at the door of Elisha's house. But Elisha sent a messenger out to him with this message: "Go and wash yourself seven times in the Jordan River. Then your skin will be restored, and you will be healed of leprosy."

But Naaman became angry and stalked away. "I thought he would surely come out to meet me!" he said. "I expected him to wave his hand over the leprosy and call on the name of the LORD his God and heal me! Aren't the Abana River and Pharpar River of Damascus better than all the rivers of Israel put together? Why shouldn't I wash in them and be healed?" So Naaman turned and went away in a rage.

But his officers tried to reason with him and said, "Sir, if the prophet had told you to do some great thing, wouldn't you have done it? So you should certainly obey him when he says simply to go and wash and be cured!" So Naaman went down to the Jordan River and dipped himself seven times, as the man of God had instructed him. And his flesh became as healthy as a young child's, and he was healed!

Then Naaman and his entire party went back to find the man of God. They stood before him, and Naaman said, "I know at last that there is no God in all the world except in Israel. Now please accept my gifts."

But Elisha replied, "As surely as the LORD lives, whom I serve, I will not accept any gifts." And though Naaman urged him to take the gifts, Elisha refused.

Take ANOTHER LOOK

Leprosy was one disease that didn't go away. During his time on Earth, Jesus cured many lepers. One time, he cured 10 at once! As with Naaman, the cure involved a step of faith. Oddly enough, one of the lepers was a man from another country—just like Naaman. While you read this story, consider a step of faith that God might want you to take. Like the lepers, are you willing to take it?

Luke 17:11-19, NLT

As Jesus continued on toward Jerusalem, he reached the border between Galilee and Samaria. As he entered a village there, ten lepers stood at a distance, crying out, "Jesus, Master, have mercy on us!"

He looked at them and said, "Go show yourselves to the priests." And as they went, their leprosy disappeared.

One of them, when he saw that he was healed, came back to Jesus, shouting, "Praise God, I'm healed!" He fell face down on the ground at Jesus' feet, thanking him for what he had done. This man was a Samaritan.

Jesus asked, "Didn't I heal ten men? Where are the other nine? Does only this foreigner return to give glory to God?" And Jesus said to the man, "Stand up and go. Your faith has made you well."

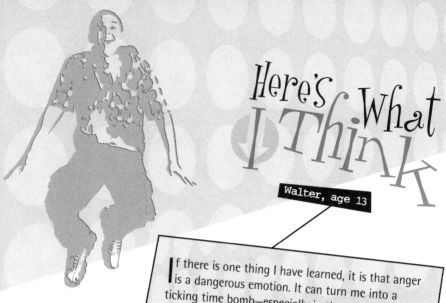

Here's What I Think

Walter, age 13

If there is one thing I have learned, it is that anger is a dangerous emotion. It can turn me into a ticking time bomb—especially in the morning. When I get up, I cannot stand to talk to anyone. I am not a morning person, but that's no excuse to show disrespect to my parents or to yell at my brother.

Sometimes when I don't control my anger, it costs me later on—the one or two hours of precious free time I have after school. Anger can cost us all big time—just like it almost did for Naaman. If he had not let his servants calm him down and persuade him to follow Elisha's orders, Naaman would have gone home angry *and* with his leprosy, missing out on his only chance to be cured. That's a good lesson for all of us—don't let our anger trip us up.

Walter

Control your anger before it controls you.

)))) A FISH STORY ((((

Ôntroduction

Many fishermen talk about the big fish that got away—the one they almost caught. In this story, Jonah was the one who got away . . . or tried to. Instead of catching a fish, a fish caught him! It all started when God tried to send Jonah to Nineveh with a message. He learned the hard way that with God, you can run, but you can't hide.

Jonah 1:1–2:10, NLT

The LORD gave this message to Jonah son of Amittai: "Get up and go to the great city of Nineveh! Announce my judgment against it because I have seen how wicked its people are."

But Jonah got up and went in the opposite direction in order to get away from the LORD. He went down to the seacoast, to the port of Joppa, where he found a ship leaving for Tarshish. He bought a ticket and went on board, hoping that by going away to the west he could escape from the LORD.

But as the ship was sailing along, suddenly the LORD flung a powerful wind over the sea, causing a violent storm that threatened to send them to the bottom. Fearing for their lives, the desperate sailors shouted to their gods for help and threw the cargo overboard to lighten the ship. And all this time Jonah was sound asleep down in the hold. So the captain went down after him. "How can you sleep at a time like this?" he shouted. "Get up and pray to your god! Maybe he will have mercy on us and spare our lives."

Then the crew cast lots to see which of them had offended the gods and caused the terrible storm. When they did this, Jonah lost the toss. "What have you done to bring this awful storm down on us?" they demanded. "Who are you? What is your line of work? What country are you from? What is your nationality?"

And Jonah answered, "I am a Hebrew, and I worship the LORD, the God of heaven, who made the sea and the land." Then he told them that he was running away from the LORD.

The sailors were terrified when they heard this. "Oh, why did you do it?" they groaned. And since the storm was getting worse all the time, they asked him, "What should we do to you to stop this storm?"

"Throw me into the sea," Jonah said, "and it will become calm again. For I know that this terrible storm is all my fault."

Instead, the sailors tried even harder to row the boat ashore. But the stormy sea was too violent for them, and they couldn't make it. Then they cried out to the LORD, Jonah's God. "O LORD," they pleaded, "don't make us die for this man's sin. And don't hold us responsible for his death, because it isn't our fault. O LORD, you have sent this storm upon him for your own good reasons."

Then the sailors picked Jonah up and threw him into the raging sea, and the storm stopped at once! The sailors were awestruck by the LORD's great power, and they offered him a sacrifice and vowed to serve him.

Now the LORD had arranged for a great fish to swallow Jonah. And Jonah was inside the fish for three days and three nights.

Jonah's Prayer, 2:1-10

Then Jonah prayed to the LORD his God from inside the fish. He said, "I cried out to the LORD in my great trouble, and he answered me. I called to you from the world of the dead, and LORD, you heard me! You threw me into the ocean depths, and I sank down to the heart of the sea. I was buried beneath your wild and stormy waves. Then I said, 'O LORD, you have driven me from your presence. How will I ever again see your holy Temple?'

"I sank beneath the waves, and death was very near. The waters closed in around me, and seaweed wrapped itself around my head. I sank down to the very roots of the mountains. I was locked out of life and imprisoned in the land of the dead. But you, O LORD my God, have snatched me from the yawning jaws of death!

"When I had lost all hope, I turned my thoughts once more to the LORD. And my earnest prayer went out to you in your holy Temple. Those who worship false gods turn their backs on all God's mercies. But I will offer sacrifices to you with songs of praise, and I will fulfill all my vows. For my salvation comes from the LORD alone."

Then the LORD ordered the fish to spit up Jonah on the beach, and it did.

Take ANOTHER LOOK

Centuries later, some leaders called Pharisees demanded proof that Jesus was the promised Savior. Jesus could have performed a miracle. But instead, he told the story of Jonah that you just read. Here's what Jesus said.

Matthew 12:38-41, NLT

One day some teachers of religious law and Pharisees came to Jesus and said, "Teacher, we want you to show us a miraculous sign to prove that you are from God."

But Jesus replied, "Only an evil, faithless generation would ask for a miraculous sign; but the only sign I will give them is the sign of the prophet Jonah. For as Jonah was in the belly of the great fish for three days and three nights, so I, the Son of Man, will be in the heart of the earth for three days and three nights.

"The people of Nineveh will rise up against this generation on judgment day and condemn it, because they repented at the preaching of Jonah. And now someone greater than Jonah is here—and you refuse to repent."

Here's What I Think

Julie, age 18

When I ought to do something—whether it's doing my homework or cleaning my room—I find excuses pretty easily. "Well," I'll say, "I have to do something *else* now." Or, "Maybe I'll do that *later*." Often, like Jonah, I run away. If my mom wants help cleaning the house, I might decide to leave on a bike ride instead.

But making excuses and running away don't make my homework and chores disappear. Jonah may have run away, but he still had to go to Nineveh in the end. Additionally, if he hadn't run away in the first place, he could have avoided a lot of trouble (namely, being swallowed by a fish)!

Is there something you ought to do? It might be anything—your homework, your chores, or even sharing Jesus' love with a friend. God doesn't want you to make excuses. Do it now. You'll be glad you did.

Julie

Don't make excuses—just do it!

»» COME CLEAN ««

Introduction

Wash your hands! You must hear that every time before you eat, right? We need to come to the table with clean hands. The people of Israel needed to clean up too, but they had to come clean before God. See what King Hezekiah did to help the people clean up their act.

2 Chronicles 29:3-11, 18-30, NLT

In the very first month of the first year of his reign, Hezekiah reopened the doors of the Temple of the LORD and repaired them. He summoned the priests and Levites to meet him at the courtyard east of the Temple. He said to them, "Listen to me, you Levites! Purify yourselves, and purify the Temple of the LORD, the God of your ancestors. Remove all the defiled things from the sanctuary. Our ancestors were unfaithful and did what was evil in the sight of the LORD our God. They abandoned the LORD and his Temple; they turned their backs on him. They also shut the doors to the Temple's foyer, and they snuffed out the lamps. They stopped burning incense and presenting burnt offerings at the sanctuary of the God of Israel. That is why the LORD's anger has fallen upon Judah and Jerusalem. He has made us an object of dread, horror, and ridicule, as you can so plainly see. Our fathers have been killed in battle, and our sons and daughters and wives are in captivity. But now I will make a covenant with the LORD, the God of Israel, so that his fierce anger will turn away from us. My dear Levites, do not neglect your duties any longer! The LORD has chosen you to stand in his presence, to minister to him, and to lead the people in worship and make offerings to him."

The Temple Rededication, 29:18-30

Then the Levites went to King Hezekiah and gave him this report: "We have purified the Temple of the LORD, the altar of burnt offering with all its utensils, and the table of the Bread of the Presence with all its utensils. We have also recovered all the utensils taken by King Ahaz when he was unfaithful and closed the Temple. They are now in front of the altar of the LORD, purified and ready for use." Early the next morning King Hezekiah gathered the city officials and went to the Temple of the LORD. They brought seven bulls, seven rams, seven lambs, and seven male goats as a sin offering for the kingdom, for the Temple, and for Judah. The king commanded the priests, who were descendants of Aaron, to sacrifice the animals on the altar of the LORD. So they killed the bulls, and the priests took the blood and sprinkled it on the altar. Next they killed the rams and sprinkled their blood on the altar. And finally, they did the same with the lambs. The male goats for the sin offering were then brought before the king and the assembly of people, who laid their hands on them. The priests then killed the goats as a sin offering and sprinkled their blood on the altar to make atonement for the sins of all Israel. The king had specifically commanded that this burnt offering and sin offering should be made for all Israel.

King Hezekiah then stationed the Levites at the Temple of the LORD with cymbals, harps, and lyres. He obeyed all the commands that the LORD had given to King David through Gad, the king's seer, and the prophet Nathan. The Levites then took their positions around the Temple with the instruments of David, and the priests took their positions with the trumpets. Then Hezekiah ordered that the burnt offering be placed on the altar. As the burnt offering was presented, songs of praise to the LORD were begun, accompanied by the trumpets and other instruments of David, king of Israel. The entire assembly worshiped the LORD as the singers sang and the trumpets blew, until all the burnt offerings were finished. Then the king and everyone with him bowed down in worship. King Hezekiah and the officials ordered the Levites to praise the LORD with the psalms of David and Asaph the seer. So they offered joyous praise and bowed down in worship.

Take ANOTHER LOOK

Now that Hezekiah had the Temple in order, it was time for him to get his own affairs in order, as the Old Testament prophet Isaiah put it. In other words, Hezekiah was going to die. But Hezekiah wasn't afraid to ask for the impossible. The God of impossibilities answered in an amazing way. As you read this story, think about whether or not you're willing to ask God for the impossible.

Isaiah 38:1-8, NLT

About that time Hezekiah became deathly ill, and the prophet Isaiah son of Amoz went to visit him. He gave the king this message: "This is what the LORD says: Set your affairs in order, for you are going to die. You will not recover from this illness."

When Hezekiah heard this, he turned his face to the wall and prayed to the LORD, "Remember, O LORD, how I have always tried to be faithful to you and do what is pleasing in your sight." Then he broke down and wept bitterly.

Then this message came to Isaiah from the LORD: "Go back to Hezekiah and tell him, 'This is what the LORD, the God of your ancestor David, says: I have heard your prayer and seen your tears. I will add fifteen years to your life, and I will rescue you and this city from the king of Assyria. Yes, I will defend this city.

"'And this is the sign that the LORD will give you to prove he will do as he promised: I will cause the sun's shadow to move ten steps backward on the sundial of Ahaz!'" So the shadow on the sundial moved backward ten steps.

Here's What I Think

Verity, age 13

For many years, the people of Jerusalem had disobeyed God and done what they wanted. So when the temple reopened, the people spent a long time trying to clean up their act. God wants us, just like the people of Jerusalem, to focus on cleaning up our act and quit doing wrong. A good time for me to really focus on that is during Communion. During that time, I think about what I've done wrong to offend Jesus, and I ask him to forgive me. When I do that, I feel as though I'm now clean again. You don't have to wait for a time like Communion, though. You can come clean before God anytime.

Verity

Clean up your act and get right before God.

A CLEAN SWEEP

»»»

Introduction

Have you ever been compared with someone? Maybe you were told you're "thoughtful like your older brother" or "a prankster like your uncle." The kings of Israel were often compared with previous kings. If a king was good, he was usually described as following the example of David—the greatest of Israel's kings. Hezekiah and his great-grandson, Josiah, were kings "like David." Josiah was still a young king when he realized that change was needed if the people were going to follow God like David did.

2 Kings 22:1-20, NLT

Josiah was eight years old when he became king, and he reigned in Jerusalem thirty-one years. His mother was Jedidah, the daughter of Adaiah from Bozkath. He did what was pleasing in the LORD's sight and followed the example of his ancestor David. He did not turn aside from doing what was right.

In the eighteenth year of his reign, King Josiah sent Shaphan son of Azaliah and grandson of Meshullam, the court secretary, to the Temple of the LORD. He told him, "Go up to Hilkiah the high priest and have him count the money the gatekeepers have collected from the people at the LORD's Temple. Entrust this money to the men assigned to supervise the Temple's restoration. Then they can use it to pay workers to repair the Temple of the LORD. They will need to hire carpenters, builders, and masons. Also have them buy the timber and the cut stone needed to repair the Temple. But there will be no need for the construction supervisors to keep account of the money they receive, for they are honest people."

Hilkiah Discovers God's Law

Hilkiah the high priest said to Shaphan the court secretary, "I have found the Book of the Law in the LORD's Temple!" Then Hilkiah gave the scroll to Shaphan, and he read it.

Shaphan returned to the king and reported, "Your officials have given the money collected at the Temple of the LORD to the workers and supervisors at the

Temple." Shaphan also said to the king, "Hilkiah the priest has given me a scroll." So Shaphan read it to the king.

When the king heard what was written in the Book of the Law, he tore his clothes in despair. Then he gave these orders to Hilkiah the priest, Ahikam son of Shaphan, Acbor son of Micaiah, Shaphan the court secretary, and Asaiah the king's personal adviser: "Go to the Temple and speak to the LORD for me and for the people and for all Judah. Ask him about the words written in this scroll that has been found. The LORD's anger is burning against us because our ancestors have not obeyed the words in this scroll. We have not been doing what this scroll says we must do."

So Hilkiah the priest, Ahikam, Acbor, Shaphan, and Asaiah went to the newer Mishneh section of Jerusalem to consult with the prophet Huldah. She was the wife of Shallum son of Tikvah and grandson of Harhas, the keeper of the Temple wardrobe. She said to them, "The LORD, the God of Israel, has spoken! Go and tell the man who sent you, 'This is what the LORD says: I will destroy this city and its people, just as I stated in the scroll you read. For my people have abandoned me and worshiped pagan gods, and I am very angry with them for everything they have done. My anger is burning against this place, and it will not be quenched.'

"But go to the king of Judah who sent you to seek the LORD and tell him: 'This is what the LORD, the God of Israel, says concerning the message you have just heard: You were sorry and humbled yourself before the LORD when you heard what I said against this city and its people, that this land would be cursed and become desolate. You tore your clothing in despair and wept before me in repentance. So I have indeed heard you, says the LORD. I will not send the promised disaster against this city until after you have died and been buried in peace. You will not see the disaster I am going to bring on this place.'" So they took her message back to the king.

Take ANOTHER LOOK

Have you ever received a letter (you know . . . those things that arrive by snail mail) with a P.S. at the end of it? A P.S., or postscript, usually contains additional news that the letter writer forgot to add earlier. The next bit of information is sort of like a P.S. It contains extra information about what actions Josiah took after he discovered God's Law.

2 Kings 23:1-3, NLT

Then the king summoned all the leaders of Judah and Jerusalem. And the king went up to the Temple of the LORD with all the people of Judah and Jerusalem, and the priests, and the prophets— all the people from the least to the greatest.

There the king read to them the entire Book of the Covenant that had been found in the LORD's Temple. The king took his place of authority beside the pillar and renewed the covenant in the LORD's presence. He pledged to obey the LORD by keeping all his commands, regulations, and laws with all his heart and soul. In this way, he confirmed all the terms of the covenant that were written in the scroll, and all the people pledged themselves to the covenant.

Here's What I Think

Walter, age 13

It's easy for me to forget what's the right thing to do. Even on youth trips, you're doing whatever you please most of the time, and then for about 20 minutes a day, you act like God means something to you. But one of our church's youth trips rocked my world. It was at a weeklong retreat in Dallas that God spoke to me through his Word. That was when God reminded me of what I needed to do: live a God-honoring life from then on. Soon after, I realized I wanted to publicly declare my heart for God. I wanted everyone to know that I believed with all my heart, soul, and mind that he is the only God and that he sent his one and only Son to die on the cross for my sins. I wanted to be baptized. In a way, I was acting like King Josiah. He proclaimed how much he loved God. He vowed to follow God for the rest of his life. And that's what I did too.

Walter

Make today your God-dependence day—
declare to follow only him!

»» A DARING DIET ««

Introduction

Ever think you're too young to make a difference? Guess what. You're not! Here you will read about three young men from Israel who refused to disobey God's laws. They won the enemy's respect—and it all came from eating vegetables! Read on.

Daniel 1:1-21, NLT

During the third year of King Jehoiakim's reign in Judah, King Nebuchadnezzar of Babylon came to Jerusalem and besieged it with his armies. The Lord gave him victory over King Jehoiakim of Judah. When Nebuchadnezzar returned to Babylon, he took with him some of the sacred objects from the Temple of God and placed them in the treasure-house of his god in the land of Babylonia.

Then the king ordered Ashpenaz, who was in charge of the palace officials, to bring to the palace some of the young men of Judah's royal family and other noble families, who had been brought to Babylon as captives. "Select only strong, healthy, and good-looking young men," he said. "Make sure they are well versed in every branch of learning, are gifted with knowledge and good sense, and have the poise needed to serve in the royal palace. Teach these young men the language and literature of the Babylonians." The king assigned them a daily ration of the best food and wine from his own kitchens. They were to be trained for a three-year period, and then some of them would be made his advisers in the royal court.

Daniel, Hananiah, Mishael, and Azariah were four of the young men chosen, all from the tribe of Judah. The chief official renamed them with these Babylonian names:

Daniel was called Belteshazzar.

Hananiah was called Shadrach.

Mishael was called Meshach.

Azariah was called Abednego.

But Daniel made up his mind not to defile himself by eating the food and wine given to them by the king. He asked the chief official for permission to eat other things instead. Now God had given the chief official great respect for Daniel. But he was alarmed by Daniel's suggestion. "My lord the king has ordered that you eat this food and wine," he said. "If you become pale and thin compared to the other youths your age, I am afraid the king will have me beheaded for neglecting my duties."

Daniel talked it over with the attendant who had been appointed by the chief official to look after Daniel, Hananiah, Mishael, and Azariah. "Test us for ten days on a diet of vegetables and water," Daniel said. "At the end of the ten days, see how we look compared to the other young men who are eating the king's rich food. Then you can decide whether or not to let us continue eating our diet." So the attendant agreed to Daniel's suggestion and tested them for ten days.

At the end of the ten days, Daniel and his three friends looked healthier and better nourished than the young men who had been eating the food assigned by the king. So after that, the attendant fed them only vegetables instead of the rich foods and wines.

God gave these four young men an unusual aptitude for learning the literature and science of the time. And God gave Daniel special ability in understanding the meanings of visions and dreams.

When the three-year training period ordered by the king was completed, the chief official brought all the young men to King Nebuchadnezzar. The king talked with each of them, and none of them impressed him as much as Daniel, Hananiah, Mishael, and Azariah. So they were appointed to his regular staff of advisers. In all matters requiring wisdom and balanced judgment, the king found the advice of these young men to be ten times better than that of all the magicians and enchanters in his entire kingdom.

Daniel remained there until the first year of King Cyrus's reign.

Take ANOTHER LOOK

Several years after Daniel was taken to Babylon, Ezekiel was chosen to be a prophet. In the book of Ezekiel, God talks about Daniel and other men who followed God wholeheartedly. Although they weren't perfect, they were obedient. But even though men like Daniel made wise choices, they couldn't save anyone. Only Jesus could.

Ezekiel 14:12-20, NLT

Then this message came to me from the LORD: "Son of man, suppose the people of a country were to sin against me, and I lifted my fist to crush them, cutting off their food supply and sending a famine to destroy both people and animals alike. Even if Noah, Daniel, and Job were there, their righteousness would save no one but themselves, declares the Sovereign LORD.

"Or suppose I were to send an invasion of dangerous wild animals to devastate the land and kill the people. Even if these three men were there, the Sovereign LORD swears that it would do no good—it wouldn't save the people from destruction. Those three alone would be saved, but the land would be devastated.

"Or suppose I were to bring war against the land, and I told enemy armies to come and destroy everything. Even if these three men were in the land, the Sovereign LORD swears that they could not save the people. They alone would be saved.

"Or suppose I were to pour out my fury by sending an epidemic of disease into the land, and the plague killed people and animals alike. Even if Noah, Daniel, and Job were living there, the Sovereign LORD swears that they could not save the people. They alone would be saved by their righteousness."

Here's What I Think

Daniel, age 15

I'm actually named after the main guy in that story. I've always been impressed with Daniel's faith. He easily could have thought, *You know what? I could be executed for disagreeing with the king's orders. I'm out.* Think about it. If you were just made a slave, do you think the first thing you would want to do is tell the king's chief official, "Your food stinks. I want some veggies—ya know, some greens—and just water, none of this wine stuff."

I know I wouldn't! But Daniel knew his No. 1 priority was to obey God without hesitation. I think that is something we all should strive for. When God tells us something, let's respond like Daniel and just do it. If God says jump, do it with all your might!

Daniel

When God speaks, jump to it!

A HOT TIME
AT THE PALACE

Introduction

If someone wanted you to do something wrong, what would you do? Suppose that person threatened your life. Would that change what you would do? Three of Daniel's friends had this experience. Nebuchadnezzar wanted them to break one of God's rules and worship a false idol. Here's what happened.

Daniel 3:1-29, NLT

King Nebuchadnezzar made a gold statue ninety feet tall and nine feet wide and set it up on the plain of Dura in the province of Babylon. Then he sent messages to the princes, prefects, governors, advisers, counselors, judges, magistrates, and all the provincial officials to come to the dedication of the statue he had set up. When all these officials had arrived and were standing before the image King Nebuchadnezzar had set up, a herald shouted out, "People of all races and nations and languages, listen to the king's command! When you hear the sound of the horn, flute, zither, lyre, harp, pipes, and other instruments, bow to the ground to worship King Nebuchadnezzar's gold statue. Anyone who refuses to obey will immediately be thrown into a blazing furnace."

So at the sound of the musical instruments, all the people, whatever their race or nation or language, bowed to the ground and worshiped the statue that King Nebuchadnezzar had set up.

But some of the astrologers went to the king and informed on the Jews. They said to King Nebuchadnezzar, "Long live the king! You issued a decree requiring all the people to bow down and worship the gold statue when they hear the sound of the musical instruments. That decree also states that those who refuse to obey must be thrown into a blazing furnace. But there are some Jews—Shadrach, Meshach, and Abednego—whom you have put in charge of the province of Babylon. They have defied Your Majesty by refusing to serve your gods or to worship the gold statue you have set up."

Then Nebuchadnezzar flew into a rage and ordered Shadrach, Meshach, and Abednego to be brought before him. When they were brought in,

Nebuchadnezzar said to them, "Is it true, Shadrach, Meshach, and Abednego, that you refuse to serve my gods or to worship the gold statue I have set up? I will give you one more chance. If you bow down and worship the statue I have made when you hear the sound of the musical instruments, all will be well. But if you refuse, you will be thrown immediately into the blazing furnace. What god will be able to rescue you from my power then?"

Shadrach, Meshach, and Abednego replied, "O Nebuchadnezzar, we do not need to defend ourselves before you. If we are thrown into the blazing furnace, the God whom we serve is able to save us. He will rescue us from your power, Your Majesty. But even if he doesn't, Your Majesty can be sure that we will never serve your gods or worship the gold statue you have set up."

The Blazing Furnace

Nebuchadnezzar was so furious with Shadrach, Meshach, and Abednego that his face became distorted with rage. He commanded that the furnace be heated seven times hotter than usual. Then he ordered some of the strongest men of his army to bind Shadrach, Meshach, and Abednego and throw them into the blaz- ing furnace. So they tied them up and threw them into the furnace, fully clothed. And because the king, in his anger, had demanded such a hot fire in the furnace, the flames leaped out and killed the soldiers as they threw the three men in! So Shadrach, Meshach, and Abednego, securely tied, fell down into the roaring flames.

But suddenly, as he was watching, Nebuchadnezzar jumped up in amazement and exclaimed to his advisers, "Didn't we tie up three men and throw them into the furnace?"

"Yes," they said, "we did indeed, Your Majesty."

"Look!" Nebuchadnezzar shouted. "I see four men, unbound, walking around in the fire. They aren't even hurt by the flames! And the fourth looks like a divine being!"

Then Nebuchadnezzar came as close as he could to the door of the flaming furnace and shouted: "Shadrach, Meshach, and Abednego, servants of the Most High God, come out! Come here!" So Shadrach, Meshach, and Abednego stepped out of the fire. Then the princes, prefects, governors, and advisers crowded around them and saw that the fire had not touched them. Not a hair on their heads was singed, and their clothing was not scorched. They didn't even smell of smoke!

Then Nebuchadnezzar said, "Praise to the God of Shadrach, Meshach, and Abednego! He sent his angel to rescue his servants who trusted in him. They defied the king's command and were willing to die rather than serve or worship any god except their own God. Therefore, I make this decree: If any people, whatever their race or nation or language, speak a word against the God of Shadrach, Meshach, and Abednego, they will be torn limb from limb, and their houses will be crushed into heaps of rubble. There is no other god who can rescue like this!"

Take ANOTHER LOOK

The Old Testament prophet Isaiah had encouraging words for people who suffer because of their faith in God. Although we may not go through "the fire of oppression" like Shadrach, Meshach, and Abednego, we can still know the comfort of God's presence.

Isaiah 43:1-3, NLT

But now, O Israel, the LORD who created you says: "Do not be afraid, for I have ransomed you. I have called you by name; you are mine. When you go through deep waters and great trouble, I will be with you. When you go through rivers of difficulty, you will not drown! When you walk through the fire of oppression, you will not be burned up; the flames will not consume you. For I am the LORD, your God, the Holy One of Israel, your Savior. I gave Egypt, Ethiopia, and Seba as a ransom for your freedom."

Here's What I Think

Janna, age 14

In this story, everyone is bowing down to the idol Nebuchadnezzar made. But Shadrach, Meshach, and Abednego refused. They knew it was wrong, even though everyone was doing it. And because of that, they got thrown into a fiery furnace! God was with them, though, and he rescued them from the flames.

Most of us probably won't face a fiery furnace when we stand up for Christ and do what is right. But we may get ridiculed for it. Or people may reject us as their friend. But we shouldn't let that stop us. I go to a Christian school. That doesn't necessarily mean that everyone who attends is a Christian. In fact, many people at our school cuss. But that is something I choose not to do. I think it is wrong, especially if you *are* a Christian. God took care of Shadrach, Meshach, and Abednego for doing the right thing. He will take care of me.

Janna

God will care for you when things get hot.

THE FALL
OF JERUSALEM

Introduction

How would you feel if your house or apartment building were suddenly torn down right before your eyes? You might feel the way the people of Israel felt in this story. Because they continually disobeyed God, he had warned them that their city of Jerusalem would be destroyed. The beautiful temple that Solomon's workers built—the place the Israelites loved the most—would also be torn down. So when an enemy army invaded, the people in Jerusalem feared that the end had finally come.

2 Kings 25:8-21, NLT

On August 14 of that year, which was the nineteenth year of Nebuchadnezzar's reign, Nebuzaradan, captain of the guard, an official of the Babylonian king, arrived in Jerusalem. He burned down the Temple of the Lord, the royal palace, and all the houses of Jerusalem. He destroyed all the important buildings in the city. Then the captain of the guard supervised the entire Babylonian army as they tore down the walls of Jerusalem. Nebuzaradan, captain of the guard, then took as exiles those who remained in the city, along with the rest of the people and the troops who had declared their allegiance to the king of Babylon. But the captain of the guard allowed some of the poorest people to stay behind in Judah to care for the vineyards and fields.

The Babylonians broke up the bronze pillars, the bronze water carts, and the bronze Sea that were at the LORD's Temple, and they carried all the bronze away to Babylon. They also took all the pots, shovels, lamp snuffers, dishes, and all the other bronze utensils used for making sacrifices at the Temple. Nebuzaradan, captain of the guard, also took the firepans and basins, and all the other utensils made of pure gold or silver.

The bronze from the two pillars, the water carts, and the Sea was too great to be weighed. These things had been made for the LORD's Temple in the days of King Solomon. Each of the pillars was 27 feet tall. The bronze capital on top of each pillar was 7 1/2 feet high and was decorated with a network of bronze pomegranates all the way around.

The captain of the guard took with him as prisoners Seraiah the chief priest, his assistant Zephaniah, and the three chief gatekeepers. And of the people still hiding in the city, he took an officer of the Judean army, five of the king's personal advisers, the army commander's chief secretary, who was in charge of recruitment, and sixty other citizens. Nebuzaradan the commander took them all to the king of Babylon at Riblah. And there at Riblah, in the land of Hamath, the king of Babylon had them all put to death. So the people of Judah were sent into exile from their land.

Take ANOTHER LOOK The news to Israel wasn't all bad. Although God's people were forced to leave their homeland, God promised to bring them back home again. As you read the passages below, consider how God's sense of "rightness" and love work together.

Ezekiel 34:11-16, NLT

For this is what the Sovereign LORD says: I myself will search and find my sheep. I will be like a shepherd looking for his scattered flock. I will find my sheep and rescue them from all the places to which they were scattered on that dark and cloudy day. I will bring them back home to their own land of Israel from among the peoples and nations. I will feed them on the mountains of Israel and by the rivers in all the places where people live. Yes, I will give them good pastureland on the high hills of Israel. There they will lie down in pleasant places and feed in lush mountain pastures. I myself will tend my sheep and cause them to lie down in peace, says the Sovereign LORD. I will search for my lost ones who strayed away, and I will bring them safely home again. I will bind up the injured and strengthen the weak. But I will destroy those who are fat and powerful. I will feed them, yes—feed them justice!

Jeremiah 29:10-13, NLT

"The truth is that you will be in Babylon for seventy years. But then I will come and do for you all the good things I have promised, and I will bring you home again. For I know the plans I have for you," says the LORD. "They are plans for good and not for disaster, to give you a future and a hope. In those days when you pray, I will listen. If you look for me in earnest, you will find me when you seek me."

Here's What I Think

Faith, age 14

Often, I take for granted how truly blessed I am to live in a place where I'm not persecuted for my beliefs. I can go to church every Sunday and attend a Christian school. I can openly share my faith with others and not worry about anything happening to me because of it.

But in places like China, Christians can't do that. The government tries to keep believers from worshiping and praying to God, from studying God's Word, and from spreading the gospel. They are tortured for their beliefs, but they still stand strong in God.

Just like the exiled people of Jerusalem discovered, others can take away your freedom of religion. They can take away your place of worship, or even your life—but they can't take God away from you.

Faith

No one can take God from you.

»» CUT DOWN TO SIZE ««

Ɵntroduction

Nebuchadnezzar thought he was king of the world. His powerful army had conquered other nations, including the nation of Israel. He had built a strong city and a beautiful palace. Yeah, he had it all—except a firm belief in the one true God of Israel. He had plenty of faith in himself—that was his problem. But God had a surprising way of cutting this "king of the world" down to size.

Daniel 4:4-34, NLT

"I, Nebuchadnezzar, was living in my palace in comfort and prosperity. But one night I had a dream that greatly frightened me; I saw visions that terrified me as I lay in my bed. So I issued an order calling in all the wise men of Babylon, so they could tell me what my dream meant. When all the magicians, enchanters, astrologers, and fortune-tellers came in, I told them the dream, but they could not tell me what it meant. At last Daniel came in before me, and I told him the dream. (He was named Belteshazzar after my god, and the spirit of the holy gods is in him.)

"I said to him, 'O Belteshazzar, master magician, I know that the spirit of the holy gods is in you and that no mystery is too great for you to solve. Now tell me what my dream means.

"'While I was lying in my bed, this is what I dreamed. I saw a large tree in the middle of the earth. The tree grew very tall and strong, reaching high into the heavens for all the world to see. It had fresh green leaves, and it was loaded with fruit for all to eat. Wild animals lived in its shade, and birds nested in its branches. All the world was fed from this tree.

"'Then as I lay there dreaming, I saw a messenger, a holy one, coming down from heaven. The messenger shouted, "Cut down the tree; lop off its branches! Shake off its leaves, and scatter its fruit! Chase the animals from its shade and the birds from its branches. But leave the stump and the roots in the ground, bound with a band of iron and bronze and surrounded by tender grass. Now let him be drenched with the dew of heaven, and let him live like an animal among the plants of the fields. For seven periods of time, let him have the mind of an animal instead of a human. For this has been decreed by the messengers; it is command-ed by the holy ones. The purpose of this decree is that the whole world may understand that the Most High rules over the kingdoms of the world and gives them to anyone he chooses—even to the lowliest of humans."

" 'O Belteshazzar, that was the dream that I, King Nebuchadnezzar, had. Now tell me what it means, for no one else can help me. All the wisest men of my kingdom have failed me. But you can tell me because the spirit of the holy gods is in you.'

Daniel Explains the Dream

"Upon hearing this, Daniel (also known as Belteshazzar) was overcome for a time, aghast at the meaning of the dream. Finally, the king said to him, 'Belteshazzar, don't be alarmed by the dream and what it means.'

"Belteshazzar replied, 'Oh, how I wish the events foreshadowed in this dream would happen to your enemies, my lord, and not to you! You saw a tree growing very tall and strong, reaching high into the heavens for all the world to see. It had fresh green leaves, and it was loaded with fruit for all to eat. Wild animals lived in its shade, and birds nested in its branches. That tree, Your Majesty, is you. For you have grown strong and great; your greatness reaches up to heaven, and your rule to the ends of the earth.

" 'Then you saw a messenger, a holy one, coming down from heaven and say-ing, "Cut down the tree and destroy it. But leave the stump and the roots in the ground, bound with a band of iron and bronze and surrounded by tender grass. Let him be drenched with the dew of heaven. Let him eat grass with the animals of the field for seven periods of time."

" 'This is what the dream means, Your Majesty, and what the Most High has declared will happen to you. You will be driven from human society, and you will live in the fields with the wild animals. You will eat grass like a cow, and you will be drenched with the dew of heaven. Seven periods of time will pass while you live this way, until you learn that the Most High rules over the kingdoms of the world and gives them to anyone he chooses. But the stump and the roots were left in the ground. This means that you will receive your kingdom back again when you have learned that heaven rules.

" 'O King Nebuchadnezzar, please listen to me. Stop sinning and do what is right. Break from your wicked past by being merciful to the poor. Perhaps then you will continue to prosper.'

The Dream's Fulfillment

"But all these things did happen to King Nebuchadnezzar. Twelve months later, he was taking a walk on the flat roof of the royal palace in Babylon. As he looked out across the city, he said, 'Just look at this great city of Babylon! I, by my own mighty power, have built this beautiful city as my royal residence and as an expression of my royal splendor.'

"While he was still speaking these words, a voice called down from heaven, 'O King Nebuchadnezzar, this message is for you! You are no longer ruler of this kingdom. You will be driven from human society. You will live in the fields with the wild animals, and you will eat grass like a cow. Seven periods of time will pass while you live this way, until you learn that the Most High rules over the kingdoms of the world and gives them to anyone he chooses.'

"That very same hour the prophecy was fulfilled, and Nebuchadnezzar was driven from human society. He ate grass like a cow, and he was drenched with the dew of heaven. He lived this way until his hair was as long as eagles' feathers and his nails were like birds' claws.

Nebuchadnezzar Praises God

"After this time had passed, I, Nebuchadnezzar, looked up to heaven. My sanity returned, and I praised and worshiped the Most High and honored the one who lives forever.

Take ANOTHER LOOK

Nebuchadnezzar's story showed how God reacted to pride. This passage from Proverbs below also shows what God thought about pride. Many of the proverbs were written and collected by Solomon, who was considered Israel's wisest and richest king. These proverbs are a warning to anyone who likes to brag.

Proverbs 16:5, 18-20, NLT

The LORD despises pride; be assured that the proud will be punished.

Pride goes before destruction, and haughtiness before a fall.
It is better to live humbly with the poor than to share plunder with the proud.
Those who listen to instruction will prosper; those who trust the LORD will be happy.

Here's What I Think

Kali, age 18

1 Peter 4:10 says, "God has given gifts to each of you from his great variety of spiritual gifts. Manage them well so that God's generosity can flow through you." God has given every one of us spiritual gifts. Isn't that amazing? When I read the story of Daniel, what comes to my mind is his amazing God-given ability to interpret dreams.

God used Daniel's spiritual gift of interpreting dreams to connect with King Nebuchadnezzar and let him know he was disobeying the Lord. It ultimately brought King Nebuchadnezzar back to God. So what gifts has God given you? Does he want you to reach out to someone today? Are you ready to accept God's challenge?

Kali

Use your God-given gifts well.

THE HANDWRITING'S
ON THE WALL

Ontroduction

One bad decision can lead to disaster. When Belshazzar became king of Babylon, he forgot the lesson in humility that God taught his great-grandfather, Nebuchadnezzar. So God had to teach him a new lesson—the last one Belshazzar would ever learn.

Daniel 5:1-31, NLT

A number of years later, King Belshazzar gave a great feast for a thousand of his nobles and drank wine with them. While Belshazzar was drinking, he gave orders to bring in the gold and silver cups that his predecessor, Nebuchadnezzar, had taken from the Temple in Jerusalem, so that he and his nobles, his wives, and his concubines might drink from them. So they brought these gold cups taken from the Temple of God in Jerusalem, and the king and his nobles, his wives, and his concubines drank from them. They drank toasts from them to honor their idols made of gold, silver, bronze, iron, wood, and stone.

At that very moment they saw the fingers of a human hand writing on the plaster wall of the king's palace, near the lampstand. The king himself saw the hand as it wrote, and his face turned pale with fear. Such terror gripped him that his knees knocked together and his legs gave way beneath him.

The king shouted for the enchanters, astrologers, and fortune-tellers to be brought before him. He said to these wise men of Babylon, "Whoever can read this writing and tell me what it means will be dressed in purple robes of royal honor and will wear a gold chain around his neck. He will become the third highest ruler in the kingdom!" But when all the king's wise men came in, none of them could read the writing or tell him what it meant. So the king grew even more alarmed, and his face turned ashen white. His nobles, too, were shaken.

But when the queen mother heard what was happening, she hurried to the banquet hall. She said to Belshazzar, "Long live the king! Don't be so pale and afraid about this. There is a man in your kingdom who has within him the spirit of the holy gods. During Nebuchadnezzar's reign, this man was found to have insight, understanding, and wisdom as though he himself were a god. Your predecessor, King Nebuchadnezzar, made him chief over all the magicians, enchanters, astrologers, and fortune-tellers of Babylon. This man Daniel, whom the king named Belteshazzar, has a sharp mind and is filled with divine knowledge and understanding. He can interpret dreams, explain riddles, and solve difficult problems. Call for Daniel, and he will tell you what the writing means."

Daniel Explains the Writing

So Daniel was brought in before the king. The king asked him, "Are you Daniel, who was exiled from Judah by my predecessor, King Nebuchadnezzar? I have heard that you have the spirit of the gods within you and that you are filled with insight, understanding, and wisdom. My wise men and enchanters have tried to read this writing on the wall, but they cannot. I am told that you can give interpretations and solve difficult problems. If you can read these words and tell me their meaning, you will be clothed in purple robes of royal honor, and you will wear a gold chain around your neck. You will become the third highest ruler in the kingdom."

Daniel answered the king, "Keep your gifts or give them to someone else, but I will tell you what the writing means. Your Majesty, the Most High God gave sovereignty, majesty, glory, and honor to your predecessor, Nebuchadnezzar. He made him so great that people of all races and nations and languages trembled before him in fear. He killed those he wanted to kill and spared those he wanted to spare. He honored those he wanted to honor and disgraced those he wanted to disgrace. But when his heart and mind were hardened with pride, he was brought down from his royal throne and stripped of his glory. He was driven from human society. He was given the mind of an animal, and he lived among the wild donkeys. He ate grass like a cow, and he was drenched with the dew of heaven, until he learned that the Most High God rules the kingdoms of the world and appoints anyone he desires to rule over them.

"You are his successor, O Belshazzar, and you knew all this, yet you have not humbled yourself. For you have defied the Lord of heaven and have had these cups from his Temple brought before you. You and your nobles and your wives and concubines have been drinking wine from them while praising gods of silver, gold, bronze, iron, wood, and stone—gods that neither see nor hear nor know anything at all. But you have not honored the God who gives you the breath of life and controls your destiny! So God has sent this hand to write a message.

"This is the message that was written: MENE, MENE, TEKEL, PARSIN. This is what these words mean:

Mene means 'numbered'—God has numbered the days of your reign and has brought it to an end.

Tekel means 'weighed'—you have been weighed on the balances and have failed the test.

Parsin means 'divided'—your kingdom has been divided and given to the Medes and Persians."

Then at Belshazzar's command, Daniel was dressed in purple robes, a gold chain was hung around his neck, and he was proclaimed the third highest ruler in the kingdom.

That very night Belshazzar, the Babylonian king, was killed. And Darius the Mede took over the kingdom at the age of sixty-two.

Take ANOTHER LOOK

God told the prophet Isaiah to speak a prophecy against Babylon more than 100 years before they conquered Israel. God knew who would conquer the Babylonians way before it happened. How did he know this? Not only does God know everything, he also "assigned this task" himself. When God says that something will happen, it happens.

Isaiah 13:1-11, NLT

Isaiah son of Amoz received this message concerning the destruction of Babylon:

"See the flags waving as the enemy attacks. Cheer them on, O Israel! Wave to them as they march against Babylon to destroy the palaces of the high and mighty. I, the LORD, have assigned this task to these armies, and they will rejoice when I am exalted. I have called them to satisfy my anger."

Hear the noise on the mountains! Listen, as the armies march! It is the noise and the shout of many nations. The LORD Almighty has brought them here to form an army. They came from countries far away. They are the LORD's weapons; they carry his anger with them and will destroy the whole land. Scream in terror, for the LORD's time has arrived—the time for the Almighty to destroy. Every arm is paralyzed with fear. Even the strongest hearts melt and are afraid. Fear grips them with terrible pangs, like those of a woman about to give birth. They look helplessly at one another as the flames of the burning city reflect on their faces. For see, the day of the LORD is coming—the terrible day of his fury and fierce anger. The land will be destroyed and all the sinners with it. The heavens will be black above them. No light will shine from stars or sun or moon.

"I, the LORD, will punish the world for its evil and the wicked for their sin. I will crush the arrogance of the proud and the haughtiness of the mighty."

Here's What I Think

Mike, age 19

So many times it seems that wrongdoing and evil go unpunished. Maybe your classmate cheats on a test and gets away with it. Maybe a bully at school picks on you every day and never gets in trouble. You know you don't deserve getting picked on, but this bully never seems to go away.

In this story, King Belshazzar performed an incredibly disrespectful act towards God. He drank out of the temple goblets while praising other gods. That makes me mad every time I read it. But then it happened. God decided that the king had gone too far, so God wrote the king's punishment on the wall. The king would die that very night, and his kingdom would be given to his enemies. So don't worry when a bully or a cheater seems to get away with it. God knows. He'll take care of it.

Mike

God will write the last word
on those who do wrong.

INTO THE LIONS' DEN

Introduction

How old are your grandparents? Could you imagine them in charge of a country? Older people are sometimes very wise like Daniel. Although Daniel was probably older than your grandparents, he was one of three people in charge of a whole kingdom. The king had great respect for Daniel's wisdom. But not everybody respected Daniel like the king did.

Daniel 6:1-24, NLT

Darius the Mede decided to divide the kingdom into 120 provinces, and he appointed a prince to rule over each province. The king also chose Daniel and two others as administrators to supervise the princes and to watch out for the king's interests. Daniel soon proved himself more capable than all the other administrators and princes. Because of his great ability, the king made plans to place him over the entire empire. Then the other administrators and princes began searching for some fault in the way Daniel was handling his affairs, but they couldn't find anything to criticize. He was faithful and honest and always responsible. So they concluded, "Our only chance of finding grounds for accusing Daniel will be in connection with the requirements of his religion."

So the administrators and princes went to the king and said, "Long live King Darius! We have unanimously agreed that Your Majesty should make a law that will be strictly enforced. Give orders that for the next thirty days anyone who prays to anyone, divine or human—except to Your Majesty—will be thrown to the lions. And let Your Majesty issue and sign this law so it cannot be changed, a law of the Medes and Persians, which cannot be revoked." So King Darius signed the law.

But when Daniel learned that the law had been signed, he went home and knelt down as usual in his upstairs room, with its windows open toward Jerusalem. He prayed three times a day, just as he had always done, giving thanks to his God. The officials went together to Daniel's house and found him praying and asking for God's help. So they went back to the king and reminded him about his law. "Did you not sign a law that for the next thirty days anyone who prays to anyone, divine or human—except to Your Majesty—will be thrown to the lions?"

"Yes," the king replied, "that decision stands; it is a law of the Medes and Persians, which cannot be revoked."

Then they told the king, "That man Daniel, one of the captives from Judah, is paying no attention to you or your law. He still prays to his God three times a day."

Hearing this, the king was very angry with himself for signing the law, and he tried to find a way to save Daniel. He spent the rest of the day looking for a way to get Daniel out of this predicament. In the evening the men went together to the king and said, "Your Majesty knows that according to the law of the Medes and the Persians, no law that the king signs can be changed."

So at last the king gave orders for Daniel to be arrested and thrown into the den of lions. The king said to him, "May your God, whom you worship continually, rescue you."

A stone was brought and placed over the mouth of the den. The king sealed the stone with his own royal seal and the seals of his nobles, so that no one could rescue Daniel from the lions. Then the king returned to his palace and spent the night fasting. He refused his usual entertainment and couldn't sleep at all that night.

Very early the next morning, the king hurried out to the lions' den. When he got there, he called out in anguish, "Daniel, servant of the living God! Was your God, whom you worship continually, able to rescue you from the lions?"

Daniel answered, "Long live the king! My God sent his angel to shut the lions' mouths so that they would not hurt me, for I have been found innocent in his sight. And I have not wronged you, Your Majesty."

The king was overjoyed and ordered that Daniel be lifted from the den. Not a scratch was found on him because he had trusted in his God. Then the king gave orders to arrest the men who had maliciously accused Daniel. He had them thrown into the lions' den, along with their wives and children. The lions leaped on them and tore them apart before they even hit the floor of the den.

Take ANOTHER LOOK

Daniel was surrounded by danger in the den of the lions. You may never be surrounded by hungry lions like Daniel, but you'll feel afraid at some point in your life. Psalm 91 provides hope for people who face scary situations. As you read the psalm, do you truly see God as your "place of safety"?

Psalm 91:1-4, NLT

Those who live in the shelter of the Most High
will find rest in the shadow of the Almighty.

This I declare of the Lord:
He alone is my refuge, my place of safety;
he is my God, and I am trusting him.
For he will rescue you from every trap
and protect you from the fatal plague.
He will shield you with his wings.
He will shelter you with his feathers.
His faithful promises are your armor and protection.

Here's What I Think

Nicee, age 14

My youth minister often jokes that we really should pray over our lunch food at school because you don't know who's in the back cooking. We just laugh when he says that. But we know that if we really did try to pray in the lunchroom, we would never hear the end of it. Well, one day I tried it. After my friends and I had gotten our food, we were at the table laughing and joking. Suddenly I stopped talking and began to say grace. As I prayed, my friends grew silent. I thought for sure that they were going to laugh at me. But surprisingly, when I finished, we just picked up where we had left off talking. I know God kept them from laughing at me because I was willing to set an example in the midst of my biggest critics. Give it a try some-time—you may be surprised at what happens!

Nicee

Pray—anytime, anywhere, for any reason.

»» REBUILDING THE TEMPLE «

Ôntroduction

Imagine returning to a land your great-grandparents may have known, but you've never seen. The people of Israel had been away from their land for 70 years. Many had been born in a foreign land and had never seen the city of Jerusalem. They had only heard stories of its beauty. Now imagine returning to that city and finding it in ruins. How would you feel? What would you do first? Two men knew what to do. The Temple—the place where God was worshiped—needed to be rebuilt.

Ezra 3:1-13, NLT

Now in early autumn, when the Israelites had settled in their towns, all the people assembled together as one person in Jerusalem. Then Jeshua son of Jehozadak with his fellow priests and Zerubbabel son of Shealtiel with his family began to rebuild the altar of the God of Israel so they could sacrifice burnt offerings on it, as instructed in the law of Moses, the man of God. Even though the people were afraid of the local residents, they rebuilt the altar at its old site. Then they immediately began to sacrifice burnt offerings on the altar to the LORD. They did this each morning and evening.

They celebrated the Festival of Shelters as prescribed in the law of Moses, sacrificing the burnt offerings specified for each day of the festival. They also offered the regular burnt offerings and the offerings required for the new moon celebrations and the other annual festivals to the LORD. Freewill offerings were also sacrificed to the LORD by the people. Fifteen days before the Festival of Shelters began, the priests had begun to sacrifice burnt offerings to the LORD. This was also before they had started to lay the foundation of the LORD's Temple.

The People Rebuild the Temple

Then they hired masons and carpenters and bought cedar logs from the people of Tyre and Sidon, paying them with food, wine, and olive oil. The logs were brought down from the Lebanon mountains and floated along the coast of the Mediterranean Sea to Joppa, for King Cyrus had given permission for this.

The construction of the Temple of God began in midspring, during the second year after they arrived in Jerusalem. The work force was made up of everyone who had returned from exile, including Zerubbabel son of Shealtiel, Jeshua son of Jehozadak and his fellow priests, and all the Levites. The Levites who were twenty years old or older were put in charge of rebuilding the LORD's Temple. The workers at the Temple of God were supervised by Jeshua with his sons and relatives, and Kadmiel and his sons, all descendants of Hodaviah. They were helped in this task by the Levites of the family of Henadad.

When the builders completed the foundation of the LORD's Temple, the priests put on their robes and took their places to blow their trumpets. And the Levites, descendants of Asaph, clashed their cymbals to praise the LORD, just as King David had prescribed. With praise and thanks, they sang this song to the LORD:

"He is so good!
His faithful love for Israel endures forever!"

Then all the people gave a great shout, praising the LORD because the foundation of the LORD's Temple had been laid.

Many of the older priests, Levites, and other leaders remembered the first Temple, and they wept aloud when they saw the new Temple's foundation. The others, however, were shouting for joy. The joyful shouting and weeping mingled together in a loud commotion that could be heard far in the distance.

Take ANOTHER LOOK

You can imagine how excited and thankful the people of Israel were to return to their land and rebuild the Temple. Rebuilding the Temple meant a lot to them. In the story you just read, the people of Israel quoted Psalm 106, part of which is below. How much does worship mean to you?

Psalm 106:1-5, NLT

Praise the Lord!
Give thanks to the Lord, for he is good!
    His faithful love endures forever.
Who can list the glorious miracles of the Lord?
    Who can ever praise him half enough?
Happy are those who deal justly with others
    and always do what is right.

Remember me, too, Lord, when you show favor to your people;
    come to me with your salvation.
Let me share in the prosperity of your chosen ones.
    Let me rejoice in the joy of your people;
    let me praise you with those who are your heritage.

Here's What I Think

Walter, age 13

About two years ago my family went on a three-week trip out West. It was awesome! We did it all: Grand Canyon, Black Canyon, Mesa Verde, Carlsbad Caverns, Tombstone, Hollywood, and Zion National Park. After we got back, we were still excited. This past summer we took another trip. It was a two-week trip up North.

We saw the Field of Dreams, Chicago, Indianapolis, and Abraham Lincoln's boyhood home. But for some reason this trip wasn't as good as the first one. There was something about that first trip. It was a lot like when the Levites rebuilt the temple. People mourned because it wasn't the original, elaborate, beautiful temple that they had remembered. The "first" anything always has a special place—but God is there for the "second," "third," or whatever!

Walter

God is in your past, your present, and your future.

THE NEW
QUEEN

Ontroduction

Remember the story of Cinderella? Esther's story is like a real-life fairy tale. When the king of Persia became angry with his wife, Queen Vashti, and decided to find a new one, the search was on. Now Esther was a poor but beautiful young woman who happened to be single. But she was also Jewish—a foreigner living in a land to which her people had been taken many years before. Her people had no status in Persia. Would the king of Persia choose her? Check it out.

Esther 2:1-20, NLT

But after Xerxes' anger had cooled, he began thinking about Vashti and what she had done and the decree he had made. So his attendants suggested, "Let us search the empire to find beautiful young virgins for the king. Let the king appoint agents in each province to bring these beautiful young women into the royal harem at Susa. Hegai, the eunuch in charge, will see that they are all given beauty treatments. After that, the young woman who pleases you most will be made queen instead of Vashti." This advice was very appealing to the king, so he put the plan into effect immediately.

Now at the fortress of Susa there was a certain Jew named Mordecai son of Jair. He was from the tribe of Benjamin and was a descendant of Kish and Shimei. His family had been exiled from Jerusalem to Babylon by King Nebuchadnezzar, along with King Jehoiachin of Judah and many others. This man had a beautiful and lovely young cousin, Hadassah, who was also called Esther. When her father and mother had died, Mordecai adopted her into his family and raised her as his own daughter. As a result of the king's decree, Esther, along with many other young women, was brought to the king's harem at the fortress of Susa and placed in Hegai's care. Hegai was very impressed with Esther and treated her kindly. He quickly ordered a special menu for her and provided her with beauty treatments. He also assigned her seven maids specially chosen from the king's palace, and he moved her and her maids into the best place in the harem.

Esther had not told anyone of her nationality and family background, for Mordecai had told her not to. Every day Mordecai would take a walk near the courtyard of the harem to ask about Esther and to find out what was happening to her.

Before each young woman was taken to the king's bed, she was given the prescribed twelve months of beauty treatments—six months with oil of myrrh, followed by six months with special perfumes and ointments. When the time came for her to go in to the king, she was given her choice of whatever clothing or jewelry she wanted to enhance her beauty. That evening she was taken to the king's private rooms, and the next morning she was brought to the second harem, where the king's wives lived. There she would be under the care of Shaashgaz, another of the king's eunuchs. She would live there for the rest of her life, never going to the king again unless he had especially enjoyed her and requested her by name.

When it was Esther's turn to go to the king, she accepted the advice of Hegai, the eunuch in charge of the harem. She asked for nothing except what he suggested, and she was admired by everyone who saw her. When Esther was taken to King Xerxes at the royal palace in early winter of the seventh year of his reign, the king loved her more than any of the other young women. He was so delighted with her that he set the royal crown on her head and declared her queen instead of Vashti. To celebrate the occasion, he gave a banquet in Esther's honor for all his princes and servants, giving generous gifts to everyone and declaring a public festival for the provinces.

Even after all the young women had been transferred to the second harem and Mordecai had become a palace official, Esther continued to keep her nationality and family background a secret. She was still following Mordecai's orders, just as she did when she was living in his home.

Take ANOTHER LOOK

Esther's not the only one who was chosen. The God of the universe chose us to belong to him. He's even more delighted in us than Xerxes was with Esther. Unlike Xerxes' kingdom, God's kingdom will last forever!

Ephesians 1:3-8, NLT

How we praise God, the Father of our Lord Jesus Christ, who has blessed us with every spiritual blessing in the heavenly realms because we belong to Christ. Long ago, even before he made the world, God loved us and chose us in Christ to be holy and without fault in his eyes. His unchanging plan has always been to adopt us into his own family by bringing us to himself through Jesus Christ. And this gave him great pleasure. So we praise God for the wonderful kindness he has poured out on us because we belong to his dearly loved Son. He is so rich in kindness that he purchased our freedom through the blood of his Son, and our sins are forgiven. He has showered his kindness on us, along with all wisdom and understanding.

Here's What I Think

Julie, age 18

I really don't like contests or competition. So when I participated in a college scholarship contest, I was *nervous*. I had to compete with more than 100 other kids and prove that I was a good enough student to earn the scholarship. I kept thinking, *These other kids are perfect! Why would the college want me, anyway?*

Esther probably felt the same way. There were hundreds of beautiful girls competing to be queen, and she was just a simple Jewish orphan. Even so, it was God's plan for her to become queen—and that's exactly what happened.

Although I felt pretty insignificant during the contest, I later found out that I had won the scholarship. I should have trusted in God's plan from the beginning (instead of being nervous) because he always knew what was best for me. In God's eyes, I'm not insignificant at all . . . and neither are you.

Julie

God chooses you!

»»» ESTHER SAVES THE DAY «««

Ôntroduction

As king of Persia, Xerxes had total control. He could even command someone to be put to death. Decisions were made only with his approval. The king approved a plan to kill all of the Jews in Persia. The king's prime minister, Haman, was jealous of Mordecai's standing and wanted to get rid of all Jews. Though Esther was the queen, she couldn't even go near the king without his permission. She could be put to death just for walking into his throne room. Would she risk her life to save her people, the Jews?

Esther 4:1-17; 5:1-8; 7:1-8, NLT

When Mordecai learned what had been done, he tore his clothes, put on sackcloth and ashes, and went out into the city, crying with a loud and bitter wail. He stood outside the gate of the palace, for no one was allowed to enter while wearing clothes of mourning. And as news of the king's decree reached all the provinces, there was great mourning among the Jews. They fasted, wept, and wailed, and many people lay in sackcloth and ashes.

When Queen Esther's maids and eunuchs came and told her about Mordecai, she was deeply distressed. She sent clothing to him to replace the sackcloth, but he refused it. Then Esther sent for Hathach, one of the king's eunuchs who had been appointed as her attendant. She ordered him to go to Mordecai and find out what was troubling him and why he was in mourning. So Hathach went out to Mordecai in the square in front of the palace gate.

Mordecai told him the whole story and told him how much money Haman had promised to pay into the royal treasury for the destruction of the Jews. Mordecai gave Hathach a copy of the decree issued in Susa that called for the death of all Jews, and he asked Hathach to show it to Esther. He also asked Hathach to explain it to her and to urge her to go to the king to beg for mercy and plead for her people. So Hathach returned to Esther with Mordecai's message.

Then Esther told Hathach to go back and relay this message to Mordecai:

"The whole world knows that anyone who appears before the king in his inner court without being invited is doomed to die unless the king holds out his gold scepter. And the king has not called for me to come to him in more than a month." So Hathach gave Esther's message to Mordecai.

Mordecai sent back this reply to Esther: "Don't think for a moment that you will escape there in the palace when all other Jews are killed. If you keep quiet at a time like this, deliverance for the Jews will arise from some other place, but you and your relatives will die. What's more, who can say but that you have been elevated to the palace for just such a time as this?"

Then Esther sent this reply to Mordecai: "Go and gather together all the Jews of Susa and fast for me. Do not eat or drink for three days, night or day. My maids and I will do the same. And then, though it is against the law, I will go in to see the king. If I must die, I am willing to die." So Mordecai went away and did as Esther told him.

Esther's Request to the King, 5:1-8

Three days later, Esther put on her royal robes and entered the inner court of the palace, just across from the king's hall. The king was sitting on his royal throne, facing the entrance. When he saw Queen Esther standing there in the inner court, he welcomed her, holding out the gold scepter to her. So Esther approached and touched its tip.

Then the king asked her, "What do you want, Queen Esther? What is your request? I will give it to you, even if it is half the kingdom!"

And Esther replied, "If it please Your Majesty, let the king and Haman come today to a banquet I have prepared for the king."

The king turned to his attendants and said, "Tell Haman to come quickly to a banquet, as Esther has requested." So the king and Haman went to Esther's banquet.

And while they were drinking wine, the king said to Esther, "Now tell me what you really want. What is your request? I will give it to you, even if it is half the kingdom!"

Esther replied, "This is my request and deepest wish. If Your Majesty is pleased with me and wants to grant my request, please come with Haman tomorrow to the banquet I will prepare for you. Then tomorrow I will explain what this is all about."

The King Executes Haman, 7:1-10

So the king and Haman went to Queen Esther's banquet. And while they were drinking wine that day, the king again asked her, "Tell me what you want, Queen Esther. What is your request? I will give it to you, even if it is half the kingdom!"

And so Queen Esther replied, "If Your Majesty is pleased with me and wants to grant my request, my petition is that my life and the lives of my people will be spared. For my people and I have been sold to those who would kill, slaughter, and annihilate us. If we had only been sold as slaves, I could remain quiet, for that would have been a matter too trivial to warrant disturbing the king."

"Who would do such a thing?" King Xerxes demanded. "Who would dare touch you?"

Esther replied, "This wicked Haman is our enemy." Haman grew pale with fright before the king and queen. Then the king jumped to his feet in a rage and went out into the palace garden.

But Haman stayed behind to plead for his life with Queen Esther, for he knew that he was doomed. In despair he fell on the couch where Queen Esther was reclining, just as the king returned from the palace garden. "Will he even assault the queen right here in the palace, before my very eyes?" the king roared. And as soon as the king spoke, his attendants covered Haman's face, signaling his doom.

Take ANOTHER LOOK

Thanks to Mordecai's warning and Esther's quick thinking, their people were saved. And even though God wasn't mentioned in the story, he was the behind-the-scenes hero who made Esther's victory possible. So a new holiday was celebrated to remember the story of Esther and the defeat of Haman.

Esther 9:20-26, NLT

Mordecai recorded these events and sent letters to the Jews near and far, throughout all the king's provinces, encouraging them to celebrate an annual festival on these two days. He told them to celebrate these days with feasting and gladness and by giving gifts to each other and to the poor. This would commemorate a time when the Jews gained relief from their enemies, when their sorrow was turned into gladness and their mourning into joy.

So the Jews adopted Mordecai's suggestion and began this annual custom. Haman son of Hammedatha the Agagite, the enemy of the Jews, had plotted to crush and destroy them on the day and month determined by casting lots (the lots were called *purim*). But when Esther came before the king, he issued a decree causing Haman's evil plot to backfire, and Haman and his sons were hanged on the gallows. (That is why this celebration is called Purim, because it is the ancient word for casting lots.)

Here's What I Think

Verity, age 13

When Esther was called upon to save the Jews from death, she made excuses at first. But then Esther realized that Mordecai was right—God had put her in a place where she was in the king's favor. At the right time, Esther could carry out her purpose in God's plan.

Often, God calls upon us to do something for him. Whether it's a simple smile or a heart-to-heart talk with a friend, God wants us to fulfill his task. Everyone in our lives is put there for a reason. We have to learn to respond to God's call, as Esther did.

I remember one day my friend and I were listening to music. Coincidentally, I had a CD with me called *Father's Love Letter*, and we listened to it together. It was very emotional for her. She cried some, and I prayed with her. It was so amazing how everything happened. God knew that we would have that moment together, and it was no accident that the CD was with me. We are all put in different situations for a specific reason. We just have to do what God wants.

Verity

Look where God has put you today.

»HOME AT LAST «

Ïntroduction

The people of Israel had finally returned home. They wanted to rebuild their land. But people from other nations living in the area put a stop to the rebuilding for a long time. Would God allow the work to continue? Ezra, a priest and scribe, hoped so.

Ezra 7:1-26, NLT

Many years later, during the reign of King Artaxerxes of Persia, there was a man named Ezra. He was the son of Seraiah, son of Azariah, son of Hilkiah, son of Shallum, son of Zadok, son of Ahitub, son of Amariah, son of Azariah, son of Meraioth, son of Zerahiah, son of Uzzi, son of Bukki, son of Abishua, son of Phinehas, son of Eleazar, son of Aaron the high priest. This Ezra was a scribe, well versed in the law of Moses, which the LORD, the God of Israel, had given to the people of Israel. He came up to Jerusalem from Babylon, and the king gave him everything he asked for, because the gracious hand of the LORD his God was on him.

Some of the people of Israel, as well as some of the priests, Levites, singers, gatekeepers, and Temple servants, traveled up to Jerusalem with him in the seventh year of King Artaxerxes' reign.

Ezra arrived in Jerusalem in August of that year. He had left Babylon on April 8 and came to Jerusalem on August 4, for the gracious hand of his God was on him. This was because Ezra had determined to study and obey the law of the LORD and to teach those laws and regulations to the people of Israel.

Artaxerxes' Letter to Ezra

King Artaxerxes had presented a copy of this letter to Ezra, the priest and scribe who studied and taught the commands and laws of the LORD to Israel:

"Greetings from Artaxerxes, the king of kings, to Ezra the priest, the teacher of the law of the God of heaven.

"I decree that any of the people of Israel in my kingdom, including the priests and Levites, may volunteer to return to Jerusalem with you. I and my Council of Seven hereby instruct you to conduct an inquiry into the situation in Judah and Jerusalem, based on your God's law, which is in your hand. We also commission you to take with you some silver and gold, which we are freely presenting as an offering to the God of Israel who lives in Jerusalem.

"Moreover you are to take any silver and gold which you may obtain from the province of Babylon, as well as the freewill offerings of the people and the priests that are presented for the Temple of their God in Jerusalem. These donations are to be used specifically for the purchase of bulls, rams, lambs, and the appropriate grain offerings and drink offerings, all of which will be offered on the altar of the Temple of your God in Jerusalem. Any money that is left over may be used in whatever way you and your colleagues feel is the will of your God. But as for the utensils we are entrusting to you for the service of the Temple of your God, deliver them in full to the God of Jerusalem. If you run short of money for anything necessary for your God's Temple or for any similar needs, you may requisition funds from the royal treasury.

"I, Artaxerxes the king, hereby send this decree to all the treasurers in the province west of the Euphrates River: 'You are to give Ezra whatever he requests of you, for he is a priest and teacher of the law of the God of heaven. You are to give him up to 7,500 pounds of silver, 500 bushels of wheat, 550 gallons of wine, 550 gallons of olive oil, and an unlimited supply of salt. Be careful to provide whatever the God of heaven demands for his Temple, for why should we risk bringing God's anger against the realm of the king and his sons? I also decree that no priest, Levite, singer, gatekeeper, Temple servant, or other worker in this Temple of God will be required to pay taxes of any kind.'

"And you, Ezra, are to use the wisdom God has given you to appoint magistrates and judges who know your God's laws to govern all the people in the province west of the Euphrates River. If the people are not familiar with those laws, you must teach them. Anyone who refuses to obey the law of your God and the law of the king will be punished immediately by death, banishment, confiscation of goods, or imprisonment."

Take ANOTHER LOOK

Like Ezra, Nehemiah was a man of Israel who had never seen his homeland. Yet God gave him the desire to return and help with the rebuilding process. But also like Ezra, Nehemiah couldn't just pack his suitcases and leave. He had to have permission from the king.

Nehemiah 2:1-6, NLT

Early the following spring, during the twentieth year of King Artaxerxes' reign, I was serving the king his wine. I had never appeared sad in his presence before this time. So the king asked me, "Why are you so sad? You aren't sick, are you? You look like a man with deep troubles."

Then I was badly frightened, but I replied, "Long live the king! Why shouldn't I be sad? For the city where my ancestors are buried is in ruins, and the gates have been burned down."

The king asked, "Well, how can I help you?"

With a prayer to the God of heaven, I replied, "If it please Your Majesty and if you are pleased with me, your servant, send me to Judah to rebuild the city where my ancestors are buried."

The king, with the queen sitting beside him, asked, "How long will you be gone? When will you return?" So the king agreed, and I set a date for my departure.

Here's What I Think

Jammeshia, age 17

There have been times when I felt far from God. At those points, I have decided that I don't have to go to God daily and pray and read his Word. And so my life seems somewhat empty. At those times, I realize that I am nothing like Ezra in this story. He studied God's Word daily and always used it in his life. It is awesome to see the ways the Lord will use us if we just seek him on a daily basis. After reading this passage, I know now that God is ready and wants to use me if I just make myself available to him.

Jammeshia

Keep connected to God so he can use you.

A JOB
WELL DONE

Before moving back to Israel, Nehemiah was the wine taster for the king of Persia. Although that was an important job, God had a different job in mind for Nehemiah. God wanted Nehemiah to lead the rebuilding project in Jerusalem, where Ezra was now living. The city wall needed to be rebuilt to allow the people to feel safe. This project would need the cooperation of all of the people of Israel to get the job done and overcome opposition. And with everyone's help, the job was completed in a record 52 days!

Nehemiah 2:11-20; 4:1-23, NLT

Three days after my arrival at Jerusalem, I slipped out during the night, taking only a few others with me. I had not told anyone about the plans God had put in my heart for Jerusalem. We took no pack animals with us, except the donkey that I myself was riding. I went out through the Valley Gate, past the Jackal's Well, and over to the Dung Gate to inspect the broken walls and burned gates. Then I went to the Fountain Gate and to the King's Pool, but my donkey couldn't get through the rubble. So I went up the Kidron Valley instead, inspecting the wall before I turned back and entered again at the Valley Gate.

The city officials did not know I had been out there or what I was doing, for I had not yet said anything to anyone about my plans. I had not yet spoken to the religious and political leaders, the officials, or anyone else in the administration. But now I said to them, "You know full well the tragedy of our city. It lies in ruins, and its gates are burned. Let us rebuild the wall of Jerusalem and rid ourselves of this disgrace!" Then I told them about how the gracious hand of God had been on me, and about my conversation with the king.

They replied at once, "Good! Let's rebuild the wall!" So they began the good work.

But when Sanballat, Tobiah, and Geshem the Arab heard of our plan, they scoffed contemptuously. "What are you doing, rebelling against the king like this?" they asked.

But I replied, "The God of heaven will help us succeed. We his servants will start rebuilding this wall. But you have no stake or claim in Jerusalem."

Enemies Oppose the Rebuilding, 4:1-23

Sanballat was very angry when he learned that we were rebuilding the wall. He flew into a rage and mocked the Jews, saying in front of his friends and the Samarian army officers, "What does this bunch of poor, feeble Jews think they are doing? Do they think they can build the wall in a day if they offer enough sacrifices? Look at those charred stones they are pulling out of the rubbish and using again!"

Tobiah the Ammonite, who was standing beside him, remarked, "That stone wall would collapse if even a fox walked along the top of it!"

Then I prayed, "Hear us, O our God, for we are being mocked. May their scoffing fall back on their own heads, and may they themselves become captives in a foreign land! Do not ignore their guilt. Do not blot out their sins, for they have provoked you to anger here in the presence of the builders."

At last the wall was completed to half its original height around the entire city, for the people had worked very hard. But when Sanballat and Tobiah and the Arabs, Ammonites, and Ashdodites heard that the work was going ahead and that the gaps in the wall were being repaired, they became furious. They all made plans to come and fight against Jerusalem and to bring about confusion there. But we prayed to our God and guarded the city day and night to protect ourselves.

Then the people of Judah began to complain that the workers were becoming tired. There was so much rubble to be moved that we could never get it done by ourselves. Meanwhile, our enemies were saying, "Before they know what's happening, we will swoop down on them and kill them and end their work."

The Jews who lived near the enemy came and told us again and again, "They will come from all directions and attack us!" So I placed armed guards behind the lowest parts of the wall in the exposed areas. I stationed the people to stand guard by families, armed with swords, spears, and bows.

Then as I looked over the situation, I called together the leaders and the people and said to them, "Don't be afraid of the enemy! Remember the Lord, who is great and glorious, and fight for your friends, your families, and your homes!"

When our enemies heard that we knew of their plans and that God had frustrated them, we all returned to our work on the wall. But from then on, only half my men worked while the other half stood guard with spears, shields, bows, and coats of mail. The officers stationed themselves behind the people of Judah who were building the wall. The common laborers carried on their work with one hand supporting their load and one hand holding a weapon. All the builders had a sword belted to their side. The trumpeter stayed with me to sound the alarm.

Then I explained to the nobles and officials and all the people, "The work is very spread out, and we are widely separated from each other along the wall. When you hear the blast of the trumpet, rush to wherever it is sounding. Then our God will fight for us!"

We worked early and late, from sunrise to sunset. And half the men were always on guard. I also told everyone living outside the walls to move into Jerusalem. That way they and their servants could go on guard duty at night as well as work during the day. During this time, none of us—not I, nor my relatives, nor my servants, nor the guards who were with me—ever took off our clothes. We carried our weapons with us at all times, even when we went for water.

Take ANOTHER LOOK

Now that all of the hard work of rebuilding had been done, Nehemiah and Ezra had one more thing to do. It was time to rebuild the people's faith in God. Ezra started the process by reading God's laws to the people. Nehemiah and the Levites, the assistants to the priests, helped the people understand what was read.

Nehemiah 8:1-8, NLT

So on October 8 Ezra the priest brought the scroll of the law before the assembly, which included the men and women and all the children old enough to understand. He faced the square just inside the Water Gate from early morning until noon and read aloud to everyone who could understand. All the people paid close attention to the Book of the Law. Ezra the scribe stood on a high wooden platform that had been made for the occasion. To his right stood Mattithiah, Shema, Anaiah, Uriah, Hilkiah, and Maaseiah. To his left stood Pedaiah, Mishael, Malkijah, Hashum, Hashbaddanah, Zechariah, and Meshullam. Ezra stood on the platform in full view of all the people. When they saw him open the book, they all rose to their feet.

Then Ezra praised the LORD, the great God, and all the people chanted, "Amen! Amen!" as they lifted their hands toward heaven. Then they bowed down and worshiped the LORD with their faces to the ground.

Now the Levites—Jeshua, Bani, Sherebiah, Jamin, Akkub, Shabbethai, Hodiah, Maaseiah, Kelita, Azariah, Jozabad, Hanan, and Pelaiah—instructed the people who were standing there. They read from the Book of the Law of God and clearly explained the meaning of what was being read, helping the people understand each passage.

Here's What I Think

Daniel, age 15

Teamwork is definitely very apparent in this story. Here the whole community, blacksmiths, gold-smiths, and the rest joined together to build a wall. I was interested to learn how the Jewish people worked in this story. For example, some Bible translations describe the people working *zealously* (with enthusiasm) to repair their section of the wall.

Lifting and carrying heavy, dirty stones had to be hard and unpleasant work. I mean that was labor-intensive stuff! That has to be one of the greatest acts of worship to God—to do something totally hard, draining, and difficult with joy in your heart. I think this is a great example for me to remember when I'm faced with a hard, boring job!

Daniel

Whatever you do for the Lord,
do it enthusiastically.

THE NEW TESTAMENT

A NEW COVENANT BEGINS

Introduction

Long ago, a herald's job was to prepare the people of a kingdom for the coming of a king or queen. Heralds would announce the major events of a ruler's life: his birth, her triumphs, his death, her marriage, and so on. Every good or bad monarch had a herald of some kind. Now, a herald's own birth was usually not front-page news. But the herald in this story had an assignment that came directly from God. And that herald would someday prepare the hearts of his people for the coming of the Savior, who would be called the King of kings. And that Savior would bring about a new agreement between God and people. This is the way the New Testament begins.

Luke 1:5-25, NLT

It all begins with a Jewish priest, Zechariah, who lived when Herod was king of Judea. Zechariah was a member of the priestly order of Abijah. His wife, Elizabeth, was also from the priestly line of Aaron. Zechariah and Elizabeth were righteous in God's eyes, careful to obey all of the Lord's commandments and regulations. They had no children because Elizabeth was barren, and now they were both very old.

One day Zechariah was serving God in the Temple, for his order was on duty that week. As was the custom of the priests, he was chosen by lot to enter the sanctuary and burn incense in the Lord's presence. While the incense was being burned, a great crowd stood outside, praying.

Zechariah was in the sanctuary when an angel of the Lord appeared, standing to the right of the incense altar. Zechariah was overwhelmed with fear. But the angel said, "Don't be afraid, Zechariah! For God has heard your prayer, and your wife, Elizabeth, will bear you a son! And you are to name him John. You will have great joy and gladness, and many will rejoice with you at his birth, for he will be great in the eyes of the Lord. He must never touch wine or hard liquor, and he will be filled with the Holy Spirit, even before his birth. And he will persuade many Israelites to turn to the Lord their God. He will be a man with the spirit and power of Elijah, the prophet of old. He will precede the coming of the Lord, preparing the people for his arrival. He will turn the hearts of the fathers to their children, and he will change disobedient minds to accept godly wisdom."

Zechariah said to the angel, "How can I know this will happen? I'm an old man now, and my wife is also well along in years."

Then the angel said, "I am Gabriel! I stand in the very presence of God. It was he who sent me to bring you this good news! And now, since you didn't believe what I said, you won't be able to speak until the child is born. For my words will certainly come true at the proper time."

Meanwhile, the people were waiting for Zechariah to come out, wondering why he was taking so long. When he finally did come out, he couldn't speak to them. Then they realized from his gestures that he must have seen a vision in the Temple sanctuary.

He stayed at the Temple until his term of service was over, and then he returned home. Soon afterward his wife, Elizabeth, became pregnant and went into seclusion for five months. "How kind the Lord is!" she exclaimed. "He has taken away my disgrace of having no children!"

Take ANOTHER LOOK

Gabriel also announced a birth to Elizabeth's cousin. This woman's child was to be the most amazing child ever. The child's birth would fulfill a prophecy spoken by the prophet Isaiah.

Luke 1:26-38, NLT

In the sixth month of Elizabeth's pregnancy, God sent the angel Gabriel to Nazareth, a village in Galilee, to a virgin named Mary. She was engaged to be married to a man named Joseph, a descendant of King David. Gabriel appeared to her and said, "Greetings, favored woman! The Lord is with you!"

Confused and disturbed, Mary tried to think what the angel could mean. "Don't be frightened, Mary," the angel told her, "for God has decided to bless you! You will become pregnant and have a son, and you are to name him Jesus. He will be very great and will be called the Son of the Most High. And the Lord God will give him the throne of his ancestor David. And he will reign over Israel forever; his Kingdom will never end!"

Mary asked the angel, "But how can I have a baby? I am a virgin."

The angel replied, "The Holy Spirit will come upon you, and the power of the Most High will overshadow you. So the baby born to you will be holy, and he will be called the Son of God. What's more, your relative Elizabeth has become pregnant in her old age! People used to say she was barren, but she's already in her sixth month. For nothing is impossible with God."

Mary responded, "I am the Lord's servant, and I am willing to accept whatever he wants. May everything you have said come true." And then the angel left.

Here's What I Think

Janna, age 14

Zechariah was known as a righteous man. He and Elizabeth prayed for a child. But Elizabeth was rather old and still had no children. Yet God miraculously sent an angel to tell Zechariah that they would have a son. God heard their prayers and answered them! God does hear our prayers too.

My sister-in-law was diagnosed with cancer. Because of the cancer, she can't have children. Many of our family and friends are praying that God will heal her so that she and my brother might be able to have kids. God will always answer our prayers, but not necessarily the way we want. God did give Zechariah and Elizabeth a son, but he might not heal my sister-in-law of her cancer. Still, God knows what is best. He has a perfect plan for us. We should remember that when we pray. Ask God to have his will done, not ours.

Janna

God hears our prayers and answers them!

»»» HIS NAME IS JOHN «««

Introduction

Long ago, the people of Israel had a tradition. They named a child after a family member. That would mean that Zechariah and Elizabeth would call their child Zechariah. But this elderly couple broke tradition to follow the angel's command. Here's how it happened.

Luke 1:57-80, NLT

Now it was time for Elizabeth's baby to be born, and it was a boy. The word spread quickly to her neighbors and relatives that the Lord had been very kind to her, and everyone rejoiced with her.

When the baby was eight days old, all the relatives and friends came for the circumcision ceremony. They wanted to name him Zechariah, after his father. But Elizabeth said, "No! His name is John!"

"What?" they exclaimed. "There is no one in all your family by that name." So they asked the baby's father, communicating to him by making gestures. He motioned for a writing tablet, and to everyone's surprise he wrote, "His name is John!" Instantly Zechariah could speak again, and he began praising God.

Wonder fell upon the whole neighborhood, and the news of what had happened spread throughout the Judean hills. Everyone who heard about it reflected on these events and asked, "I wonder what this child will turn out to be? For the hand of the Lord is surely upon him in a special way."

Zechariah's Prophecy

Then his father, Zechariah, was filled with the Holy Spirit and gave this prophecy:
"Praise the Lord, the God of Israel,
  because he has visited his people and redeemed them.
He has sent us a mighty Savior
  from the royal line of his servant David,
just as he promised
  through his holy prophets long ago.
Now we will be saved from our enemies
  and from all who hate us.

He has been merciful to our ancestors
by remembering his sacred covenant with them,
the covenant he gave to our ancestor Abraham.
We have been rescued from our enemies,
so we can serve God without fear,
in holiness and righteousness forever.

"And you, my little son,
will be called the prophet of the Most High,
because you will prepare the way for the Lord.
You will tell his people how to find salvation
through forgiveness of their sins.
Because of God's tender mercy,
the light from heaven is about to break upon us,
to give light to those who sit in darkness and in the shadow of death,
and to guide us to the path of peace."

John grew up and became strong in spirit. Then he lived out in the wilderness until he began his public ministry to Israel.

Take ANOTHER LOOK

From birth, John was set apart for special service to God. He may have been forbidden to drink wine as part of the Nazirite vow—a special vow taken by individuals who were called to serve God in a specific way. Samson was under the Nazirite vow, and Samuel may have been also. Here is what was included in the vow.

Numbers 6:1-8, NLT

Then the LORD said to Moses, "Speak to the people of Israel and give them these instructions: If some of the people, either men or women, take the special vow of a Nazirite, setting themselves apart to the LORD in a special way, they must give up wine and other alcoholic drinks. They must not use vinegar made from wine, they must not drink other fermented drinks or fresh grape juice, and they must not eat grapes or raisins. As long as they are bound by their Nazirite vow, they are not allowed to eat or drink anything that comes from a grapevine, not even the grape seeds or skins.

"They must never cut their hair throughout the time of their vow, for they are holy and set apart to the LORD. That is why they must let their hair grow long. And they may not go near a dead body during the entire period of their vow to the LORD, even if their own father, mother, brother, or sister has died. They must not defile the hair on their head, because it is the symbol of their separation to God. This applies as long as they are set apart to the LORD.

Here's What I Think

Faith, age 14

I often wonder what I'll do with my life. I know God says he has a plan for my life, but the future seems so unclear. How in the world could he know exactly what's in store for me? Then I read about John the Baptist's birth. I saw that from the moment John was born, God's plan was being played out in John's life. God even used John's dad, Zechariah, to give John his name and to tell others about what God had planned for John. This story helps me to realize that God is working in my life right now to fulfill his incredible plan for me! All I have to do is trust God and let God continue his work in me. "For I know the plans I have for you" says the LORD. "They are plans for good and not for disaster, to give you a hope and a future" (Jeremiah 29:11). What an amazing promise!

Faith

God has great plans for you!

BC | 4,000 | 2,000 | 1,000 | 500 | 0 | 25 | 50 | 75 | 100 | 125 | AD

»» JOY TO THE WORLD ««

Introduction

Some birth announcements are printed in the newspaper. Some are written on cards. One special birth announcement was "written" in the sky by a star and a chorus of angels. Jesus was that special child. He was the Son of God, but he wasn't born in a fancy hospital (there weren't any back then) or even in a comfortable room.

Luke 2:1-20, NLT

At that time the Roman emperor, Augustus, decreed that a census should be taken throughout the Roman Empire. (This was the first census taken when Quirinius was governor of Syria.) All returned to their own towns to register for this census. And because Joseph was a descendant of King David, he had to go to Bethlehem in Judea, David's ancient home. He traveled there from the village of Nazareth in Galilee. He took with him Mary, his fiancée, who was obviously pregnant by this time.

And while they were there, the time came for her baby to be born. She gave birth to her first child, a son. She wrapped him snugly in strips of cloth and laid him in a manger, because there was no room for them in the village inn.

The Shepherds and Angels

That night some shepherds were in the fields outside the village, guarding their flocks of sheep. Suddenly, an angel of the Lord appeared among them, and the radiance of the Lord's glory surrounded them. They were terribly frightened, but the angel reassured them. "Don't be afraid!" he said. "I bring you good news of great joy for everyone! The Savior—yes, the Messiah, the Lord—has been born tonight in Bethlehem, the city of David! And this is how you will recognize him: You will find a baby lying in a manger, wrapped snugly in strips of cloth!"

Suddenly, the angel was joined by a vast host of others—the armies of heaven—praising God:

"Glory to God in the highest heaven,
and peace on earth to all whom God favors."

When the angels had returned to heaven, the shepherds said to each other, "Come on, let's go to Bethlehem! Let's see this wonderful thing that has happened, which the Lord has told us about."

They ran to the village and found Mary and Joseph. And there was the baby, lying in the manger. Then the shepherds told everyone what had happened and what the angel had said to them about this child. All who heard the shepherds' story were astonished, but Mary quietly treasured these things in her heart and thought about them often. The shepherds went back to their fields and flocks, glorifying and praising God for what the angels had told them, and because they had seen the child, just as the angel had said.

Take ANOTHER LOOK

Before Jesus was born, Mary made up her own song of praise to God. Her song told all about the great things God did for his people. God had remembered his promise to send the Savior, and now that Savior was finally here.

Luke 1:46-55, NLT

Mary responded,
"Oh, how I praise the Lord.
    How I rejoice in God my Savior!
For he took notice of his lowly servant girl,
    and now generation after generation
        will call me blessed.
For he, the Mighty One, is holy,
    and he has done great things for me.
    His mercy goes on from generation to generation,
        to all who fear him.
His mighty arm does tremendous things!
    How he scatters the proud and haughty ones!
He has taken princes from their thrones
    and exalted the lowly.
He has satisfied the hungry with good things
    and sent the rich away with empty hands.
And how he has helped his servant Israel!
    He has not forgotten his promise to be merciful.
For he promised our ancestors—Abraham and his children—
    to be merciful to them forever."

Here's What I Think

Kali, age 18

When I read this story again, it hit me that Jesus was a servant his entire life. Although he was called King of kings, Jesus never desired a position of royalty or power. Jesus was like this from the very moment of his birth! Since he was the king of everything, you would think that Jesus would have been born in a nicer place instead of a smelly stable.

You would think that his parents would be "somebodies"—not a lowly carpenter or a no-name young woman. You would think that his first visitors would be kings or high-powered officials—not a bunch of unimportant shepherds. But Jesus' whole purpose in coming to Earth was to do his Father's will and serve us. Shouldn't we, in turn, serve each other too? How can you serve someone else today?

Kali

Learn from the baby born in a stable—live to serve others!

»»» A LIGHT FOR ALL PEOPLE ««

Introduction

When God gave Moses the rules that he wanted the people to follow, God included some rules for parents. Special offerings were to be given for a firstborn son at the temple. This child was usually dedicated to God for his service. There was even a rule for poor people like Joseph and Mary who couldn't afford to give an expensive offering. So, in obedience to the Law, Mary and Joseph traveled to Jerusalem to visit the temple.

Luke 2:21-40, NLT

Eight days later, when the baby was circumcised, he was named Jesus, the name given him by the angel even before he was conceived.

Then it was time for the purification offering, as required by the law of Moses after the birth of a child; so his parents took him to Jerusalem to present him to the Lord. The law of the Lord says, "If a woman's first child is a boy, he must be dedicated to the Lord." So they offered a sacrifice according to what was required in the law of the Lord—"either a pair of turtledoves or two young pigeons."

The Prophecy of Simeon

Now there was a man named Simeon who lived in Jerusalem. He was a righteous man and very devout. He was filled with the Holy Spirit, and he eagerly expected the Messiah to come and rescue Israel. The Holy Spirit had revealed to him that he would not die until he had seen the Lord's Messiah. That day the Spirit led him to the Temple. So when Mary and Joseph came to present the baby Jesus to the Lord as the law required, Simeon was there. He took the child in his arms and praised God, saying,

"Lord, now I can die in peace!
As you promised me,
I have seen the Savior
you have given to all people.
He is a light to reveal God to the nations,
and he is the glory of your people Israel!"

Joseph and Mary were amazed at what was being said about Jesus. Then Simeon blessed them, and he said to Mary, "This child will be rejected by many in Israel, and it will be their undoing. But he will be the greatest joy to many others. Thus, the deepest thoughts of many hearts will be revealed. And a sword will pierce your very soul."

The Prophecy of Anna

Anna, a prophet, was also there in the Temple. She was the daughter of Phanuel, of the tribe of Asher, and was very old. She was a widow, for her husband had died when they had been married only seven years. She was now eighty-four years old. She never left the Temple but stayed there day and night, worshiping God with fasting and prayer. She came along just as Simeon was talking with Mary and Joseph, and she began praising God. She talked about Jesus to everyone who had been waiting for the promised King to come and deliver Jerusalem.

When Jesus' parents had fulfilled all the requirements of the law of the Lord, they returned home to Nazareth in Galilee. There the child grew up healthy and strong. He was filled with wisdom beyond his years, and God placed his special favor upon him.

Take ANOTHER LOOK

Many prophets like Isaiah talked about the coming Savior. Even though Isaiah never saw the Savior in person like Simeon and Anna did, he believed that God would send the Messiah someday. And Simeon's words echoed Isaiah's prophecy that the Savior would be a light for all people.

Isaiah 9:2-7, NLT

The people who walk in darkness will see a great light—a light that will shine on all who live in the land where death casts its shadow. Israel will again be great, and its people will rejoice as people rejoice at harvesttime. They will shout with joy like warriors dividing the plunder. For God will break the chains that bind his people and the whip that scourges them, just as he did when he destroyed the army of Midian with Gideon's little band. In that day of peace, battle gear will no longer be issued. Never again will uniforms be bloodstained by war. All such equipment will be burned.

For a child is born to us, a son is given to us. And the government will rest on his shoulders. These will be his royal titles: Wonderful Counselor, Mighty God, Everlasting Father, Prince of Peace. His ever expanding, peaceful government will never end. He will rule forever with fairness and justice from the throne of his ancestor David. The passionate commitment of the LORD Almighty will guarantee this!

Here's What I Think

Mike, age 19

More than anything else, God wants us to be obedient. In this passage we see Simeon waiting at the temple, watching for Jesus. Simeon had been there for years, patiently waiting day in and out until God finally fulfilled his promise. What if Simeon had decided to take the day off? Or what if he had gone for a coffee break? Simeon would have missed the greatest moment of his life—seeing Jesus, the promised Messiah. Likewise, Mary and Joseph also had to be obedient so God could fulfill his promise to Simeon. If they had decided not to present Jesus at the temple on that very day, then Simeon might have had to wait even longer before seeing Jesus. By being obedient to God, we allow God to fulfill his will in our lives *and* in the lives of others.

Michel

God is counting on your obedience!

STAR SEARCH

Introduction

Imagine someone coming from a foreign country just to see you. Maybe you can easily imagine that if you have relatives living in another country. But can you imagine that a person you've never met would willingly travel thousands of miles just to catch a glimpse of you? In this story, men from the East searched for Jesus. Their only map to Jesus' location was a star and a Scripture verse. They were the Magi—wise men, men who studied the stars. They believed that a new star in the sky represented the birth of a king. Unfortunately, the wise men picked a bad location to stop and ask for directions.

Matthew 2:1-12, NLT

Jesus was born in the town of Bethlehem in Judea, during the reign of King Herod. About that time some wise men from eastern lands arrived in Jerusalem, asking, "Where is the newborn king of the Jews? We have seen his star as it arose, and we have come to worship him."

Herod was deeply disturbed by their question, as was all of Jerusalem. He called a meeting of the leading priests and teachers of religious law. "Where did the prophets say the Messiah would be born?" he asked them.

"In Bethlehem," they said, "for this is what the prophet wrote:
'O Bethlehem of Judah,
    you are not just a lowly village in Judah,
for a ruler will come from you
    who will be the shepherd for my people Israel.' "

Then Herod sent a private message to the wise men, asking them to come see him. At this meeting he learned the exact time when they first saw the star. Then he told them, "Go to Bethlehem and search carefully for the child. And when you find him, come back and tell me so that I can go and worship him, too!"

After this interview the wise men went their way. Once again the star appeared to them, guiding them to Bethlehem. It went ahead of them and stopped over the place where the child was. When they saw the star, they were filled with joy! They entered the house where the child and his mother, Mary, were, and they fell down before him and worshiped him. Then they opened their treasure chests and gave him gifts of gold, frankincense, and myrrh.

But when it was time to leave, they went home another way, because God had warned them in a dream not to return to Herod.

Take ANOTHER LOOK

The prophet Micah foretold the birthplace of the Savior hundreds of years beforehand, which the wise men quoted in the following passage. Bethlehem was the hometown of David, the great Old Testament king of Israel. Jesus came from David's family line to become the greatest king of all.

Micah 5:2, NLT

But you, O Bethlehem Ephrathah, are only a small village in Judah. Yet a ruler of Israel will come from you, one whose origins are from the distant past.

Here's What I Think

Nicee, age 14

I used to feel like I wasn't giving enough back to God. He had done so much for me on a regular basis, and I couldn't even pray for five minutes! I asked myself, How can I expect God to give me what I want when I never give him what he wants? I wanted God to wake me up in the morning, yet I never prayed in the morning. I never spent time reading my Bible, yet I expected him to meet my every request. It wasn't until I realized that, when I gave more of my time, I got more from spending time with him. That's when I rearranged my daily schedule around him. God is God, and he deserves my time even when I don't feel like it. My commitment is like a gift—it pleases God. What gift of time can you give to God today?

Nicee

Give God the gift of your time today.

»» ESCAPE TO EGYPT «««

Introduction

Herod had an evil a plan—to kill all of the boys in Bethlehem who were two years old and under. But Herod didn't want to stop the Israelite population from growing. He was trying to prevent any potential threat—even from a little baby—to the taking of his throne. Herod didn't realize that God would not let anything happen to his Son. As usual, God had a plan.

Matthew 2:13-23, NLT

After the wise men were gone, an angel of the Lord appeared to Joseph in a dream. "Get up and flee to Egypt with the child and his mother," the angel said. "Stay there until I tell you to return, because Herod is going to try to kill the child."

That night Joseph left for Egypt with the child and Mary, his mother, and they stayed there until Herod's death. This fulfilled what the Lord had spoken through the prophet: "I called my Son out of Egypt."

Herod was furious when he learned that the wise men had outwitted him. He sent soldiers to kill all the boys in and around Bethlehem who were two years old and under, because the wise men had told him the star first appeared to them about two years earlier. Herod's brutal action fulfilled the prophecy of Jeremiah:

"A cry of anguish is heard in Ramah—
weeping and mourning unrestrained.
Rachel weeps for her children,
refusing to be comforted—for they are dead."

The Return to Nazareth

When Herod died, an angel of the Lord appeared in a dream to Joseph in Egypt and told him, "Get up and take the child and his mother back to the land of Israel, because those who were trying to kill the child are dead."

So Joseph returned immediately to Israel with Jesus and his mother. But when he learned that the new ruler was Herod's son Archelaus, he was afraid. Then, in another dream, he was warned to go to Galilee. So they went and lived in a town called Nazareth. This fulfilled what was spoken by the prophets concerning the Messiah: "He will be called a Nazarene."

Take ANOTHER LOOK

This wasn't the first time that Joseph was warned through a dream. Before Jesus was born, even before Joseph and Mary were married, Joseph faced a tough decision. After finding out that Mary was going to have a child, Joseph wondered how to break their engagement. A public announcement would mean embarrassment and possibly even death for Mary. But God had just the right answer for Joseph.

Matthew 1:18-25, NLT

Now this is how Jesus the Messiah was born. His mother, Mary, was engaged to be married to Joseph. But while she was still a virgin, she became pregnant by the Holy Spirit. Joseph, her fiancé, being a just man, decided to break the engagement quietly, so as not to disgrace her publicly.

As he considered this, he fell asleep, and an angel of the Lord appeared to him in a dream. "Joseph, son of David," the angel said, "do not be afraid to go ahead with your marriage to Mary. For the child within her has been conceived by the Holy Spirit. And she will have a son, and you are to name him Jesus, for he will save his people from their sins."

All of this happened to fulfill the Lord's message through his prophet:

"Look! The virgin will conceive a child!
She will give birth to a son,
and he will be called Immanuel
(meaning, God is with us)."

When Joseph woke up, he did what the angel of the Lord commanded. He brought Mary home to be his wife, but she remained a virgin until her son was born. And Joseph named him Jesus.

Here's What I Think

Walter, age 13

On Monday morning I woke up. I walked into school. I ate lunch. I got home and did my homework. I went to bed. Tuesday, September 11, 2001, was the same as any other day—or was it?

That very morning, two planes crashed into the twin towers of the World Trade Center in New York City that were filled with thousands of people. Just because some terrorists hated the United States, they decided to kill a bunch of innocent people. Satan was behind that event, I assure you. In the same way, Herod was so hateful and angry that he killed innocent people. He had everyone age two and under killed. Satan can do some bad stuff. But God is bigger than anything or anybody. If he could keep Jesus and his parents safe, then he can keep me safe.

Walter

Nothing—and no one—is bigger than God.

»»» AN OBEDIENT SON «««

Introduction

Jesus never did anything wrong—even as a child. But that didn't mean that Jesus didn't from time to time do things that caused his parents to worry. Wondering what Jesus could have done to make his parents worry? It happened during a family trip to Jerusalem for the Passover. Every year, Jesus' family went on a trip to Jerusalem with relatives and other families in their community. Traveling together was a good safety measure because of bandits in the area. Mary and Joseph didn't meet any outlaws, but the couple would always remember this trip. You can find this story only in the Gospel of Luke.

Luke 2:41-52, NLT

Every year Jesus' parents went to Jerusalem for the Passover festival. When Jesus was twelve years old, they attended the festival as usual. After the celebration was over, they started home to Nazareth, but Jesus stayed behind in Jerusalem. His parents didn't miss him at first, because they assumed he was with friends among the other travelers. But when he didn't show up that evening, they started to look for him among their relatives and friends.

When they couldn't find him, they went back to Jerusalem to search for him there. Three days later they finally discovered him. He was in the Temple, sitting among the religious teachers, discussing deep questions with them. And all who heard him were amazed at his understanding and his answers.

His parents didn't know what to think. "Son!" his mother said to him. "Why have you done this to us? Your father and I have been frantic, searching for you everywhere."

"But why did you need to search?" he asked. "You should have known that I would be in my Father's house." But they didn't understand what he meant.

Then he returned to Nazareth with them and was obedient to them; and his mother stored all these things in her heart.

So Jesus grew both in height and in wisdom, and he was loved by God and by all who knew him.

Take ANOTHER LOOK

During the time of Moses, God had established certain festivals at which all the men of Israel had to appear before the Lord. Because Jesus was 12, he was almost at the age of adulthood. Jesus and his family were required by God's law to attend this festival.

Exodus 23:14-17, NLT

"Each year you must celebrate three festivals in my honor. The first is the Festival of Unleavened Bread. For seven days you are to eat bread made without yeast, just as I commanded you before. This festival will be an annual event at the appointed time in early spring, for that is the anniversary of your exodus from Egypt. Everyone must bring me a sacrifice at that time. You must also celebrate the Festival of Harvest, when you bring me the first crops of your harvest. Finally, you are to celebrate the Festival of the Final Harvest at the end of the harvest season. At these three times each year, every man in Israel must appear before the Sovereign LORD.

Here's What I Think

Julie, age 18

He was just a small-town carpenter's son—a kid who probably liked to play games, explore new things, and ask lots of questions. Maybe, once or twice, he faced a school bully or was teased for being a little different. If you think about it, Jesus was a lot like you and me.

I love this story because it shows that when Jesus was still a kid, he was already doing great things for God. There he was, sitting in the temple, asking questions and sharing *his* knowledge. Jesus was really teaching the teachers. Do you ever think that you're too young to make a difference? (I've felt that way sometimes.) Next time you feel shy about sharing Christ with your friends or doing something for God, remember to follow Jesus' example from this story. Even though you're just a kid, God can still use you.

Julie

There are no age requirements for serving God!

A VOICE IN THE WILDERNESS

Introduction

Eighteen years passed. When an all-grown-up Jesus was ready to start his ministry, his cousin John went before him to preach about Jesus' coming. John may have worn strange clothes and eaten strange things, but he did the job that he was sent to do. He became known as John the Baptist because he baptized people in the Jordan River. Usually, the people he baptized had sins that needed forgiveness. But one of the people John baptized was surprising: Jesus, who had never done anything wrong.

Mark 1:1-11, NLT

Here begins the Good News about Jesus the Messiah, the Son of God. In the book of the prophet Isaiah, God said,

"Look, I am sending my messenger before you,
and he will prepare your way.
He is a voice shouting in the wilderness:
'Prepare a pathway for the Lord's coming!
Make a straight road for him!'"

This messenger was John the Baptist. He lived in the wilderness and was preaching that people should be baptized to show that they had turned from their sins and turned to God to be forgiven. People from Jerusalem and from all over Judea traveled out into the wilderness to see and hear John. And when they confessed their sins, he baptized them in the Jordan River. His clothes were woven from camel hair, and he wore a leather belt; his food was locusts and wild honey.

He announced: "Someone is coming soon who is far greater than I am—so much greater that I am not even worthy to be his slave. I baptize you with water, but he will baptize you with the Holy Spirit!"

The Baptism of Jesus

One day Jesus came from Nazareth in Galilee, and he was baptized by John in the Jordan River. And when Jesus came up out of the water, he saw the heavens split open and the Holy Spirit descending like a dove on him. And a voice came from heaven saying, "You are my beloved Son, and I am fully pleased with you."

Take ANOTHER LOOK

There was a time when John the Baptist wasn't sure whether or not Jesus was the Savior. John was in prison for telling the truth to King Herod, and he was feeling discouraged. But Jesus didn't criticize John for his doubts. Instead, he told a crowd of listeners all about John. You can read all about it below.

Matthew 11:1-15, NLT

When Jesus had finished giving these instructions to his twelve disciples, he went off teaching and preaching in towns throughout the country.

John the Baptist, who was now in prison, heard about all the things the Messiah was doing. So he sent his disciples to ask Jesus, "Are you really the Messiah we've been waiting for, or should we keep looking for someone else?"

Jesus told them, "Go back to John and tell him about what you have heard and seen—the blind see, the lame walk, the lepers are cured, the deaf hear, the dead are raised to life, and the Good News is being preached to the poor. And tell him: 'God blesses those who are not offended by me.'"

When John's disciples had gone, Jesus began talking about him to the crowds. "Who is this man in the wilderness that you went out to see? Did you find him weak as a reed, moved by every breath of wind? Or were you expecting to see a man dressed in expensive clothes? Those who dress like that live in palaces, not out in the wilderness. Were you looking for a prophet? Yes, and he is more than a prophet. John is the man to whom the Scriptures refer when they say,

'Look, I am sending my messenger before you,
   and he will prepare your way before you.'

"I assure you, of all who have ever lived, none is greater than John the Baptist. Yet even the most insignificant person in the Kingdom of Heaven is greater than he is! And from the time John the Baptist began preaching and baptizing until now, the Kingdom of Heaven has been forcefully advancing, and violent people attack it. For before John came, all the teachings of the Scriptures looked forward to this present time. And if you are willing to accept what I say, he is Elijah, the one the prophets said would come. Anyone who is willing to hear should listen and understand!"

Here's What I Think

Verity, age 13

John helped people turn from their sinful ways. They admitted their sins and he baptized them. This was an act of repentance, which means to turn from your sins. When Jesus came, he had John baptize him even though he had no sins to confess. Why?

Jesus wanted to set an example for people back then and for us today. As sinners, we also need to repent and confess our sins, asking God to forgive us. Almost every night while praying, I try to remember distinctly any sins of that day. I ask God to forgive me. I want to be right with God.

Verity

Listen to John—confess and turn away from sin.

JESUS' BIG TEST

Introduction

Immediately after his baptism, Jesus spent time with his Father in prayer. But before Jesus could start his ministry, the Holy Spirit allowed him to go through a period of temptation. During this time, Jesus was feeling weak from hunger. Because of that, Satan hoped that he could easily get Jesus to give in to temptation. Now, being tempted is not the same as doing something wrong. The wrong comes when a person gives in to temptation. As this story shows, Jesus was tempted, but overcame the temptation with a powerful weapon—the Word of God.

Luke 4:1-13, NLT

Then Jesus, full of the Holy Spirit, left the Jordan River. He was led by the Spirit to go out into the wilderness, where the Devil tempted him for forty days. He ate nothing all that time and was very hungry.

Then the Devil said to him, "If you are the Son of God, change this stone into a loaf of bread." But Jesus told him, "No! The Scriptures say, 'People need more than bread for their life.'"

Then the Devil took him up and revealed to him all the kingdoms of the world in a moment of time. The Devil told him, "I will give you the glory of these kingdoms and authority over them—because they are mine to give to anyone I please. I will give it all to you if you will bow down and worship me."

Jesus replied, "The Scriptures say,
'You must worship the Lord your God;
    serve only him.'"

Then the Devil took him to Jerusalem, to the highest point of the Temple, and said, "If you are the Son of God, jump off! For the Scriptures say,
'He orders his angels to protect and guard you.
And they will hold you with their hands
    to keep you from striking your foot on a stone.'"

Jesus responded, "The Scriptures also say, 'Do not test the Lord your God.'"

When the Devil had finished tempting Jesus, he left him until the next opportunity came.

Take ANOTHER LOOK

The story of Jesus' temptation and this passage below from the book of Hebrews remind us that Jesus understands what it feels like to be tempted. Jesus is called a high priest because he offered a sacrifice to God for wrongdoing. Unlike Aaron and other high priests in the Bible, Jesus offered himself as the sacrifice. He did this out of love. So the next time you're tempted, maybe you'll remember that the ultimate high priest is on your side.

Hebrews 4:14-16, NLT

That is why we have a great High Priest who has gone to heaven, Jesus the Son of God. Let us cling to him and never stop trusting him. This High Priest of ours understands our weaknesses, for he faced all of the same temptations we do, yet he did not sin. So let us come boldly to the throne of our gracious God. There we will receive his mercy, and we will find grace to help us when we need it.

Here's What I Think

Jammeshia, age 17

I don't have to look far to find something in this world that tempts me. Walking through the mall, I always seem to want more. It makes me sad because I feel like giving in so often. Then I remember how Jesus was tempted, and yet, he did not give in. This is so encouraging because God gives me the same ways to escape and defeat those temptations that he gave to Jesus. For example, I can memorize Scripture. I never thought it was that important, but look how Jesus used it against Satan. Now in every area where I know I am weak, I try to find some Scripture to memorize so that I can resist the Devil's temptations. Try it!

Jammeshia

Arm yourself with God's Word to fight temptation.

FISHING FOR DISCIPLES

Introduction

Every good leader needs followers. Knowing that his time on Earth was limited, Jesus wanted to train a group of followers to carry on his work. But instead of choosing highly educated men or popular people, Jesus chose the most unlikely group of followers. Some were even poor fishermen. This unlikely group would have a unique mission—to fish for people.

Luke 5:1-11, NLT

One day as Jesus was preaching on the shore of the Sea of Galilee, great crowds pressed in on him to listen to the word of God. He noticed two empty boats at the water's edge, for the fishermen had left them and were washing their nets. Stepping into one of the boats, Jesus asked Simon, its owner, to push it out into the water. So he sat in the boat and taught the crowds from there.

When he had finished speaking, he said to Simon, "Now go out where it is deeper and let down your nets, and you will catch many fish."

"Master," Simon replied, "we worked hard all last night and didn't catch a thing. But if you say so, we'll try again." And this time their nets were so full they began to tear! A shout for help brought their partners in the other boat, and soon both boats were filled with fish and on the verge of sinking.

When Simon Peter realized what had happened, he fell to his knees before Jesus and said, "Oh, Lord, please leave me—I'm too much of a sinner to be around you." For he was awestruck by the size of their catch, as were the others with him. His partners, James and John, the sons of Zebedee, were also amazed.

Jesus replied to Simon, "Don't be afraid! From now on you'll be fishing for people!" And as soon as they landed, they left everything and followed Jesus.

Would you have chosen Matthew for a disciple? He wasn't popular. As a tax collector, he was even a cheat. But as you can read below, Jesus picked him. Matthew wrote about his own experience in the Gospel that bears his name.

Matthew 9:9-13, NLT

As Jesus was going down the road, he saw Matthew sitting at his tax-collection booth. "Come, be my disciple," Jesus said to him. So Matthew got up and followed him.

That night Matthew invited Jesus and his disciples to be his dinner guests, along with his fellow tax collectors and many other notorious sinners. The Pharisees were indignant. "Why does your teacher eat with such scum?" they asked his disciples.

When he heard this, Jesus replied, "Healthy people don't need a doctor—sick people do." Then he added, "Now go and learn the meaning of this Scripture: 'I want you to be merciful; I don't want your sacrifices.' For I have come to call sinners, not those who think they are already good enough."

Matthew 10:2-4, NLT

Here are the names of the twelve apostles:
first Simon (also called Peter),
then Andrew (Peter's brother),
James (son of Zebedee),
John (James's brother),
Philip,
Bartholomew,
Thomas,
Matthew (the tax collector),
James (son of Alphaeus),
Thaddaeus,
Simon (the Zealot),
Judas Iscariot (who later betrayed him).

Here's What I Think

Daniel, age 15

I love to fish. I'm not the best fisherman, but Peter was a professional! The nights when he caught absolutely nothing were probably few and far between. When I'm fishing, I don't like being told how to fish by someone less experienced than I am. I think, *Who's this kid to tell me that I'm fishing wrong?* That's not really the right attitude to have.

I think Peter may have had similar thoughts: *Jesus, this carpenter, is going to tell me that after a night of unsuccessful fishing I should take my cleaned fishing gear and go back out for one more cast.* Yet, Peter trusted Jesus. Even though Peter probably thought it was pretty pointless, he did as Jesus said. And because he did, Peter was rewarded with the biggest catch he probably ever had. So what does that mean to me? God honors our obedience, even if we think it is pointless or a waste of time.

Daniel

Obeying God is never a waste of time.

»»» WATER INTO WINE «««

Introduction

Jesus' first recorded miracle occurred at a wedding. Now, this miracle might seem an odd choice for the Savior just beginning his ministry. But it wasn't really. Jesus saved the host of the wedding from a great deal of humiliation. In a society where hospitality was valued, running out of wine would have been a huge embarrassment.

John 2:1-12, NLT

The next day Jesus' mother was a guest at a wedding celebration in the village of Cana in Galilee. Jesus and his disciples were also invited to the celebration. The wine supply ran out during the festivities, so Jesus' mother spoke to him about the problem. "They have no more wine," she told him.

"How does that concern you and me?" Jesus asked. "My time has not yet come."

But his mother told the servants, "Do whatever he tells you."

Six stone waterpots were standing there; they were used for Jewish ceremonial purposes and held twenty to thirty gallons each. Jesus told the servants, "Fill the jars with water." When the jars had been filled to the brim, he said, "Dip some out and take it to the master of ceremonies." So they followed his instructions. When the master of ceremonies tasted the water that was now wine, not knowing where it had come from (though, of course, the servants knew), he called the bridegroom over. "Usually a host serves the best wine first," he said. "Then, when everyone is full and doesn't care, he brings out the less expensive wines. But you have kept the best until now!"

This miraculous sign at Cana in Galilee was Jesus' first display of his glory. And his disciples believed in him.

After the wedding he went to Capernaum for a few days with his mother, his brothers, and his disciples.

Maybe you're wondering why huge water jars were at the wedding in the first place. The people of Israel had many rules about washing their hands. Of course, we also wash our hands before a meal. But the people of Israel washed before, during, and after the meal. The Pharisees believed that the washing made a person spiritually clean. Jesus would have known all about that when he turned the water into wine at the wedding. In the previous story and in the next one from the Gospel of Mark, Jesus showed that he cared more about people than about tradition.

Mark 7:1-8, NLT

One day some Pharisees and teachers of religious law arrived from Jerusalem to confront Jesus. They noticed that some of Jesus' disciples failed to follow the usual Jewish ritual of hand washing before eating. (The Jews, especially the Pharisees, do not eat until they have poured water over their cupped hands, as required by their ancient traditions. Similarly, they eat nothing bought from the market unless they have immersed their hands in water. This is but one of many traditions they have clung to—such as their ceremony of washing cups, pitchers, and kettles.) So the Pharisees and teachers of religious law asked him, "Why don't your disciples follow our age-old customs? For they eat without first performing the hand-washing ceremony."

Jesus replied, "You hypocrites! Isaiah was prophesying about you when he said,

'These people honor me with their lips,
 but their hearts are far away.
Their worship is a farce,
 for they replace God's commands with their own man-made teachings.'

For you ignore God's specific laws and substitute your own traditions."

Here's What I Think

Janna, age 14

This wedding at Cana was Jesus' very first miracle. It would have been so cool to be there. This was obviously a miracle because Jesus made something unnatural happen. Some people today think that God doesn't perform miracles. But that is not true.

God is doing miracles every day. I have a friend, and he had cancer in his leg. About a month ago he was cleared of the cancer and is now in remission. I consider that a miracle! God is working all the time in our lives. We just need to be aware of what he is doing and give him thanks for the big miracles and the small ones.

Janna

God's miracles do happen—look for them.

»»» NICODEMUS VISITS JESUS «««

Introduction

Jesus was popular with the regular people of Palestine (another name for the land of Israel), but he was hated by the Pharisees. Who were they? The Pharisees were a Jewish religious group who carefully obeyed the Law of Moses and made sure everyone knew it. Their bad opinion of someone could ruin that person's life. In the Pharisees' opinion, Jesus was a nobody from an unimportant region (Nazareth). But Nicodemus was one Pharisee who had second thoughts about Jesus. What if Jesus really was who John the Baptist said he was—the promised Savior? Would Nicodemus risk his reputation to talk to Jesus?

John 3:1-21, NLT

After dark one evening, a Jewish religious leader named Nicodemus, a Pharisee, came to speak with Jesus. "Teacher," he said, "we all know that God has sent you to teach us. Your miraculous signs are proof enough that God is with you."

Jesus replied, "I assure you, unless you are born again, you can never see the Kingdom of God."

"What do you mean?" exclaimed Nicodemus. "How can an old man go back into his mother's womb and be born again?"

Jesus replied, "The truth is, no one can enter the Kingdom of God without being born of water and the Spirit. Humans can reproduce only human life, but the Holy Spirit gives new life from heaven. So don't be surprised at my statement that you must be born again. Just as you can hear the wind but can't tell where it comes from or where it is going, so you can't explain how people are born of the Spirit."

"What do you mean?" Nicodemus asked.

Jesus replied, "You are a respected Jewish teacher, and yet you don't understand these things? I assure you, I am telling you what we know and have seen, and yet you won't believe us. But if you don't even believe me when I tell you about things that happen here on earth, how can you possibly believe if I tell you what is going on in heaven? For only I, the Son of Man, have come to earth and will return to heaven again. And as Moses lifted up the bronze snake on a pole in the wilderness, so I, the Son of Man, must be lifted up on a pole, so that everyone who believes in me will have eternal life.

"For God so loved the world that he gave his only Son, so that everyone who believes in him will not perish but have eternal life. God did not send his Son into the world to condemn it, but to save it.

"There is no judgment awaiting those who trust him. But those who do not trust him have already been judged for not believing in the only Son of God. Their judgment is based on this fact: The light from heaven came into the world, but they loved the darkness more than the light, for their actions were evil. They hate the light because they want to sin in the darkness. They stay away from the light for fear their sins will be exposed and they will be punished. But those who do what is right come to the light gladly, so everyone can see that they are doing what God wants."

Take ANOTHER Look

Jesus reminded Nicodemus about a story you can find in the Old Testament book of Numbers. Because of the disobedience of the people of Israel, God sent poisonous snakes to bite them. But God had an unusual remedy to heal those who had been bitten. God ordered the people to look at a bronze snake that he had lifted on a pole. One day, Jesus would be "lifted" on a cross to die for the wrongdoings of all people. Those who looked to him would have unending life. As you read this story, consider Jesus' willingness to die for the sins of all people, including you.

Numbers 21:4-9, NLT

Then the people of Israel set out from Mount Hor, taking the road to the Red Sea to go around the land of Edom. But the people grew impatient along the way, and they began to murmur against God and Moses. "Why have you brought us out of Egypt to die here in the wilderness?" they complained. "There is nothing to eat here and nothing to drink. And we hate this wretched manna!"

So the LORD sent poisonous snakes among them, and many of them were bitten and died. Then the people came to Moses and cried out, "We have sinned by speaking against the LORD and against you. Pray that the LORD will take away the snakes." So Moses prayed for the people.

Then the LORD told him, "Make a replica of a poisonous snake and attach it to the top of a pole. Those who are bitten will live if they simply look at it!" So Moses made a snake out of bronze and attached it to the top of a pole. Whenever those who were bitten looked at the bronze snake, they recovered!

Here's What I Think

Faith, age 14

G rowing up in a Christian family, I was always told that God loved me, that Jesus died on the cross for my sins, and that he hears me when I pray. As a little kid, I accepted it because I knew I was supposed to and I had no reason to doubt what my parents were telling me.

It wasn't until the last several years that God really started deepening my faith. Before, I could tell you the entire story of Jesus' life, death, and resurrection. Now I can tell you how knowing Jesus has changed my life. I was a lot like Nicodemus. He knew the Old Testament, but when Jesus tried to show him the deeper meaning behind the Scriptures, Nicodemus didn't get it. I'm also learning that just being familiar with the Bible isn't enough. I need to figure out what it *really* means to me.

Faith

**Where's your knowledge of Jesus?
In your head or heart?**

»»» A THIRST FOR KNOWLEDGE «««

Introduction

Jesus often shocked people by his actions. Take his conversation with a woman at a well in a Samaritan village. What's shocking about that? In those days, Jewish men didn't talk to women in public. Also, this woman was a lowly Samaritan with a bad reputation. A triple whammy! Although the Samaritans were partially related to the people of Israel, they were considered outcasts. Many Jews even went out of their way to avoid traveling through the Samaritans' land! But not Jesus.

John 4:1-30, NLT

Jesus learned that the Pharisees had heard, "Jesus is baptizing and making more disciples than John" (though Jesus himself didn't baptize them—his disciples did). So he left Judea to return to Galilee.

He had to go through Samaria on the way. Eventually he came to the Samaritan village of Sychar, near the parcel of ground that Jacob gave to his son Joseph. Jacob's well was there; and Jesus, tired from the long walk, sat wearily beside the well about noontime. Soon a Samaritan woman came to draw water, and Jesus said to her, "Please give me a drink." He was alone at the time because his disciples had gone into the village to buy some food.

The woman was surprised, for Jews refuse to have anything to do with Samaritans. She said to Jesus, "You are a Jew, and I am a Samaritan woman. Why are you asking me for a drink?"

Jesus replied, "If you only knew the gift God has for you and who I am, you would ask me, and I would give you living water."

"But sir, you don't have a rope or a bucket," she said, "and this is a very deep well. Where would you get this living water? And besides, are you greater than our ancestor Jacob who gave us this well? How can you offer better water than he and his sons and his cattle enjoyed?"

Jesus replied, "People soon become thirsty again after drinking this water. But the water I give them takes away thirst altogether. It becomes a perpetual spring within them, giving them eternal life."

"Please, sir," the woman said, "give me some of that water! Then I'll never be thirsty again, and I won't have to come here to haul water."

"Go and get your husband," Jesus told her.

"I don't have a husband," the woman replied. Jesus said, "You're right! You don't have a husband—for you have had five husbands, and you aren't even married to the man you're living with now."

"Sir," the woman said, "you must be a prophet. So tell me, why is it that you Jews insist that Jerusalem is the only place of worship, while we Samaritans claim it is here at Mount Gerizim, where our ancestors worshiped?"

Jesus replied, "Believe me, the time is coming when it will no longer matter whether you worship the Father here or in Jerusalem. You Samaritans know so little about the one you worship, while we Jews know all about him, for salvation comes through the Jews. But the time is coming and is already here when true worshipers will worship the Father in spirit and in truth. The Father is looking for anyone who will worship him that way. For God is Spirit, so those who worship him must worship in spirit and in truth."

The woman said, "I know the Messiah will come—the one who is called Christ. When he comes, he will explain everything to us."

Then Jesus told her, "I am the Messiah!"

Just then his disciples arrived. They were astonished to find him talking to a woman, but none of them asked him why he was doing it or what they had been discussing. The woman left her water jar beside the well and went back to the village and told everyone, "Come and meet a man who told me everything I ever did! Can this be the Messiah?" So the people came streaming from the village to see him.

Later, during the Festival of Shelters (one of the festivals Jewish men had to attend), Jesus talked to a crowd at the temple about "living water." As this story from the Gospel of John explains, Jesus was talking about the Holy Spirit. His words amazed some people but angered others. When the Pharisees thought about having Jesus arrested, Nicodemus (remember him from the last story?) spoke up for him. Would you have done that?

John 7:37-52, NLT

On the last day, the climax of the festival, Jesus stood and shouted to the crowds, "If you are thirsty, come to me! If you believe in me, come and drink! For the Scriptures declare that rivers of living water will flow out from within." (When he said "living water," he was speaking of the Spirit, who would be given to everyone believing in him. But the Spirit had not yet been given, because Jesus had not yet entered into his glory.)

Division and Unbelief

When the crowds heard him say this, some of them declared, "This man surely is the Prophet." Others said, "He is the Messiah." Still others said, "But he can't be! Will the Messiah come from Galilee? For the Scriptures clearly state that the Messiah will be born of the royal line of David, in Bethlehem, the village where King David was born." So the crowd was divided in their opinion about him. And some wanted him arrested, but no one touched him.

The Temple guards who had been sent to arrest him returned to the leading priests and Pharisees. "Why didn't you bring him in?" they demanded.

"We have never heard anyone talk like this!" the guards responded.

"Have you been led astray, too?" the Pharisees mocked. "Is there a single one of us rulers or Pharisees who believes in him? These ignorant crowds do, but what do they know about it? A curse on them anyway!"

Nicodemus, the leader who had met with Jesus earlier, then spoke up. "Is it legal to convict a man before he is given a hearing?" he asked.

They replied, "Are you from Galilee, too? Search the Scriptures and see for yourself—no prophet ever comes from Galilee!"

Here's What I Think

I became a Christian when I was six years old, but throughout my walk of faith I have stumbled many times. I struggle with jealousy, peer pressure, anger, and so much more. It amazes me how God continually loves and forgives everyone. Sometimes I just don't get it.

When I read this passage, it hit me that God loves me no matter who I am, what I've done, or where I've been. The same goes for the woman at the well. She was a Samaritan woman who was despised by the Jews, yet Jesus loved her. She had sinned within some relationships she had, yet Jesus loved her. And no matter where she had been on her journey through life, Jesus still loved her and he offered her "living water" so she would never thirst again. What an amazing God we have who loves us so much, no matter what!

Kali

Quench your "thirst" with "living water."

»» A DOUBLE
HEALING ««

Introduction

Because of his miracles, Jesus gained popularity almost overnight. Crowds followed him everywhere he went, just like people follow their favorite celebrities today. So you can imagine the size of the crowd waiting to see Jesus in Capernaum, Jesus' home base. He often returned there after being on the road, and the crowds knew it. They brought their sick friends and family to be healed by Jesus. That's what four men did for their paralyzed friend. They wanted him to walk again, but Jesus had a deeper healing in mind for this man.

Mark 2:1-12, NLT

Several days later Jesus returned to Capernaum, and the news of his arrival spread quickly through the town. Soon the house where he was staying was so packed with visitors that there wasn't room for one more person, not even outside the door. And he preached the word to them. Four men arrived carrying a paralyzed man on a mat. They couldn't get to Jesus through the crowd, so they dug through the clay roof above his head. Then they lowered the sick man on his mat, right down in front of Jesus. Seeing their faith, Jesus said to the paralyzed man, "My son, your sins are forgiven."

But some of the teachers of religious law who were sitting there said to themselves, "What? This is blasphemy! Who but God can forgive sins!"

Jesus knew what they were discussing among themselves, so he said to them, "Why do you think this is blasphemy? Is it easier to say to the paralyzed man, 'Your sins are forgiven' or 'Get up, pick up your mat, and walk'? I will prove that I, the Son of Man, have the authority on earth to forgive sins." Then Jesus turned to the paralyzed man and said, "Stand up, take your mat, and go on home, because you are healed!"

The man jumped up, took the mat, and pushed his way through the stunned onlookers. Then they all praised God. "We've never seen anything like this before!" they exclaimed.

The man in the story above wasn't the only paralyzed man that Jesus healed. He also healed a man at a pool called Bethesda in Jerusalem. Jesus asked this man a strange question—one that Jesus didn't ask anyone else. But Jesus had a reason for asking this question. He knew that people sometimes made excuses rather than asking for help. Sure enough, the man at the pool was ready with an excuse. But as you read in the story below from the book of John, Jesus didn't let the man's excuse stop him from helping.

John 5:1-15, NLT

Afterward Jesus returned to Jerusalem for one of the Jewish holy days. Inside the city, near the Sheep Gate, was the pool of Bethesda, with five covered porches. Crowds of sick people—blind, lame, or paralyzed—lay on the porches. One of the men lying there had been sick for thirty-eight years. When Jesus saw him and knew how long he had been ill, he asked him, "Would you like to get well?"

"I can't, sir," the sick man said, "for I have no one to help me into the pool when the water is stirred up. While I am trying to get there, someone else always gets in ahead of me."

Jesus told him, "Stand up, pick up your sleeping mat, and walk!"

Instantly, the man was healed! He rolled up the mat and began walking! But this miracle happened on the Sabbath day. So the Jewish leaders objected. They said to the man who was cured, "You can't work on the Sabbath! It's illegal to carry that sleeping mat!"

He replied, "The man who healed me said to me, 'Pick up your sleeping mat and walk.' "

"Who said such a thing as that?" they demanded.

The man didn't know, for Jesus had disappeared into the crowd. But afterward Jesus found him in the Temple and told him, "Now you are well; so stop sinning, or something even worse may happen to you." Then the man went to find the Jewish leaders and told them it was Jesus who had healed him.

Here's What I Think

Mike, age 19

The men in the story we just read felt a need for their friend to see Jesus. Their thoughts produced action. Look at what they did. Their sick friend could not go see Jesus on his own, so they carried him on a mat.

Then, when the house was too crowded for them to get inside, these men dug a hole through the roof and lowered their sick friend down to Jesus. What a great example for me. I have friends who need Jesus too. Instead of feeling bad that my friends don't know Jesus, I should be doing something about it! Instead of just wishing they will ask me to go to church or talk about Jesus, I should bring it up in conversation and invite them to come to church with me.

Mike

What friends can you bring to meet Jesus?

»» LISTEN UP! ««

Introduction

During the second year of his three-year ministry, Jesus preached the longest of his recorded sermons. This sermon is called the Sermon on the Mount. Jesus loved to tell people about the kingdom of God. Citizens of this kingdom (people who believe and follow Jesus) would be known by certain characteristics or attitudes. What are these characteristics? Humility, mercy, purity of heart, suffering, and more. Jesus' listeners were probably shocked by this list. After all, no one would have thought that a person who suffers is "blessed." But Jesus looked at life differently. The misery of this world is temporary, but the kingdom of God will last forever.

Matthew 5:1-12, NLT

One day as the crowds were gathering, Jesus went up the mountainside with his disciples and sat down to teach them.

This is what he taught them:

"God blesses those who realize their need for him,
for the Kingdom of Heaven is given to them."

"God blesses those who mourn,
for they will be comforted."

"God blesses those who are gentle and lowly,
for the whole earth will belong to them."

"God blesses those who are hungry and thirsty for justice,
for they will receive it in full."

"God blesses those who are merciful,
for they will be shown mercy."

"God blesses those whose hearts are pure,
for they will see God."

"God blesses those who work for peace,
for they will be called the children of God."

"God blesses those who are persecuted because they live for God,
for the Kingdom of Heaven is theirs."

"God blesses you when you are mocked and persecuted and lied about because you are my followers. Be happy about it! Be very glad! For a great reward awaits you in heaven. And remember, the ancient prophets were persecuted, too."

Take ANOTHER LOOK

Paul, who was a follower of Jesus, also talked about the kingdom of God. Like Jesus, Paul wanted to explain what being a citizen of heaven is like. Paul wanted to comfort those who were suffering because of their belief in Jesus. As you read these two passages from Paul's letter to the Philippians, think about where your citizenship lies.

Philippians 1:27-30, NLT

But whatever happens to me, you must live in a manner worthy of the Good News about Christ, as citizens of heaven. Then, whether I come and see you again or only hear about you, I will know that you are standing side by side, fighting together for the Good News. Don't be intimidated by your enemies. This will be a sign to them that they are going to be destroyed, but that you are going to be saved, even by God himself. For you have been given not only the privilege of trusting in Christ but also the privilege of suffering for him. We are in this fight together. You have seen me suffer for him in the past, and you know that I am still in the midst of this great struggle.

Philippians 3:20,21, NLT

But we are citizens of heaven, where the Lord Jesus Christ lives. And we are eagerly waiting for him to return as our Savior. He will take these weak mortal bodies of ours and change them into glorious bodies like his own, using the same mighty power that he will use to conquer everything, everywhere.

Here's What I Think

Nicee, age 14

Once in class, I was talking about a book I was reading. The book explained how Christians shouldn't act like non-Christians, or people who don't believe in God. As soon as I began to speak, my classmates began to laugh at me. Usually, I get mad and argue when that happens, but on that particular morning I had read Matthew 5.

So I decided to silently pray before I reacted. Then, I told my classmates that every time they mocked me, I would be blessed. As soon as I said that, my classmates stopped! Who knows? Maybe they didn't want me to get *too many* blessings! God's words are always true, because later on that day I received a great blessing—a good friend of mine accepted Christ!

Nicee

Make sure you have the right attitudes.

»»» JESUS TEACHES
ABOUT PRAYER «««

Ôntroduction

During the Sermon on the Mount, Jesus gave his disciples a pattern for prayer. Throughout the years, this pattern has become known as the Lord's Prayer. Maybe it should have been called the "disciples' prayer" instead, because Jesus used it to teach his followers how to pray. But more than that, Jesus taught them how to think about God. This holy and powerful God wanted to be known in a far more personal way: as our Father.

Matthew 6:5-15, NLT

"And now about prayer. When you pray, don't be like the hypocrites who love to pray publicly on street corners and in the synagogues where everyone can see them. I assure you, that is all the reward they will ever get. But when you pray, go away by yourself, shut the door behind you, and pray to your Father secretly. Then your Father, who knows all secrets, will reward you.

"When you pray, don't babble on and on as people of other religions do. They think their prayers are answered only by repeating their words again and again. Don't be like them, because your Father knows exactly what you need even before you ask him! Pray like this:

Our Father in heaven,
may your name be honored.

May your Kingdom come soon.
May your will be done here on earth,
just as it is in heaven.

Give us our food for today,
and forgive us our sins,
just as we have forgiven those who have sinned against us.

And don't let us yield to temptation,
but deliver us from the evil one.

"If you forgive those who sin against you, your heavenly Father will forgive you. But if you refuse to forgive others, your Father will not forgive your sins."

Jesus later told a story about two men who prayed. Jesus wanted to make a point about praying with an attitude that recognizes our need for God. Many of the religious leaders prayed long prayers, hoping to be overheard and admired. Maybe they expected God to admire them too. But another man in the story talked to God with a humble attitude. Is that the kind of attitude you have?

Luke 18:9-14, NLT

Then Jesus told this story to some who had great self-confidence and scorned everyone else: "Two men went to the Temple to pray. One was a Pharisee, and the other was a dishonest tax collector. The proud Pharisee stood by himself and prayed this prayer: 'I thank you, God, that I am not a sinner like everyone else, especially like that tax collector over there! For I never cheat, I don't sin, I don't commit adultery, I fast twice a week, and I give you a tenth of my income.'

"But the tax collector stood at a distance and dared not even lift his eyes to heaven as he prayed. Instead, he beat his chest in sorrow, saying, 'O God, be merciful to me, for I am a sinner.' I tell you, this sinner, not the Pharisee, returned home justified before God. For the proud will be humbled, but the humble will be honored."

Here's What I Think

Walter, age 13

The scary thing about prayer is that most of us want to make sure that our prayers *sound* really good rather than simply pouring our hearts into them. I fit right into this category. Sometimes while praying in a group, I don't listen to other people while they are praying. I'm too busy worrying about *my* prayer to listen to what others are praying about.

Jesus made it clear how he wants us to pray: Don't try to sound good, and just pray from the heart. That's easier for me to do in the comfort of my own room. When I get in front of a huge group of people, I start focusing on *what* I'm going to say rather than *who* I'm going to say it to. That's why I need to remember to pray as if it's Jesus and me, no matter how many people are there.

Walter

Talk to God from your heart!

A SOLDIER'S
AMAZING FAITH

Introduction

In Jesus' day, the **people** of Israel were used to seeing Roman soldiers. Since Rome ruled the known world, Roman soldiers were **stationed** in Jerusalem. Some soldiers treated the people of Israel cruelly. But others, like **the** centurion in the story below, were different. So, this centurion had authority and recognized it **when** he saw it, and he knew that Jesus had a special **kind of** authority.

Luke 7:1-10, NLT

When Jesus had finished saying all this, he went back to Capernaum. Now the highly valued slave of a Roman officer was sick and near death. When the officer heard about Jesus, he sent some respected Jewish leaders to ask him to come and heal his slave. So they earnestly begged Jesus to come with them and help the man. "If anyone deserves your help, it is he," they said, "for he loves the Jews and even built a synagogue for us."

So Jesus went with them. But just before they arrived at the house, the officer sent some friends to say, "Lord, don't trouble yourself by coming to my home, for I am not worthy of such an honor. I am not even worthy to come and meet you. Just say the word from where you are, and my servant will be healed. I know because I am under the authority of my superior officers, and I have authority over my soldiers. I only need to say, 'Go,' and they go, or 'Come,' and they come. And if I say to my slaves, 'Do this or that,' they do it."

When Jesus heard this, he was amazed. Turning to the crowd, he said, "I tell you, I haven't seen faith like this in all the land of Israel!" And when the officer's friends returned to his house, they found the slave completely healed.

Take ANOTHER LOOK

Jesus had an encounter with another Gentile (a non-Jewish person) whose faith delighted him. In the story below, some of Jesus' words might seem a little harsh at first. However, Jesus was not insulting the woman. Rather he was contrasting how the Jewish people regarded the Gentiles with his own attitude of acceptance and compassion. Instead of getting angry at Jesus' words, the woman responded humbly and persistently. So Jesus rewarded her faith. As you read this story from the book of Matthew, consider how you would have responded if you had been this woman.

Matthew 15:21-28, NLT

Jesus then left Galilee and went north to the region of Tyre and Sidon. A Gentile woman who lived there came to him, pleading, "Have mercy on me, O Lord, Son of David! For my daughter has a demon in her, and it is severely tormenting her."

But Jesus gave her no reply—not even a word. Then his disciples urged him to send her away. "Tell her to leave," they said. "She is bothering us with all her begging."

Then he said to the woman, "I was sent only to help the people of Israel—God's lost sheep—not the Gentiles."

But she came and worshiped him and pleaded again, "Lord, help me!"

"It isn't right to take food from the children and throw it to the dogs," he said.

"Yes, Lord," she replied, "but even dogs are permitted to eat crumbs that fall beneath their master's table."

"Woman," Jesus said to her, "your faith is great. Your request is granted." And her daughter was instantly healed.

Here's What I Think

Julie, age 18

What would happen if you had faith in no one? It sure wouldn't be a very safe and secure world. If you didn't have faith in your teachers, you would always wonder if they taught the truth. No faith in your friends? You'd be afraid to tell them secrets. And if you had no faith in your parents, you'd constantly worry if they would be there to take care of you.

Faith in people allows us to live without too much anxiety and worrying. But even more important is our faith in God. After all, people will let us down and disappoint us. God never will. With faith in God, I can pray confidently—knowing that he will do what is best for me. It's easy to be anxious about all the things that go on in my life . . . but faith in God, *trusting* him to work in my life, allows me to have peace.

Julie

Put your faith in the one who will not disappoint.

A GIFT OF LOVE

Introduction

Ever hear the phrase, "Never judge a book by its cover"? On the outside, the woman in this story had a bad "cover"—a bad reputation. Maybe you know someone like that. Many people probably judged and avoided this woman because of her reputation. On the other hand, they wouldn't have avoided the Pharisee—the man who invited Jesus to his home. The Pharisees were important and treated with respect. But Jesus soon discovered that this woman had one important quality that the Pharisee lacked. See if you can figure out what it is.

Luke 7:36-50, NLT

One of the Pharisees asked Jesus to come to his home for a meal, so Jesus accepted the invitation and sat down to eat. A certain immoral woman heard he was there and brought a beautiful jar filled with expensive perfume. Then she knelt behind him at his feet, weeping. Her tears fell on his feet, and she wiped them off with her hair. Then she kept kissing his feet and putting perfume on them.

When the Pharisee who was the host saw what was happening and who the woman was, he said to himself, "This proves that Jesus is no prophet. If God had really sent him, he would know what kind of woman is touching him. She's a sinner!"

Then Jesus spoke up and answered his thoughts. "Simon," he said to the Pharisee, "I have something to say to you."

"All right, Teacher," Simon replied, "go ahead."

Then Jesus told him this story: "A man loaned money to two people—five hundred pieces of silver to one and fifty pieces to the other. But neither of them could repay him, so he kindly forgave them both, canceling their debts. Who do you suppose loved him more after that?"

Simon answered, "I suppose the one for whom he canceled the larger debt."

"That's right," Jesus said. Then he turned to the woman and said to Simon, "Look at this woman kneeling here. When I entered your home, you didn't offer me water to wash the dust from my feet, but she has washed them with her tears and wiped them with her hair. You didn't give me a kiss of greeting, but she has kissed my feet again and again from the time I first came in. You neglected the courtesy of olive oil to anoint my head, but she has anointed my feet with rare perfume. I tell you, her sins—and they are many—have been forgiven, so she has shown me much love. But a person who is forgiven little shows only little love." Then Jesus said to the woman, "Your sins are forgiven."

The men at the table said among themselves, "Who does this man think he is, going around forgiving sins?"

And Jesus said to the woman, "Your faith has saved you; go in peace."

Take ANOTHER LOOK

Years later, a week before Jesus was arrested and put to death, another woman anointed Jesus' feet. This woman was Mary of Bethany, one of Jesus' friends. (See page 282.) She did this to honor Jesus, but he knew that her action had an even greater meaning. Check out this passage from the book of John.

John 12:1-8, NLT

Six days before the Passover ceremonies began, Jesus arrived in Bethany, the home of Lazarus—the man he had raised from the dead. A dinner was prepared in Jesus' honor. Martha served, and Lazarus sat at the table with him. Then Mary took a twelve-ounce jar of expensive perfume made from essence of nard, and she anointed Jesus' feet with it and wiped his feet with her hair. And the house was filled with fragrance.

But Judas Iscariot, one of his disciples—the one who would betray him—said, "That perfume was worth a small fortune. It should have been sold and the money given to the poor." Not that he cared for the poor—he was a thief who was in charge of the disciples' funds, and he often took some for his own use.

Jesus replied, "Leave her alone. She did it in preparation for my burial. You will always have the poor among you, but I will not be here with you much longer."

Here's What I Think

Verity, age 13

As Jesus ate in Simon's house, a prostitute came and continuously kissed his feet and poured expensive perfume over his feet. Yet, the host Simon did not bother to give Jesus this basic courtesy of washing his feet. This sinful woman wanted forgiveness, and in the end, her faith saved her.

If only we were like her. I always take for granted my relationship with God and never completely appreciate my forgiveness from Christ. This story is a good reminder for me of how I should treat Jesus each day. Do I show him the love and respect and honor due him, like the woman did? Or am I more like Simon and show Jesus nothing? How about you?

Verity

Give Jesus your gift of love today.

»»» BE STILL!

Introduction

Ever been surprised by someone? Maybe you discovered a hidden talent in someone you've known all your life. Or maybe you doubted that person's abilities until you saw him or her do something cool. Even after seeing miracle after miracle, Jesus' disciples sometimes doubted that Jesus was the Savior whom the Old Testament prophets talked about. After all, Jesus probably looked like an ordinary man. But one day, Jesus did something so amazing, they could only conclude that this ordinary man was also the extraordinary Son of God.

Mark 4:35-41, NLT

As evening came, Jesus said to his disciples, "Let's cross to the other side of the lake."

He was already in the boat, so they started out, leaving the crowds behind (although other boats followed). But soon a fierce storm arose. High waves began to break into the boat until it was nearly full of water.

Jesus was sleeping at the back of the boat with his head on a cushion. Frantically they woke him up, shouting, "Teacher, don't you even care that we are going to drown?"

When he woke up, he rebuked the wind and said to the water, "Quiet down!" Suddenly the wind stopped, and there was a great calm. And he asked them, "Why are you so afraid? Do you still not have faith in me?"

And they were filled with awe and said among themselves, "Who is this man, that even the wind and waves obey him?"

Take ANOTHER LOOK

In this portion of Psalm 65, David spoke about the power of God. Only God had the power to calm "raging oceans." Jesus demonstrated that power in the story above. Sometimes problems in our lives can seem like raging oceans. As you read this part of Psalm 65, consider asking God to calm the raging oceans in your life.

Psalm 65:5-8, NLT

You faithfully answer our prayers with awesome deeds,
 O God our savior.
You are the hope of everyone on earth,
 even those who sail on distant seas.
You formed the mountains by your power
 and armed yourself with mighty strength.
You quieted the raging oceans
 with their pounding waves
 and silenced the shouting of the nations.
Those who live at the ends of the earth
 stand in awe of your wonders.
From where the sun rises to where it sets,
 you inspire shouts of joy.

Here's What I Think

Jammeshia, age 17

Can you think of any storms in your life? Wow, I know I can! I can think of times when I am worried about getting homework finished on time, or worried if a friend is mad at me, or worried about cleaning up after myself on time so I can go hang out with my friends. (Can you tell that I worry a lot?) But, no matter what the situation is, Jesus is always waiting for me to say, *Hey, I need you, God!* When I do that, Jesus is right there willing to calm me down. The worst thing I could do in those situations is to worry. Worrying is just like saying *I'm not sure that God can do his job!* I know that's not true, so from now on I am going to let Jesus calm my storms!

Jammeshia

Let Jesus calm your storms.

»»» DELIVER US FROM EVIL «««

Ôntroduction

Maybe you've thought that demon possession is something that only happens in old movies like *The Exorcist* or on TV shows. But demon possession wasn't invented by Hollywood. In Jesus' day, it was all too real—a sad reminder of the presence of evil in the world. Right after Jesus calmed the storm, he met a man possessed by many evil spirits. These spirits controlled the man's actions, making him violent and dangerous. Would the Son of God, who had authority over wind and waves, have authority over demons too?

Luke 8:26-39, NLT

So they arrived in the land of the Gerasenes, across the lake from Galilee. As Jesus was climbing out of the boat, a man who was possessed by demons came out to meet him. Homeless and naked, he had lived in a cemetery for a long time. As soon as he saw Jesus, he shrieked and fell to the ground before him, screaming, "Why are you bothering me, Jesus, Son of the Most High God? Please, I beg you, don't torture me!" For Jesus had already commanded the evil spirit to come out of him. This spirit had often taken control of the man. Even when he was shackled with chains, he simply broke them and rushed out into the wilderness, completely under the demon's power.

"What is your name?" Jesus asked.

"Legion," he replied—for the man was filled with many demons. The demons kept begging Jesus not to send them into the Bottomless Pit. A large herd of pigs was feeding on the hillside nearby, and the demons pleaded with him to let them enter into the pigs. Jesus gave them permission. So the demons came out of the man and entered the pigs, and the whole herd plunged down the steep hillside into the lake, where they drowned.

When the herdsmen saw it, they fled to the nearby city and the surrounding countryside, spreading the news as they ran. A crowd soon gathered around Jesus, for they wanted to see for themselves what had happened. And they saw the man who had been possessed by demons sitting quietly at Jesus' feet, clothed and sane. And the whole crowd was afraid. Then those who had seen what happened told the others how the demon-possessed man had been healed. And all the people in that region begged Jesus to go away and leave them alone, for a great wave of fear swept over them.

So Jesus returned to the boat and left, crossing back to the other side of the lake. The man who had been demon possessed begged to go, too, but Jesus said, "No, go back to your family and tell them all the wonderful things God has done for you." So he went all through the city telling about the great thing Jesus had done for him.

Take ANOTHER LOOK

The man above wasn't the only demon-possessed person whom Jesus helped. This passage from Matthew describes another time when Jesus helped drive out demons. Stories about demons aren't in the Bible to terrify people. They serve as a reminder that God has the power over everything, including evil.

Matthew 8:14-17, NLT

When Jesus arrived at Peter's house, Peter's mother-in-law was in bed with a high fever. But when Jesus touched her hand, the fever left her. Then she got up and prepared a meal for him.

That evening many demon-possessed people were brought to Jesus. All the spirits fled when he commanded them to leave; and he healed all the sick. This fulfilled the word of the Lord through Isaiah, who said, "He took our sicknesses and removed our diseases."

Here's What I Think

Daniel, age 15

My mom and I recently went to a restaurant. On our way in, we passed a homeless man. As we were seated, my mom asked if I had seen the homeless man outside and if I thought we should invite him to eat with us. I hadn't thought twice about him.

My mom's compassion resembled Jesus' kindness toward the naked, homeless, crazy man in this story. If I were in that situation I probably would have been a little more than concerned about what was happening. But Jesus didn't show any concern or fear or even rejection. Instead, Jesus compassionately freed this demon-possessed man. Imagine yourself in his position. If it were me, I would probably rush into the nearest building, but Jesus helped the man. I feel that Jesus' example in this story is a personal challenge for me. To whom can I show compassion like Jesus?

Daniel

Follow Jesus' example—and show others his compassion.

JESUS FEEDS
FIVE THOUSAND

Introduction

This account of Jesus feeding the 5,000 is the only miracle of Jesus that is told in all four Gospels. From all four accounts, we know that Jesus and his disciples were looking for a place to be alone and rest. The people, some of whom had been following Jesus for miles, had other ideas. When Jesus saw the crowd, he had only one response: compassion. Jesus asked Philip where they could find food, probably because Philip was from the area. Philip did a quick calculation and estimated that it would cost more than six month's wages to feed such a crowd. But Jesus wanted to teach Philip a greater lesson—faith is more important than financial resources.

John 6:1-15, NLT

After this, Jesus crossed over the Sea of Galilee, also known as the Sea of Tiberias. And a huge crowd kept following him wherever he went, because they saw his miracles as he healed the sick. Then Jesus went up into the hills and sat down with his disciples around him. (It was nearly time for the annual Passover celebration.) Jesus soon saw a great crowd of people climbing the hill, looking for him. Turning to Philip, he asked, "Philip, where can we buy bread to feed all these people?" He was testing Philip, for he already knew what he was going to do.

Philip replied, "It would take a small fortune to feed them!"

Then Andrew, Simon Peter's brother, spoke up. "There's a young boy here with five barley loaves and two fish. But what good is that with this huge crowd?"

"Tell everyone to sit down," Jesus ordered. So all of them—the men alone numbered five thousand—sat down on the grassy slopes. Then Jesus took the loaves, gave thanks to God, and passed them out to the people. Afterward he did the same with the fish. And they all ate until they were full. "Now gather the leftovers," Jesus told his disciples, "so that nothing is wasted." There were only five barley loaves to start with, but twelve baskets were filled with the pieces of bread the people did not eat!

When the people saw this miraculous sign, they exclaimed, "Surely, he is the Prophet we have been expecting!" Jesus saw that they were ready to take him by force and make him king, so he went higher into the hills alone.

Take ANOTHER LOOK

The following morning, many of the crowd were still waiting to see Jesus. But Jesus knew that they were following him only because he had given them food. He wanted them to see that they had a greater need—spiritual hunger—which could be satisfied only through faith in him. In the following verses, Jesus calls himself the bread of life. Read on to discover what Jesus had to say about our need for daily bread.

John 6:35-51, NLT

Jesus replied, "I am the bread of life. No one who comes to me will ever be hungry again. Those who believe in me will never thirst. But you haven't believed in me even though you have seen me. However, those the Father has given me will come to me, and I will never reject them. For I have come down from heaven to do the will of God who sent me, not to do what I want. And this is the will of God, that I should not lose even one of all those he has given me, but that I should raise them to eternal life at the last day. For it is my Father's will that all who see his Son and believe in him should have eternal life—that I should raise them at the last day."

Then the people began to murmur in disagreement because he had said, "I am the bread from heaven." They said, "This is Jesus, the son of Joseph. We know his father and mother. How can he say, 'I came down from heaven'?"

But Jesus replied, "Don't complain about what I said. For people can't come to me unless the Father who sent me draws them to me, and at the last day I will raise them from the dead. As it is written in the Scriptures, 'They will all be taught by God.' Everyone who hears and learns from the Father comes to me. (Not that anyone has ever seen the Father; only I, who was sent from God, have seen him.)

"I assure you, anyone who believes in me already has eternal life. Yes, I am the bread of life! Your ancestors ate manna in the wilderness, but they all died. However, the bread from heaven gives eternal life to everyone who eats it. I am the living bread that came down out of heaven. Anyone who eats this bread will live forever; this bread is my flesh, offered so the world may live."

Here's What I Think

Janna, age 14

Consider the scene. Here is this multitude of people following Jesus to hear his teachings. And it is pretty close to lunchtime. You know these people have to be hungry. There is a young boy with five small loaves of bread and two small fish. Jesus takes the food, divides it, and feeds the entire crowd! Amazing!

Even though the little boy was probably hungry, he was willing to give up his lunch. The boy didn't give part of his lunch to Jesus. He gave everything he had to Jesus. We need to be the same way. We should surrender our lives completely to God. That includes money, clothes, sports, friends, *everything*. That is not an easy thing to do. It is hard to let go of things we enjoy. But Jesus says in Luke 9:23, "If any of you wants to be my follower, you must put aside your selfish ambition, shoulder your cross daily, and follow me."

Janna

Give your all to the one who can do it all!

»» A STEP OF FAITH ««

Ðntroduction

Out of all of Jesus' disciples, Peter was probably the one most willing to take a risk. Early one morning, after seeing Jesus doing something astounding, Peter wanted to follow in his master's footsteps. But Peter quickly learned that he needed more than enthusiasm to follow Jesus—he needed faith.

Matthew 14:22-33, NLT

Immediately after this, Jesus made his disciples get back into the boat and cross to the other side of the lake while he sent the people home. Afterward he went up into the hills by himself to pray. Night fell while he was there alone. Meanwhile, the disciples were in trouble far away from land, for a strong wind had risen, and they were fighting heavy waves.

About three o'clock in the morning Jesus came to them, walking on the water. When the disciples saw him, they screamed in terror, thinking he was a ghost. But Jesus spoke to them at once. "It's all right," he said. "I am here! Don't be afraid."

Then Peter called to him, "Lord, if it's really you, tell me to come to you by walking on water."

"All right, come," Jesus said.

So Peter went over the side of the boat and walked on the water toward Jesus. But when he looked around at the high waves, he was terrified and began to sink. "Save me, Lord!" he shouted.

Instantly Jesus reached out his hand and grabbed him. "You don't have much faith," Jesus said. "Why did you doubt me?" And when they climbed back into the boat, the wind stopped.

Then the disciples worshiped him. "You really are the Son of God!" they exclaimed.

Take ANOTHER LOOK

The previous story shows the importance of faith. Faith was one subject Jesus never grew tired of mentioning. He wanted his disciples to know what amazing things faith in God could accomplish. Maybe that's why Jesus chose the most immovable thing around—a mountain—to explain how the impossible could be made possible in the following passage. But before you pray for your house to move or for your dog to start speaking, remember this: God has the right to say "yes" or "no" to any prayer.

Mark 11:22,23, NLT

Then Jesus said to the disciples, "Have faith in God. I assure you that you can say to this mountain, 'May God lift you up and throw you into the sea,' and your command will be obeyed. All that's required is that you really believe and do not doubt in your heart."

Here's What I Think

Faith, age 14

The principal of our Christian school was talking to us about when Jesus walked on water. He said that we're going to have storms, and we're going to have calm times in our lives. It dawned on me that my life is a lot like Peter's in this story. I obey God, but I still find myself alone in the middle of a storm with nowhere to turn and no one to save me. Then Jesus appears. Before he'll rescue me, I need to believe that he can. I put my trust in him, and Jesus draws close to me. But when I look around at my situation, I get scared again. Just when I think I'm going to drown in my problems, Jesus reaches down and helps me remember to turn to him. It's like a cycle. But I'm learning to put my faith in him in the storms—and in the calm.

Faith

Keep your eyes on Jesus.

»»» PHONY WORSHIP «««

Introduction

The Pharisees liked making and keeping rules. They wanted everyone to believe that they were good people who truly loved God. But Jesus wasn't fooled by their behavior. He knew that they cared more about rules than they did about God or other people. So, when the Pharisees decided to talk to Jesus about what his disciples weren't doing, Jesus had some hard words for them. He called them hypocrites—people who say one thing, but do another.

Matthew 15:1-20, NLT

Some Pharisees and teachers of religious law now arrived from Jerusalem to interview Jesus. "Why do your disciples disobey our age-old traditions?" they demanded. "They ignore our tradition of ceremonial hand washing before they eat."

Jesus replied, "And why do you, by your traditions, violate the direct commandments of God? For instance, God says, 'Honor your father and mother,' and 'Anyone who speaks evil of father or mother must be put to death.' But you say, 'You don't need to honor your parents by caring for their needs if you give the money to God instead.' And so, by your own tradition, you nullify the direct commandment of God. You hypocrites! Isaiah was prophesying about you when he said,

'These people honor me with their lips,
    but their hearts are far away.
Their worship is a farce,
    for they replace God's commands
    with their own man-made teachings.' "

Then Jesus called to the crowds and said, "Listen to what I say and try to understand. You are not defiled by what you eat; you are defiled by what you say and do."

Then the disciples came to him and asked, "Do you realize you offended the Pharisees by what you just said?"

Jesus replied, "Every plant not planted by my heavenly Father will be rooted up, so ignore them. They are blind guides leading the blind, and if one blind person guides another, they will both fall into a ditch."

Then Peter asked Jesus, "Explain what you meant when you said people aren't defiled by what they eat."

"Don't you understand?" Jesus asked him. "Anything you eat passes through the stomach and then goes out of the body. But evil words come from an evil heart and defile the person who says them. For from the heart come evil thoughts, murder, adultery, all other sexual immorality, theft, lying, and slander. These are what defile you. Eating with unwashed hands could never defile you and make you unacceptable to God!"

Take ANOTHER LOOK

The passage Jesus quoted in the story above comes from Isaiah 29. Like Jesus, Isaiah confronted the hypocrites of his day. The people of Judah only pretended to worship God. But God knew that their rule-keeping was as meaningless as that of the Pharisees. True worship comes from the heart.

Isaiah 29:13,14, NLT

And so the Lord says, "These people say they are mine. They honor me with their lips, but their hearts are far away. And their worship of me amounts to nothing more than human laws learned by rote. Because of this, I will do wonders among these hypocrites. I will show that human wisdom is foolish and even the most brilliant people lack understanding."

Here's What I Think

Kali, age 18

In Jesus' time the Pharisees thought that, by keeping all the rules and following all the traditions, they would be considered good or "clean" before God. But in this passage, Jesus says it is "the thought-life that defiles you," not what you eat, or what rules you keep, or what traditions you choose to follow.

In other words, it is what's inside you that counts. A friend of mine once told me that what you put in your mind comes out in your behavior or attitudes. So by watching bad movies or listening to bad music, I am defiling myself. I am filling my mind and heart with things unacceptable to God. But if I choose to fill my heart with God and his will for me, that's what will come out in my everyday life. By doing this I will live the way God wants me to live.

Kali

Fill yourself with God-things,
not world-things.

»»» AT THE CROSSROADS «««

Ôntroduction

Jesus came to Earth with a mission: to die for the sins of the whole world. But this was not what the Jewish people expected of the Savior. They had hoped he would come as a conqueror to rescue them from the Romans. Instead, Jesus came to conquer a kingdom that had been in place for far longer: the kingdom of darkness.

Luke 9:18-27, NLT

One day as Jesus was alone, praying, he came over to his disciples and asked them, "Who do people say I am?"

"Well," they replied, "some say John the Baptist, some say Elijah, and others say you are one of the other ancient prophets risen from the dead."

Then he asked them, "Who do you say I am?"

Peter replied, "You are the Messiah sent from God!"

Jesus Predicts His Death

Jesus warned them not to tell anyone about this. "For I, the Son of Man, must suffer many terrible things," he said. "I will be rejected by the leaders, the leading priests, and the teachers of religious law. I will be killed, but three days later I will be raised from the dead."

Then he said to the crowd, "If any of you wants to be my follower, you must put aside your selfish ambition, shoulder your cross daily, and follow me. If you try to keep your life for yourself, you will lose it. But if you give up your life for me, you will find true life. And how do you benefit if you gain the whole world but lose or forfeit your own soul in the process? If a person is ashamed of me and my message, I, the Son of Man, will be ashamed of that person when I return in my glory and in the glory of the Father and the holy angels. And I assure you that some of you standing here right now will not die before you see the Kingdom of God."

Take ANOTHER LOOK

Long before Jesus came to Earth, a prophet wrote about his life. That prophet was Isaiah. In chapter 53 of his book, you'll see a preview of the "coming attractions" in the life of the Savior. His life definitely wouldn't be easy.

Isaiah 53:3-6, NLT

He was despised and rejected—a man of sorrows, acquainted with bitterest grief. We turned our backs on him and looked the other way when he went by. He was despised, and we did not care.

Yet it was our weaknesses he carried; it was our sorrows that weighed him down. And we thought his troubles were a punishment from God for his own sins! But he was wounded and crushed for our sins. He was beaten that we might have peace. He was whipped, and we were healed! All of us have strayed away like sheep. We have left God's paths to follow our own. Yet the LORD laid on him the guilt and sins of us all.

Here's What I Think

Mike, age 19

One of the most important foundations of our faith is that Jesus Christ *is* the Son of God. Why is it, then, that so many times we allow opportunities to share our faith pass without mentioning the name of our Savior? In this passage, Peter gives the first declaration of who Jesus is. It was not his wisdom that led him to this conclusion, but the working of the Holy Spirit speaking through him. In our lives, we should never pass up the opportunity to speak the name of Jesus as our Lord and Savior. It is by our witness that others can come to know Jesus in the same way we do.

Mike

Who do you say Jesus is? Tell someone!

»»» THE REAL JESUS «««

Introduction

Think about how you are around your closest friends. Do your friends see the "real you"? Peter, James, and John hung out with Jesus more than any of the other nine disciples. You might say that they were three of his closest friends. So it's only natural that Jesus would want them to know the "real" him. Since he was the Son of God, he wanted to demonstrate this to them in a spectacular way. Imagine actually seeing this happen before your eyes. How would you have reacted?

Matthew 17:1-13, NLT

Six days later Jesus took Peter and the two brothers, James and John, and led them up a high mountain. As the men watched, Jesus' appearance changed so that his face shone like the sun, and his clothing became dazzling white. Suddenly, Moses and Elijah appeared and began talking with Jesus. Peter blurted out, "Lord, this is wonderful! If you want me to, I'll make three shrines, one for you, one for Moses, and one for Elijah."

But even as he said it, a bright cloud came over them, and a voice from the cloud said, "This is my beloved Son, and I am fully pleased with him. Listen to him." The disciples were terrified and fell face down on the ground.

Jesus came over and touched them. "Get up," he said, "don't be afraid." And when they looked, they saw only Jesus with them. As they descended the mountain, Jesus commanded them, "Don't tell anyone what you have seen until I, the Son of Man, have been raised from the dead."

His disciples asked, "Why do the teachers of religious law insist that Elijah must return before the Messiah comes?"

Jesus replied, "Elijah is indeed coming first to set everything in order. But I tell you, he has already come, but he wasn't recognized, and he was badly mistreated. And soon the Son of Man will also suffer at their hands." Then the disciples realized he had been speaking of John the Baptist.

Long after Jesus returned to heaven, Peter wrote about his experience on the mountain with Jesus. The experience had helped Peter understand and believe the Scriptures. That's why stories about Jesus like one we just read are included in the Bible. These stories help us to have faith in Jesus. As you read the story below, take Peter's advice and "pay close attention" to what he wrote.

2 Peter 1:16-21, NLT

For we were not making up clever stories when we told you about the power of our Lord Jesus Christ and his coming again. We have seen his majestic splendor with our own eyes. And he received honor and glory from God the Father when God's glorious, majestic voice called down from heaven, "This is my beloved Son; I am fully pleased with him." We ourselves heard the voice when we were there with him on the holy mountain.

Because of that, we have even greater confidence in the message proclaimed by the prophets. Pay close attention to what they wrote, for their words are like a light shining in a dark place—until the day Christ appears and his brilliant light shines in your hearts. Above all, you must understand that no prophecy in Scripture ever came from the prophets themselves or because they wanted to prophesy. It was the Holy Spirit who moved the prophets to speak from God.

Here's What I Think

Nicee, age 14

A lot of people mock my commitment to God. They call me things like "holier than thou." Well, I simply laugh and tell them that Christians are supposed to be Christlike, right? They talk about me behind my back and in my face, but instead of getting angry, I pray for them.

In a way, it's like what John the Baptist experienced. Many people saw what John was doing, but few understood why. I understand that many will treat me any old kind of way because they don't understand *why* I act like I do. That's OK. My job is to live for God regardless of whether others understand or not.

Nicee

Keep living for Jesus
whether others get it or not.

THE GOOD SAMARITAN

Introduction

Like stories? Jesus often told stories to help people understand spiritual truths. These stories were called parables. The Gospel of Luke has more of Jesus' parables than any other Gospel. The story you're about to read is one of the most well known of Jesus' parables. You may have heard this story before. But you may not be aware of how shocking it was to Jesus' listeners. The surprising thing about Jesus' story was the fact that the hero was a Samaritan. As you remember, the Jews and the Samaritans didn't get along. But Jesus wanted to make a point about helping others in need, whether they are an enemy or not. As you read this story about a Samaritan, think about the one person who is hard for you to help. You'll have some idea of the impact of this simple story.

Luke 10:25-37, NLT

One day an expert in religious law stood up to test Jesus by asking him this question: "Teacher, what must I do to receive eternal life?"

Jesus replied, "What does the law of Moses say? How do you read it?"

The man answered, "'You must love the Lord your God with all your heart, all your soul, all your strength, and all your mind.' And, 'Love your neighbor as yourself.'"

"Right!" Jesus told him. "Do this and you will live!"

The man wanted to justify his actions, so he asked Jesus, "And who is my neighbor?"

Story of the Good Samaritan

Jesus replied with an illustration: "A Jewish man was traveling on a trip from Jerusalem to Jericho, and he was attacked by bandits. They stripped him of his clothes and money, beat him up, and left him half dead beside the road.

"By chance a Jewish priest came along; but when he saw the man lying there, he crossed to the other side of the road and passed him by. A Temple assistant walked over and looked at him lying there, but he also passed by on the other side.

"Then a despised Samaritan came along, and when he saw the man, he felt deep pity. Kneeling beside him, the Samaritan soothed his wounds with medicine and bandaged them. Then he put the man on his own donkey and took him to an inn, where he took care of him. The next day he handed the innkeeper two pieces of silver and told him to take care of the man. 'If his bill runs higher than that,' he said, 'I'll pay the difference the next time I am here.'

"Now which of these three would you say was a neighbor to the man who was attacked by bandits?" Jesus asked.

The man replied, "The one who showed him mercy."

Then Jesus said, "Yes, now go and do the same."

Take ANOTHER LOOK

The Pharisees and the Sadducees—another group of religious leaders—looked for ways to embarrass Jesus. But Jesus was always one step ahead of them. In one encounter with them that is recorded in the book of Matthew, Jesus talked about loving one's neighbors. That's what he talked about in the Parable of the Good Samaritan.

Matthew 22:34-40, NLT

But when the Pharisees heard that he had silenced the Sadducees with his reply, they thought up a fresh question of their own to ask him. One of them, an expert in religious law, tried to trap him with this question: "Teacher, which is the most important commandment in the law of Moses?"

Jesus replied, " 'You must love the Lord your God with all your heart, all your soul, and all your mind.' This is the first and greatest commandment. A second is equally important: 'Love your neighbor as yourself.' All the other commandments and all the demands of the prophets are based on these two commandments."

Here's What I Think

Walter, age 13

If you travel a lot, you might have noticed occasionally some cars run out of gas, or suffer some type of mechanical failure in the middle of nowhere. *Most* of these car owners did not do anything wrong; their cars just broke down. I don't know about y'all (sorry, I'm from the South), but my family has never stopped to help one of these unfortunate people. I'm not saying all of these stranded people on the side of the road are nice, wholesome people, but most of them probably are.

In the Parable of the Good Samaritan, the traveler who got beat up was a lot like the people who get stuck on the side of the road every day. Too often, people just ignore the cries for help from people who are hurt. And it doesn't have to be car trouble. It could be loneliness or illness or something like that. But people are hesitant to get involved. My family is too. We need to work on that. I'm not saying that we have to run out and help everyone who's in trouble. But we sure need to be ready and willing to help someone and not just ignore him. That hurting person is my "neighbor."

Walter

How can you show Jesus' kindness to someone crying for help?

ONE GOOD
THING

Introduction

If you've ever thought that a brother or sister was being unfair, you'll understand how Martha feels in this story. Mary, Martha, and Lazarus were a family and also three of Jesus' good friends. Jesus probably spent a lot of time in their home in Bethany. But during a visit to their house, a problem arose between Mary and Martha. Martha turned to Jesus to make things right. But Jesus' response surprised her.

Luke 10:38-42, NLT

As Jesus and the disciples continued on their way to Jerusalem, they came to a village where a woman named Martha welcomed them into her home. Her sister, Mary, sat at the Lord's feet, listening to what he taught. But Martha was worrying over the big dinner she was preparing. She came to Jesus and said, "Lord, doesn't it seem unfair to you that my sister just sits here while I do all the work? Tell her to come and help me."

But the Lord said to her, "My dear Martha, you are so upset over all these details! There is really only one thing worth being concerned about. Mary has discovered it—and I won't take it away from her."

Take ANOTHER LOOK

Mary and Martha invited Jesus to come to their home. Until we get to heaven, we cannot physically be with Jesus like Mary and Martha. But Jesus can live in our hearts and our lives through the presence of the Holy Spirit. Check out these verses from Revelation 3 and 1 Corinthians.

Revelation 3:20, NLT

"Look! Here I stand at the door and knock. If you hear me calling and open the door, I will come in, and we will share a meal as friends."

1 Corinthians 3:16,17, NLT

Don't you realize that all of you together are the temple of God and that the Spirit of God lives in you? God will bring ruin upon anyone who ruins this temple. For God's temple is holy, and you Christians are that temple.

1 Corinthians 6:19,20, NLT

Or don't you know that your body is the temple of the Holy Spirit, who lives in you and was given to you by God? You do not belong to yourself, for God bought you with a high price. So you must honor God with your body.

Here's What I Think

Julie, age 18

I have a confession to make: I'm a perfectionist. I want everything I do to be *perfect*. I want to get all As; I want to be friends with everybody; I want to look my best all the time. Unfortunately, I'm sometimes so intent on being perfect that I miss out on being happy! Instead of having fun, I'm often worrying about staying on schedule or getting lunch for everyone in a group. Like Martha, I tend to forget what is really important in life—the enjoyment of Jesus.

It's not bad to work hard and strive for perfection . . . but don't forget to sit down and enjoy what God has done for you. Spend quiet, restful time listening to Jesus like Mary did. When we follow Mary's example, our friendship with Jesus will grow into something magnificent.

Julie

Take time to be with Jesus.

THE GOOD SHEPHERD

Introduction

Jesus often used stories to teach a spiritual truth about himself or about God the Father. (See, for example, page 279.) In this passage, Jesus wanted to show the difference between the kind of leadership offered by the Pharisees and the kind he offered. A good shepherd would give his life to protect his sheep. And that was what Jesus was preparing to do.

John 10:1-21, NLT

"I assure you, anyone who sneaks over the wall of a sheepfold, rather than going through the gate, must surely be a thief and a robber! For a shepherd enters through the gate. The gatekeeper opens the gate for him, and the sheep hear his voice and come to him. He calls his own sheep by name and leads them out. After he has gathered his own flock, he walks ahead of them, and they follow him because they recognize his voice. They won't follow a stranger; they will run from him because they don't recognize his voice."

Those who heard Jesus use this illustration didn't understand what he meant, so he explained it to them. "I assure you, I am the gate for the sheep," he said. "All others who came before me were thieves and robbers. But the true sheep did not listen to them. Yes, I am the gate. Those who come in through me will be saved. Wherever they go, they will find green pastures. The thief's purpose is to steal and kill and destroy. My purpose is to give life in all its fullness.

"I am the good shepherd. The good shepherd lays down his life for the sheep. A hired hand will run when he sees a wolf coming. He will leave the sheep because they aren't his and he isn't their shepherd. And so the wolf attacks them and scatters the flock. The hired hand runs away because he is merely hired and has no real concern for the sheep.

"I am the good shepherd; I know my own sheep, and they know me, just as my Father knows me and I know the Father. And I lay down my life for the sheep. I have other sheep, too, that are not in this sheepfold. I must bring them also, and they will listen to my voice; and there will be one flock with one shepherd.

"The Father loves me because I lay down my life that I may have it back again. No one can take my life from me. I lay down my life voluntarily. For I have the right to lay it down when I want to and also the power to take it again. For my Father has given me this command."

When he said these things, the people were again divided in their opinions about him. Some of them said, "He has a demon, or he's crazy. Why listen to a man like that?" Others said, "This doesn't sound like a man possessed by a demon! Can a demon open the eyes of the blind?"

Take ANOTHER LOOK

The Old Testament has a number of passages where God calls himself a shepherd. The passage below from Ezekiel 34 is one example. Hundreds of years before Jesus told the previous parable, God spoke to the prophet Ezekiel about God's disobedient people. Although God planned to punish the Israelites by allowing them to be taken away to another country, one day he would gather "his scattered flock."

Ezekiel 34:11-16, NLT

For this is what the Sovereign LORD says: I myself will search and find my sheep. I will be like a shepherd looking for his scattered flock. I will find my sheep and rescue them from all the places to which they were scattered on that dark and cloudy day. I will bring them back home to their own land of Israel from among the peoples and nations. I will feed them on the mountains of Israel and by the rivers in all the places where people live. Yes, I will give them good pastureland on the high hills of Israel. There they will lie down in pleasant places and feed in lush mountain pastures. I myself will tend my sheep and cause them to lie down in peace, says the Sovereign LORD. I will search for my lost ones who strayed away, and I will bring them safely home again. I will bind up the injured and strengthen the weak. But I will destroy those who are fat and powerful. I will feed them, yes—feed them justice!

Here's What I Think

Verity, age 13

I love the picture of Jesus as my good shepherd. It helps me understand who I am—one of his sheep. As part of Jesus' flock, I answer to the familiar voice of Jesus, who loves and protects me, and died for me.

I love picking up my Bible and reading through the passages that reflect my needs at the time. Reading and learning the Scriptures comforts me and makes me feel at peace. As I read, I feel God with me. His presence is so welcoming. Wouldn't you also want to follow a comforting, loving leader like Jesus? The Lord *is* our shepherd, and we need to follow him as his flock of sheep.

Verity

Follow the voice of your shepherd.

»» COUNT THE COST ««

Introduction

With any commitment, there is a cost. If you want to play a musical instrument well, you might have to give up some free time in order to practice. If you want to excel at sports, you probably will have to spend countless hours in training. Jesus warned his disciples about the cost of being his disciple. He knew that one day his followers' lives would be in danger, just as his own life soon would be. Were they willing to risk their reputations, their relationships with their families, or even their lives to continue as his followers?

Luke 14:25-35, NLT

Great crowds were following Jesus. He turned around and said to them, "If you want to be my follower you must love me more than your own father and mother, wife and children, brothers and sisters—yes, more than your own life. Otherwise, you cannot be my disciple. And you cannot be my disciple if you do not carry your own cross and follow me.

"But don't begin until you count the cost. For who would begin construction of a building without first getting estimates and then checking to see if there is enough money to pay the bills? Otherwise, you might complete only the foundation before running out of funds. And then how everyone would laugh at you! They would say, 'There's the person who started that building and ran out of money before it was finished!'

"Or what king would ever dream of going to war without first sitting down with his counselors and discussing whether his army of ten thousand is strong enough to defeat the twenty thousand soldiers who are marching against him? If he is not able, then while the enemy is still far away, he will send a delegation to discuss terms of peace. So no one can become my disciple without giving up everything for me.

"Salt is good for seasoning. But if it loses its flavor, how do you make it salty again? Flavorless salt is good neither for the soil nor for fertilizer. It is thrown away. Anyone who is willing to hear should listen and understand!"

Take ANOTHER LOOK

There were some people who wanted their stuff (possessions, money, etc.) more than they wanted to follow Jesus. In this passage, Jesus met a young man like that. Jesus wasn't upset because this man was wealthy, but he knew that the young man loved his stuff more than he loved God. As you read the story from the book of Mark, put yourself in the young man's place. What would you have done?

Mark 10:17-23, NLT

As he was starting out on a trip, a man came running up to Jesus, knelt down, and asked, "Good Teacher, what should I do to get eternal life?"

"Why do you call me good?" Jesus asked. "Only God is truly good. But as for your question, you know the commandments: 'Do not murder. Do not commit adultery. Do not steal. Do not testify falsely. Do not cheat. Honor your father and mother.' "

"Teacher," the man replied, "I've obeyed all these commandments since I was a child."

Jesus felt genuine love for this man as he looked at him. "You lack only one thing," he told him. "Go and sell all you have and give the money to the poor, and you will have treasure in heaven. Then come, follow me." At this, the man's face fell, and he went sadly away because he had many possessions.

Jesus looked around and said to his disciples, "How hard it is for rich people to get into the Kingdom of God!"

Here's What I Think

Jammeshia, age 17

*J*esus freak! Teacher's pet! Goodie-goodie! I can remember being called quite a few more names. I used to think I could live a Christian life halfway and it would be easy. I thought I could get excited in church, but then act like I did not know God during the week.

When I read this passage from Luke, I know that's not true. Jesus is calling every one of us to totally surrender our lives to him—not once, but daily! He does not promise that the road will be easy, but Jesus does promise that he will be there with us along the way. This is encouraging to me because, even though I might get mocked for being a Christian, Jesus will reward me for totally living for him.

Jammeshia

What do you need to give up today for Jesus?

LOST AND FOUND

Introduction

As usual, when the Pharisees challenged Jesus, he responded with a story. Remember how Jesus described himself as a good shepherd two stories ago? Now, Jesus returns to the subject of sheep with a parable about lost sheep. But he wasn't really talking about the animals. He was talking about people. To really emphasize the point about things that are lost, Jesus included a story about a lost coin. So what's the big deal about lost items? Jesus wanted his listeners to understand how God feels about lost people. How do people become lost? By doing wrong things and forgetting about God. Some lost people know absolutely nothing about God. But Jesus came to seek out and find these lost people.

Luke 15:1-10, NLT

Tax collectors and other notorious sinners often came to listen to Jesus teach. This made the Pharisees and teachers of religious law complain that he was associating with such despicable people—even eating with them!

So Jesus used this illustration: "If you had one hundred sheep, and one of them strayed away and was lost in the wilderness, wouldn't you leave the ninety-nine others to go and search for the lost one until you found it? And then you would joyfully carry it home on your shoulders. When you arrived, you would call together your friends and neighbors to rejoice with you because your lost sheep was found. In the same way, heaven will be happier over one lost sinner who returns to God than over ninety-nine others who are righteous and haven't strayed away!

"Or suppose a woman has ten valuable silver coins and loses one. Won't she light a lamp and look in every corner of the house and sweep every nook and cranny until she finds it? And when she finds it, she will call in her friends and neighbors to rejoice with her because she has found her lost coin. In the same way, there is joy in the presence of God's angels when even one sinner repents."

Paul knew exactly what it meant to be a lost sinner and to be found by God! In his letter to Timothy, a young church leader, Paul explained the basic truth of the good news—Jesus came into the world to seek sinners and to save them. No one is beyond Jesus' love and forgiveness. And that is good news!

1 Timothy 1:12-16, NLT

How thankful I am to Christ Jesus our Lord for considering me trustworthy and appointing me to serve him, even though I used to scoff at the name of Christ. I hunted down his people, harming them in every way I could. But God had mercy on me because I did it in ignorance and unbelief. Oh, how kind and gracious the Lord was! He filled me completely with faith and the love of Christ Jesus.

This is a true saying, and everyone should believe it: Christ Jesus came into the world to save sinners—and I was the worst of them all. But that is why God had mercy on me, so that Christ Jesus could use me as a prime example of his great patience with even the worst sinners. Then others will realize that they, too, can believe in him and receive eternal life.

Here's What I Think

Daniel, age 15

The depth of Jesus' forgiveness really amazes me. I do so many things of which I'm ashamed, but these stories tell me God is so great and forgiving that he parties when I come back to him! Often I get discouraged because my life just isn't going how I think it should.

So I get down and slip farther away from God. I wonder how God could still have patience to deal with me again. That's when I need to remember Jesus' words. When I do, I realize: *I'm that lost sheep. I'm that missing coin.* And God can't wait to "find" me again. It just makes me feel ecstatic to have a God so great that he would throw a party because I came back to him. GOD IS GREAT! PRAISE GOD!

Daniel

Feeling lost? Remember,
God wants to find you.

»»» A LOST SON «««

Introduction

Jesus continued his stories of the lost by telling one of a lost son. Some Bibles call this story the Parable of the Prodigal Son. A prodigal is someone—like the younger son—who spends recklessly and acts wild. But this story also can be called the story of a loving father. Jesus told this story to help people understand how much God cares about people—even the people who disobey him.

Luke 15:11-32, NLT

To illustrate the point further, Jesus told them this story: "A man had two sons. The younger son told his father, 'I want my share of your estate now, instead of waiting until you die.' So his father agreed to divide his wealth between his sons.

"A few days later this younger son packed all his belongings and took a trip to a distant land, and there he wasted all his money on wild living. About the time his money ran out, a great famine swept over the land, and he began to starve. He persuaded a local farmer to hire him to feed his pigs. The boy became so hungry that even the pods he was feeding the pigs looked good to him. But no one gave him anything.

"When he finally came to his senses, he said to himself, 'At home even the hired men have food enough to spare, and here I am, dying of hunger! I will go home to my father and say, "Father, I have sinned against both heaven and you, and I am no longer worthy of being called your son. Please take me on as a hired man."'

"So he returned home to his father. And while he was still a long distance away, his father saw him coming. Filled with love and compassion, he ran to his son, embraced him, and kissed him. His son said to him, 'Father, I have sinned against both heaven and you, and I am no longer worthy of being called your son.'

"But his father said to the servants, 'Quick! Bring the finest robe in the house and put it on him. Get a ring for his finger, and sandals for his feet. And kill the calf we have been fattening in the pen. We must celebrate with a feast, for this son of mine was dead and has now returned to life. He was lost, but now he is found.' So the party began.

"Meanwhile, the older son was in the fields working. When he returned home, he heard music and dancing in the house, and he asked one of the servants what was going on. 'Your brother is back,' he was told, 'and your father has killed the calf we were fattening and has prepared a great feast. We are celebrating because of his safe return.'

"The older brother was angry and wouldn't go in. His father came out and begged him, but he replied, 'All these years I've worked hard for you and never once refused to do a single thing you told me to. And in all that time you never gave me even one young goat for a feast with my friends. Yet when this son of yours comes back after squandering your money on prostitutes, you celebrate by killing the finest calf we have.'

"His father said to him, 'Look, dear son, you and I are very close, and everything I have is yours. We had to celebrate this happy day. For your brother was dead and has come back to life! He was lost, but now he is found!'"

Take ANOTHER LOOK

The son in the story could not help himself. He had to return home. In the same way, we can't help ourselves. The wrong things we do cause us to need a Savior. That's why God sent his Son, Jesus. Paul talks about this in the book of Romans. If we accept the fact that Jesus died for us, then we're considered "found." Then we can celebrate like the father and son in this story.

Romans 5:6-11, NLT

When we were utterly helpless, Christ came at just the right time and died for us sinners. Now, no one is likely to die for a good person, though someone might be willing to die for a person who is especially good. But God showed his great love for us by sending Christ to die for us while we were still sinners. And since we have been made right in God's sight by the blood of Christ, he will certainly save us from God's judgment. For since we were restored to friendship with God by the death of his Son while we were still his enemies, we will certainly be delivered from eternal punishment by his life. So now we can rejoice in our wonderful new relationship with God—all because of what our Lord Jesus Christ has done for us in making us friends of God.

Here's What I Think

Janna, age 14

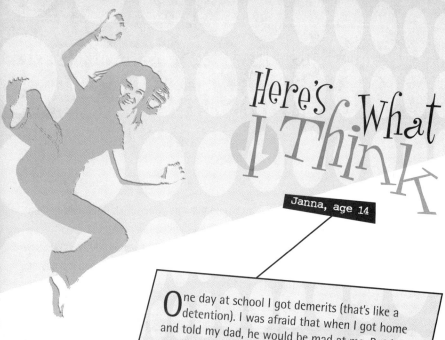

One day at school I got demerits (that's like a detention). I was afraid that when I got home and told my dad, he would be mad at me. But he wasn't; he understood that I make mistakes.

That is what happens in this story. The young man is afraid of going back home. The son thinks his dad won't accept him after the son took his inheritance and wasted it. But the father lovingly welcomes his son back. God is the same way. Many times when I sin, I wonder why or how God could ever forgive me. But God loves us so much that he sent his Son to die for us. No matter how big the sin, God will forgive us. He is always willing to take us back into his arms if we are truly sorry. And that's worth celebrating!

Janna

Come home to God—he will forgive you.

| BC | 4,000 | 2,000 | 1,000 | 500 | 0 | 25 | 50 | 75 | 100 | 125 | AD |

LAZARUS LIVES . . . AGAIN

Introduction

If one of Jesus' close friends were sick, you would think he would rush right over to help him. That's what Mary and Martha counted on when their brother, Lazarus, became ill. But instead of rushing over to their home in the town of Bethany, Jesus waited. You see, he knew something that Mary and Martha didn't know. Jesus knew that he had the power to do more than just heal a sick man. He had power over life and death.

John 11:17-44, NLT

When Jesus arrived at Bethany, he was told that Lazarus had already been in his grave for four days. Bethany was only a few miles down the road from Jerusalem, and many of the people had come to pay their respects and console Martha and Mary on their loss. When Martha got word that Jesus was coming, she went to meet him. But Mary stayed at home. Martha said to Jesus, "Lord, if you had been here, my brother would not have died. But even now I know that God will give you whatever you ask."

Jesus told her, "Your brother will rise again."

"Yes," Martha said, "when everyone else rises, on resurrection day."

Jesus told her, "I am the resurrection and the life. Those who believe in me, even though they die like everyone else, will live again. They are given eternal life for believing in me and will never perish. Do you believe this, Martha?"

"Yes, Lord," she told him. "I have always believed you are the Messiah, the Son of God, the one who has come into the world from God."

Then she left him and returned to Mary. She called Mary aside from the mourners and told her, "The Teacher is here and wants to see you." So Mary immediately went to him.

Now Jesus had stayed outside the village, at the place where Martha met him. When the people who were at the house trying to console Mary saw her leave so hastily, they assumed she was going to Lazarus's grave to weep. So they followed

296

her there. When Mary arrived and saw Jesus, she fell down at his feet and said, "Lord, if you had been here, my brother would not have died."

When Jesus saw her weeping and saw the other people wailing with her, he was moved with indignation and was deeply troubled. "Where have you put him?" he asked them.

They told him, "Lord, come and see." Then Jesus wept. The people who were standing nearby said, "See how much he loved him." But some said, "This man healed a blind man. Why couldn't he keep Lazarus from dying?"

Jesus Raises Lazarus from the Dead

And again Jesus was deeply troubled. Then they came to the grave. It was a cave with a stone rolled across its entrance. "Roll the stone aside," Jesus told them.

But Martha, the dead man's sister, said, "Lord, by now the smell will be terrible because he has been dead for four days."

Jesus responded, "Didn't I tell you that you will see God's glory if you believe?" So they rolled the stone aside. Then Jesus looked up to heaven and said, "Father, thank you for hearing me. You always hear me, but I said it out loud for the sake of all these people standing here, so they will believe you sent me." Then Jesus shouted, "Lazarus, come out!" And Lazarus came out, bound in grave-clothes, his face wrapped in a headcloth. Jesus told them, "Unwrap him and let him go!"

Take ANOTHER LOOK Lazarus wasn't the only person whom Jesus brought back to life. After healing the servant of a centurion (see page 255), Jesus once brought back the son of a widow. Luke, a doctor who became one of Jesus' followers, included this story in his Gospel.

Luke 7:11-15, NLT

Soon afterward Jesus went with his disciples to the village of Nain, with a great crowd following him. A funeral procession was coming out as he approached the village gate. The boy who had died was the only son of a widow, and many mourners from the village were with her. When the Lord saw her, his heart overflowed with compassion. "Don't cry!" he said. Then he walked over to the coffin and touched it, and the bearers stopped. "Young man," he said, "get up." Then the dead boy sat up and began to talk to those around him! And Jesus gave him back to his mother.

Here's What I Think

Faith, age 13

I've always felt like I had a lot of friends, but not one really close friend. The closest friend I had wasn't a Christian and because of that, there was always something separating us. After a big disagreement about God, I realized that I needed one good, solid Christian friend to support me.

All through elementary school, I prayed that God would provide someone, but he kept saying "no." Then, as I got into junior high, God blessed me with not just one good friend, but five or six incredible girls who I could confide in and who could hold me accountable. At first I couldn't see why God didn't show them to me earlier, but now I see that it taught me to trust him. Mary and Martha also couldn't understand why Jesus had waited so long to help Lazarus, but in the long run, it brought more glory to God.

Faith

Have faith in God's timing.

»»» LET THE CHILDREN COME ««

Ϙntroduction

There's an unfortunate old saying that says, "Children should be seen and not heard." Now, Jesus' disciples didn't know anything about that saying, but in this particular situation, they had a similar attitude. When a group of parents came, wanting their children to be blessed by Jesus, the disciples did all they could to prevent them from "bothering" Jesus. See how Jesus responded.

Mark 10:13-16, NLT

One day some parents brought their children to Jesus so he could touch them and bless them, but the disciples told them not to bother him. But when Jesus saw what was happening, he was very displeased with his disciples. He said to them, "Let the children come to me. Don't stop them! For the Kingdom of God belongs to such as these. I assure you, anyone who doesn't have their kind of faith will never get into the Kingdom of God." Then he took the children into his arms and placed his hands on their heads and blessed them.

Take ANOTHER LOOK

Instead of bringing a child to Jesus, another parent chose to bring Jesus to his sick child. As in the previous story, Jesus didn't ignore the man or tell him to go away. He willingly went with this desperate father, even though he knew that the child was dead. But, if you've read the previous story (page 296), you know what Jesus had the power to do.

Mark 5:21-23, 35-42, NLT

When Jesus went back across to the other side of the lake, a large crowd gathered around him on the shore. A leader of the local synagogue, whose name was Jairus, came and fell down before him, pleading with him to heal his little daughter. "She is about to die," he said in desperation. "Please come and place your hands on her; heal her so she can live."

While he was still speaking to her, messengers arrived from Jairus's home with the message, "Your daughter is dead. There's no use troubling the Teacher now."

But Jesus ignored their comments and said to Jairus, "Don't be afraid. Just trust me." Then Jesus stopped the crowd and wouldn't let anyone go with him except Peter and James and John. When they came to the home of the synagogue leader, Jesus saw the commotion and the weeping and wailing. He went inside and spoke to the people. "Why all this weeping and commotion?" he asked. "The child isn't dead; she is only asleep."

The crowd laughed at him, but he told them all to go outside. Then he took the girl's father and mother and his three disciples into the room where the girl was lying. Holding her hand, he said to her, "Get up, little girl!" And the girl, who was twelve years old, immediately stood up and walked around! Her parents were absolutely overwhelmed.

Here's What I Think

Kali, age 18

Mark 10:15 says, "I assure you, anyone who doesn't have their kind of faith will never get into the Kingdom of God." If I were standing there when Jesus said this, I might have thought, *I'm not a child, so does that mean I can't get into God's kingdom?* What I believe Jesus is really saying is that only those who are completely dependent on him for salvation can enter the kingdom of God. Salvation is God's gift and can't be achieved by doing good deeds or acting really nice. Children are completely dependent on their parents. They trust their parents and are honest about it. That is what Christ wants from me. I need to depend on him, be honest with him, and trust him totally and completely with my life—just like a child.

Kali

Come to Jesus like a child—dependent and trusting.

»» SEEING IS BELIEVING «««

Ôntroduction

Time was slowly running out for Jesus. As he continued to make his way toward Jerusalem, he continued teaching and healing people. Jericho was less than 20 miles from Jerusalem. Along the way, blind and disabled people could be seen begging for money. But one man wanted something besides coins—he wanted a miracle.

Mark 10:46-52, NLT

Later, as Jesus and his disciples left town, a great crowd was following. A blind beggar named Bartimaeus (son of Timaeus) was sitting beside the road as Jesus was going by. When Bartimaeus heard that Jesus from Nazareth was nearby, he began to shout out, "Jesus, Son of David, have mercy on me!"

"Be quiet!" some of the people yelled at him.

But he only shouted louder, "Son of David, have mercy on me!"

When Jesus heard him, he stopped and said, "Tell him to come here." So they called the blind man. "Cheer up," they said. "Come on, he's calling you!"

Bartimaeus threw aside his coat, jumped up, and came to Jesus. "What do you want me to do for you?" Jesus asked.

"Teacher," the blind man said, "I want to see!"

And Jesus said to him, "Go your way. Your faith has healed you." And instantly the blind man could see! Then he followed Jesus down the road.

Take ANOTHER LOOK

Just as Jesus was beginning his job of teaching, preaching, and healing, he was asked to read the Scriptures in a synagogue one Sabbath. The passage chosen was Isaiah 61—a book written hundreds of years before Jesus was even born. This passage talked about the amazing things that the Messiah would do when he came. One of these was to give sight to the blind. As the story with Bartimaeus later proved, Jesus was the promised Savior.

Luke 4:16-21, NLT

When he came to the village of Nazareth, his boyhood home, he went as usual to the synagogue on the Sabbath and stood up to read the Scriptures. The scroll containing the messages of Isaiah the prophet was handed to him, and he unrolled the scroll to the place where it says:

"The Spirit of the Lord is upon me,
    for he has appointed me to preach Good News to the poor.
He has sent me to proclaim
    that captives will be released,
    that the blind will see,
    that the downtrodden will be freed from their oppressors,
    and that the time of the Lord's favor has come."

He rolled up the scroll, handed it back to the attendant, and sat down. Everyone in the synagogue stared at him intently. Then he said, "This Scripture has come true today before your very eyes!"

Here's What I Think

Mike, age 19

Why is it that when we see someone who does not have nice clothes or who is somewhat unattractive, we try to keep them out of the spotlight? Are they less important than someone who looks nice and has the newest and most stylish outfits? In this story, the crowd that gathered around Jesus was trying to keep Bartimaeus from getting Jesus' attention. It's apparent that the crowd was embarrassed by Bartimaeus. They didn't want Jesus to have to deal with such a lowly citizen. But Jesus came to heal the sick and save the lost. He was not scared of people whom others may have looked down upon. We shouldn't be scared of them either.

Mike

Whom can you befriend for Jesus today?

»»» TO SEEK AND TO SAVE «««

Ôntroduction

Many people think of Zacchaeus as the "wee little man" from the Sunday school song. It was a fun song to sing, but it's also true. Zacchaeus was too short to see over the crowds that followed Jesus wherever he went. But Zacchaeus wasn't about to let a height problem keep him from seeing Jesus. All he needed was a tree.

Luke 19:1–10, NLT

Jesus entered Jericho and made his way through the town. There was a man there named Zacchaeus. He was one of the most influential Jews in the Roman tax-collecting business, and he had become very rich. He tried to get a look at Jesus, but he was too short to see over the crowds. So he ran ahead and climbed a sycamore tree beside the road, so he could watch from there.

When Jesus came by, he looked up at Zacchaeus and called him by name. "Zacchaeus!" he said. "Quick, come down! For I must be a guest in your home today."

Zacchaeus quickly climbed down and took Jesus to his house in great excitement and joy. But the crowds were displeased. "He has gone to be the guest of a notorious sinner," they grumbled.

Meanwhile, Zacchaeus stood there and said to the Lord, "I will give half my wealth to the poor, Lord, and if I have overcharged people on their taxes, I will give them back four times as much!"

Jesus responded, "Salvation has come to this home today, for this man has shown himself to be a son of Abraham. And I, the Son of Man, have come to seek and save those like him who are lost."

Take ANOTHER LOOK

Jesus was wrongly judged by many people. The Pharisees accused him of being a frlend of "sinners" like tax collectors. They considered themselves too good to hang out with these "sinners." But since Jesus came to seek the lost, he sometimes hung out with these types of people. In the following passage from the book of Luke, Jesus sadly considers what others had to say about him.

Luke 7:31-35, NLT

"How shall I describe this generation?" Jesus asked. "With what will I compare them? They are like a group of children playing a game in the public square. They complain to their friends, 'We played wedding songs, and you weren't happy, so we played funeral songs, but you weren't sad.' For John the Baptist didn't drink wine and he often fasted, and you say, 'He's demon possessed.' And I, the Son of Man, feast and drink, and you say, 'He's a glutton and a drunkard, and a friend of the worst sort of sinners!' But wisdom is shown to be right by the lives of those who follow it."

Here's What I Think

Nicee, age 14

As much as I try to live right, there are still many times that I fall short. I know I am not perfect, and I feel unworthy of any of God's kindness and love. But in spite of my wrongdoings and my feelings about myself, God still sees something in me that I don't even recognize. He still gives me good things and longs to be close to me. I've found that, although I make mistakes, God looks at my heart and sees my sincerity for him and others. Jesus loves me regardless, just as he did Zacchaeus. Although Zacchaeus was a sinner, Jesus saw his sincerity, forgave him, and then blessed him. God can look past all my mistakes and see what's in my heart too.

Nicee

God loves us despite our shortcomings.

)))RETURN OF THE KING (((

Introduction

The final week of Jesus' life began with Jesus entering Jerusalem. Imagine entering a city where people are looking for reasons to arrest you and put you to death. But Jesus didn't sneak into Jerusalem that Sunday hoping that no one would notice him. He entered the way that a king would—riding on the back of an animal. But he didn't ride a horse like a triumphant king would. He rode a donkey as a sign of peace and humility.

Matthew 21:1-11, NLT

As Jesus and the disciples approached Jerusalem, they came to the town of Bethphage on the Mount of Olives. Jesus sent two of them on ahead. "Go into the village over there," he said, "and you will see a donkey tied there, with its colt beside it. Untie them and bring them here. If anyone asks what you are doing, just say, 'The Lord needs them,' and he will immediately send them." This was done to fulfill the prophecy,

"Tell the people of Israel,
   'Look, your King is coming to you.
He is humble, riding on a donkey—
   even on a donkey's colt.'"

The two disciples did as Jesus said. They brought the animals to him and threw their garments over the colt, and he sat on it.

Most of the crowd spread their coats on the road ahead of Jesus, and others cut branches from the trees and spread them on the road. He was in the center of the procession, and the crowds all around him were shouting,

"Praise God for the Son of David!
Bless the one who comes in the name of the Lord!
Praise God in highest heaven!"

The entire city of Jerusalem was stirred as he entered. "Who is this?" they asked.

And the crowds replied, "It's Jesus, the prophet from Nazareth in Galilee."

Messages written in the Scriptures long ago came true when Jesus entered Jerusalem. The Old Testament prophet Zechariah mentioned that the Messiah would enter Jerusalem on a donkey. And that's exactly what happened. Also, the words that the people shouted while Jesus rode into Jerusalem can be found in Psalm 118 and Jeremiah 31.

Zechariah 9:9, NLT

Rejoice greatly, O people of Zion! Shout in triumph, O people of Jerusalem! Look, your king is coming to you. He is righteous and victorious, yet he is humble, riding on a donkey—even on a donkey's colt.

Psalm 118:25,26, NLT

Please, Lord, please save us.
Please, Lord, please give us success.
Bless the one who comes in the name of the Lord.
We bless you from the house of the Lord.

Jeremiah 31:7, NLT

Now this is what the LORD says: "Sing with joy for Israel! Shout for the greatest of nations! Shout out with praise and joy: 'Save your people, O LORD, the remnant of Israel!' "

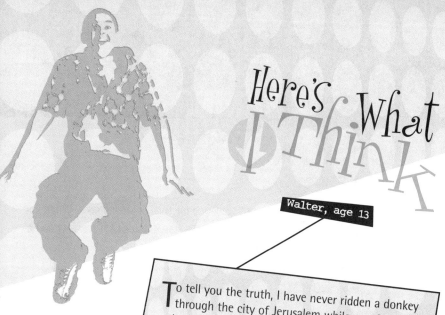

Here's What I Think

Walter, age 13

To tell you the truth, I have never ridden a donkey through the city of Jerusalem while people put palm leaves all over the street. But I *have* driven into summer camp near my hometown. When you pull in, all the counselors yell and cheer in order to welcome you to camp. It makes you feel pretty good.

But when Jesus rode through Jerusalem with people on either side of the street cheering and laying down palm branches in front of him, I don't think he felt quite so good. (Jesus knew what was going to happen a few days later—he would be arrested and then killed.) The people expected Jesus to be a conquering military leader, but instead they got a soul-saving servant. And that's a whole lot better!

Walter

Three cheers for the soul-saving servant!

CLEANING HOUSE

Introduction

What angers you the most? When you see someone mistreat someone else? When you don't get your way? Right after Jesus triumphantly entered Jerusalem, he saw something that made him really angry—angry enough to do something about it.

Matthew 21:12-17, NLT

Jesus entered the Temple and began to drive out the merchants and their customers. He knocked over the tables of the money changers and the stalls of those selling doves. He said, "The Scriptures declare, 'My Temple will be called a place of prayer,' but you have turned it into a den of thieves!"

The blind and the lame came to him, and he healed them there in the Temple. The leading priests and the teachers of religious law saw these wonderful miracles and heard even the little children in the Temple shouting, "Praise God for the Son of David." But they were indignant and asked Jesus, "Do you hear what these children are saying?"

"Yes," Jesus replied. "Haven't you ever read the Scriptures? For they say, 'You have taught children and infants to give you praise.'" Then he returned to Bethany, where he stayed overnight.

Take ANOTHER LOOK

In the previous story, Jesus quoted from two Old Testament prophets: Isaiah and Jeremiah. Jesus used the Scriptures to remind people that God's house was a special place and was not to be disrespected.

Isaiah 56:7, NLT

"I will bring them also to my holy mountain of Jerusalem and will fill them with joy in my house of prayer. I will accept their burnt offerings and sacrifices, because my Temple will be called a house of prayer for all nations."

Jeremiah 7:11, NLT

Do you think this Temple, which honors my name, is a den of thieves? I see all the evil going on there, says the LORD.

Here's What I Think

Julie, age 18

The evil queen in *Snow White* makes me mad! So do a lot of bad characters . . . like Cinderella's stepmother or the Big Bad Wolf. Reading about those bad guys can really get me angry! How *dare* they try to trick, hurt, or kill the good characters?

Although being angry is often something we need to avoid, "righteous anger" toward evil and sin is actually a noble thing. In the Bible story, Jesus was *furious* because of the sin that the money changers had brought into the temple. Jesus' anger filled him with the holy desire to fight what was wrong.

Are you "righteously angry" at things that are unjust, wrong, and sinful? If you ever feel outraged by sin and wickedness like Jesus was in the temple (or like I am when reading certain stories!), you can fight against evil by doing what you know is right! When God is on our side, bad guys won't stand a chance!

Julie

Fight evil by doing what is right!

»» JESUS IS ANOINTED ««

Ôntroduction

In Bible times, there were different reasons to anoint someone. Some hosts poured oil on their guests' heads as a sign of hospitality. Kings were anointed as a sign of their authority. But on the day before his betrayal Jesus was anointed for a totally different reason—because he was about to die.

Mark 14:1-11, NLT

It was now two days before the Passover celebration and the Festival of Unleavened Bread. The leading priests and the teachers of religious law were still looking for an opportunity to capture Jesus secretly and put him to death. "But not during the Passover," they agreed, "or there will be a riot."

Meanwhile, Jesus was in Bethany at the home of Simon, a man who had leprosy. During supper, a woman came in with a beautiful jar of expensive perfume. She broke the seal and poured the perfume over his head. Some of those at the table were indignant. "Why was this expensive perfume wasted?" they asked. "She could have sold it for a small fortune and given the money to the poor!" And they scolded her harshly.

But Jesus replied, "Leave her alone. Why berate her for doing such a good thing to me? You will always have the poor among you, and you can help them whenever you want to. But I will not be here with you much longer. She has done what she could and has anointed my body for burial ahead of time. I assure you, wherever the Good News is preached throughout the world, this woman's deed will be talked about in her memory."

Judas Agrees to Betray Jesus

Then Judas Iscariot, one of the twelve disciples, went to the leading priests to arrange to betray Jesus to them. The leading priests were delighted when they heard why he had come, and they promised him a reward. So he began looking for the right time and place to betray Jesus.

Zechariah, an Old Testament prophet, had something in common with Jesus and Judas. Like Jesus, Zechariah was considered a faithful shepherd, and this prophet, like Jesus, was rejected by his countrymen. The people considered Zechariah worth about 30 pieces of silver—the standard price for a Hebrew slave. This was the price Judas accepted to betray Jesus. Judas would later, as Zechariah did, throw away the money in the Temple.

Zechariah 11:11-13, NLT

That was the end of my covenant with them. Those who bought and sold sheep were watching me, and they knew that the LORD was speaking to them through my actions. And I said to them, "If you like, give me my wages, whatever I am worth; but only if you want to." So they counted out for my wages thirty pieces of silver.

And the LORD said to me, "Throw it to the potters"—this magnificent sum at which they valued me! So I took the thirty coins and threw them to the potters in the Temple of the LORD.

Here's What I Think

Verity, age 13

Jesus praised the woman for pouring the perfume over his head as an act of worship. The perfume was thought to be worth at least a year's wages. When the woman used it to anoint him, Jesus' critics were quick to react. Why not spend the money to help the poor rather than waste it on such an expensive gift, they said. But did you see how Jesus reacted? He was pleased with her gift rather than upset. Jesus wants us to be like the woman and worship him with gifts that show how much he means to us. If necessary, we need to be willing to give up our most precious possessions and worship him completely. We should love Jesus with all our hearts—not halfheartedly.

Verity

Give Jesus the gift of yourself.

FOLLOW MY EXAMPLE

Introduction

The clock was ticking. The time of Jesus' betrayal drew near. With only hours left to be with his disciples, Jesus spent the moments doing what he always did—teaching them. This last lesson was to be a lesson in humility, which means to have an attitude that considers others more important than yourself. This time, Jesus taught by example and shocked his followers. Jesus did something that only a slave would do in those days. And what's more, he expected his disciples to do the same.

John 13:1-20, NLT

Before the Passover celebration, Jesus knew that his hour had come to leave this world and return to his Father. He now showed the disciples the full extent of his love. It was time for supper, and the Devil had already enticed Judas, son of Simon Iscariot, to carry out his plan to betray Jesus. Jesus knew that the Father had given him authority over everything and that he had come from God and would return to God. So he got up from the table, took off his robe, wrapped a towel around his waist, and poured water into a basin. Then he began to wash the disciples' feet and to wipe them with the towel he had around him.

When he came to Simon Peter, Peter said to him, "Lord, why are you going to wash my feet?"

Jesus replied, "You don't understand now why I am doing it; someday you will."

"No," Peter protested, "you will never wash my feet!"

Jesus replied, "But if I don't wash you, you won't belong to me."

Simon Peter exclaimed, "Then wash my hands and head as well, Lord, not just my feet!"

Jesus replied, "A person who has bathed all over does not need to wash, except for the feet, to be entirely clean. And you are clean, but that isn't true of everyone here." For Jesus knew who would betray him. That is what he meant when he said, "Not all of you are clean."

After washing their feet, he put on his robe again and sat down and asked, "Do you understand what I was doing? You call me 'Teacher' and 'Lord,' and you are right, because it is true. And since I, the Lord and Teacher, have washed your feet, you ought to wash each other's feet. I have given you an example to follow. Do as I have done to you. How true it is that a servant is not greater than the master. Nor are messengers more important than the one who sends them. You know these things—now do them! That is the path of blessing.

Jesus Predicts His Betrayal

"I am not saying these things to all of you; I know so well each one of you I chose. The Scriptures declare, 'The one who shares my food has turned against me,' and this will soon come true. I tell you this now, so that when it happens you will believe I am the Messiah. Truly, anyone who welcomes my messenger is welcoming me, and anyone who welcomes me is welcoming the Father who sent me."

Take ANOTHER LOOK

Jesus offers us more than just clean feet. He offers to make us spiritually clean. Wondering how that's done? When we tell God we're sorry for the wrong things we've done, God forgives us and makes us clean inside. That's what this passage from the first book of John promises.

1 John 1:8-10, NLT

If we say we have no sin, we are only fooling ourselves and refusing to accept the truth. But if we confess our sins to him, he is faithful and just to forgive us and to cleanse us from every wrong. If we claim we have not sinned, we are calling God a liar and showing that his word has no place in our hearts.

Here's What I Think

Jammeshia, age 17

Imagine doing the lowest job possible. Maybe washing your friend's floors with a toothbrush, or cleaning all the dirty socks right after gym class. Yuck! Yet, sometimes I get upset when I have to do the smallest chore, like taking out the trash, washing the dishes, or even helping someone.

In this story, Jesus became the ultimate servant by washing his disciples' feet—not a very fun job. Reading this story helps me to see the areas in my life where I could become more like Jesus. Now I understand *how* he wants me to show love to others. So when I do something as small as taking out the trash for someone, it makes me excited because I know I am pleasing God *and* acting like Jesus.

Jammeshia

Want to be like Jesus? Serve others!

»»» A MEAL TO REMEMBER «««

Introduction

This was Jesus' last meal with his disciples before his arrest and death. The time was Passover, the holiday that began during the time of Moses. At the Passover celebration, a lamb was killed for each family as a way of remembering the terrible night when death passed over the homes of the people of Israel. Now, during Jesus' day, the ultimate lamb was about to be killed to save people from death. This lamb was actually Jesus, the Son of God. But before his suffering took place, Jesus had some final instructions for his disciples. He wanted them to remember him in a special way.

Matthew 26:17-30, NLT

On the first day of the Festival of Unleavened Bread, the disciples came to Jesus and asked, "Where do you want us to prepare the Passover supper?"

"As you go into the city," he told them, "you will see a certain man. Tell him, 'The Teacher says, My time has come, and I will eat the Passover meal with my disciples at your house.'" So the disciples did as Jesus told them and prepared the Passover supper there.

When it was evening, Jesus sat down at the table with the twelve disciples. While they were eating, he said, "The truth is, one of you will betray me."

Greatly distressed, one by one they began to ask him, "I'm not the one, am I, Lord?"

He replied, "One of you who is eating with me now will betray me. For I, the Son of Man, must die, as the Scriptures declared long ago. But how terrible it will be for my betrayer. Far better for him if he had never been born!"

Judas, the one who would betray him, also asked, "Teacher, I'm not the one, am I?" And Jesus told him, "You have said it yourself."

As they were eating, Jesus took a loaf of bread and asked God's blessing on it. Then he broke it in pieces and gave it to the disciples, saying, "Take it and eat it, for this is my body." And he took a cup of wine and gave thanks to God for it. He gave it to them and said, "Each of you drink from it, for this is my blood, which seals the covenant between God and his people. It is poured out to forgive the sins of many. Mark my words—I will not drink wine again until the day I drink it new with you in my Father's Kingdom." Then they sang a hymn and went out to the Mount of Olives.

Take ANOTHER Look

Many years after Jesus returned to heaven, the apostle Paul wrote about Jesus' last meal with his disciples. In 1 Corinthians, Paul talks about Communion—the bread and cup used to remember Jesus' death. For centuries Christians have kept this tradition.

1 Corinthians 11:23-26, NLT

For this is what the Lord himself said, and I pass it on to you just as I received it. On the night when he was betrayed, the Lord Jesus took a loaf of bread, and when he had given thanks, he broke it and said, "This is my body, which is given for you. Do this in remembrance of me." In the same way, he took the cup of wine after supper, saying, "This cup is the new covenant between God and you, sealed by the shedding of my blood. Do this in remembrance of me as often as you drink it." For every time you eat this bread and drink this cup, you are announcing the Lord's death until he comes again.

Daniel, age 15

The Lord's Supper is a symbol of the new promise that God made with us through the body and blood of Jesus. The Lord's Supper helps us remember what Jesus did for us when he died on the cross for our sins. He became a living sacrifice so that we can freely accept his forgiveness and love.

For me, the Lord's Supper reminds me that God loved *me* enough that he came down to Earth to live as one of us. Not only that, but Jesus came to save *my* life as *my* sin nailed him to the cross, just as he did for you. Jesus' sacrifice is awe-inspiring. Take a few minutes to think about what Jesus did for you and me right now. Jesus loves us so much, and his love is poured out on us constantly—no strings attached.

Daniel

Give thanks for Jesus, the Lamb.

»»» A NIGHT OF PRAYER «««

Introduction

What's the worst night you've ever spent? The worst night of Jesus' life had to be the one described below. Imagine how you would feel, knowing that you would soon be betrayed by someone you love and be taken away by force. What would you do? Maybe you would do what Jesus did—pray.

Matthew 26:36-46, NLT

Then Jesus brought them to an olive grove called Gethsemane, and he said, "Sit here while I go on ahead to pray." He took Peter and Zebedee's two sons, James and John, and he began to be filled with anguish and deep distress. He told them, "My soul is crushed with grief to the point of death. Stay here and watch with me."

He went on a little farther and fell face down on the ground, praying, "My Father! If it is possible, let this cup of suffering be taken away from me. Yet I want your will, not mine." Then he returned to the disciples and found them asleep. He said to Peter, "Couldn't you stay awake and watch with me even one hour? Keep alert and pray. Otherwise temptation will overpower you. For though the spirit is willing enough, the body is weak!"

Again he left them and prayed, "My Father! If this cup cannot be taken away until I drink it, your will be done." He returned to them again and found them sleeping, for they just couldn't keep their eyes open.

So he went back to pray a third time, saying the same things again. Then he came to the disciples and said, "Still sleeping? Still resting? Look, the time has come. I, the Son of Man, am betrayed into the hands of sinners. Up, let's be going. See, my betrayer is here!"

Jesus' prayer can be found in John 17. Part of it appears below. He didn't spend his last hours in self-pity, begging God to make things easier for him. Instead, he prayed that God would be honored. He also prayed for his followers. Would you have done the same?

John 17:1-19, NLT

When Jesus had finished saying all these things, he looked up to heaven and said, "Father, the time has come. Glorify your Son so he can give glory back to you. For you have given him authority over everyone in all the earth. He gives eternal life to each one you have given him. And this is the way to have eternal life—to know you, the only true God, and Jesus Christ, the one you sent to earth. I brought glory to you here on earth by doing everything you told me to do. And now, Father, bring me into the glory we shared before the world began.

"I have told these men about you. They were in the world, but then you gave them to me. Actually, they were always yours, and you gave them to me; and they have kept your word. Now they know that everything I have is a gift from you, for I have passed on to them the words you gave me; and they accepted them and know that I came from you, and they believe you sent me."

"My prayer is not for the world, but for those you have given me, because they belong to you. And all of them, since they are mine, belong to you; and you have given them back to me, so they are my glory! Now I am departing the world; I am leaving them behind and coming to you. Holy Father, keep them and care for them—all those you have given me—so that they will be united just as we are. During my time here, I have kept them safe. I guarded them so that not one was lost, except the one headed for destruction, as the Scriptures foretold.

"And now I am coming to you. I have told them many things while I was with them so they would be filled with my joy. I have given them your word. And the world hates them because they do not belong to the world, just as I do not. I'm not asking you to take them out of the world, but to keep them safe from the evil one. They are not part of this world any more than I am. Make them pure and holy by teaching them your words of truth. As you sent me into the world, I am sending them into the world. And I give myself entirely to you so they also might be entirely yours."

Here's What I Think

Janna, age 14

Friends are important. Look how much Jesus' friends meant to him. Even though he was God and even though he knew what was going to happen, Jesus still needed his friends' support and prayer before his arrest. We need to be helpful and support our friends as well.

I started attending a Christian school in fifth grade. A girl from Romania started attending also. She wasn't what most people would consider normal, and some people made fun of her. Some friends and I reached out to her and made her feel welcome. She needed us then, and we were willing to help. Maybe you know someone who is being teased. Or maybe a friend is just having a bad day. Do what you can to reach out to them and show them God's love.

Janna

Look for ways you can reach out to your friends.

»»» ONE TERRIBLE NIGHT «««

Introduction

You've probably heard about or seen criminals arrested on television. Sometimes, we later discover that innocent people have been arrested and unjustly accused. This was the case for Jesus one terrible night in a garden. In this beautiful setting, a gesture of friendship—a kiss—became an ugly sign of betrayal.

Matthew 26:47-56, NLT

And even as he said this, Judas, one of the twelve disciples, arrived with a mob that was armed with swords and clubs. They had been sent out by the leading priests and other leaders of the people. Judas had given them a prearranged signal: "You will know which one to arrest when I go over and give him the kiss of greeting." So Judas came straight to Jesus. "Greetings, Teacher!" he exclaimed and gave him the kiss.

Jesus said, "My friend, go ahead and do what you have come for." Then the others grabbed Jesus and arrested him. One of the men with Jesus pulled out a sword and slashed off an ear of the high priest's servant.

"Put away your sword," Jesus told him. "Those who use the sword will be killed by the sword. Don't you realize that I could ask my Father for thousands of angels to protect us, and he would send them instantly? But if I did, how would the Scriptures be fulfilled that describe what must happen now?"

Then Jesus said to the crowd, "Am I some dangerous criminal, that you have come armed with swords and clubs to arrest me? Why didn't you arrest me in the Temple? I was there teaching every day. But this is all happening to fulfill the words of the prophets as recorded in the Scriptures." At that point, all the disciples deserted him and fled.

Take ANOTHER LOOK

Zechariah, an Old Testament prophet, predicted what would happen to Jesus. Jesus quoted from this passage just before his arrest.

Zechariah 13:7, NLT

Awake, O sword, against my shepherd, the man who is my partner, says the Lord Almighty. Strike down the shepherd, and the sheep will be scattered, and I will turn against the lambs.

Here's What I Think

Verity, age 13

Have you ever told a good friend a secret? Then you find out one day that the whole school knows your secret because your friend told a bunch of people. It's an awful feeling. You feel so let down and bitter inside. Sometimes, you don't really want to talk to that friend you once trusted. Imagine how Jesus must have felt when he knew Judas was going to betray him. Jesus must have been so sad and longing for Judas to make the right decision. Even though Jesus was full of sorrow, he still loved Judas. When we are betrayed by those who are closest to us, we still need to love them, like Jesus did. After all, we are also guilty of betraying Jesus from time to time. How does that happen? What about the long weeks that we do not bother to talk to Jesus? Or when we remain silent when others mock Jesus? Yet Jesus still loves us. Remember that the next time a friend disappoints you.

Verity

Love those who let you down.

»»» TRIAL AND ERROR «««

Introduction

Jesus' horrible night continued as he faced a series of six trials. The high priest and the Sanhedrin, a council of Jewish leaders, had the power to rule on his case. But this first set of trials would be anything but fair. For one thing, since some of the trials were held at night, they weren't exactly legal. For another, the Jewish leaders already knew what their decision would be. Meanwhile, Peter followed the crowd to see what would happen to Jesus. Little did Peter know that his own trial—his time of testing—had also just begun.

Matthew 26:57-75, NLT

Then the people who had arrested Jesus led him to the home of Caiaphas, the high priest, where the teachers of religious law and other leaders had gathered. Meanwhile, Peter was following far behind and eventually came to the courtyard of the high priest's house. He went in, sat with the guards, and waited to see what was going to happen to Jesus.

Inside, the leading priests and the entire high council were trying to find witnesses who would lie about Jesus, so they could put him to death. But even though they found many who agreed to give false witness, there was no testimony they could use. Finally, two men were found who declared, "This man said, 'I am able to destroy the Temple of God and rebuild it in three days.'"

Then the high priest stood up and said to Jesus, "Well, aren't you going to answer these charges? What do you have to say for yourself?" But Jesus remained silent. Then the high priest said to him, "I demand in the name of the living God that you tell us whether you are the Messiah, the Son of God."

Jesus replied, "Yes, it is as you say. And in the future you will see me, the Son of Man, sitting at God's right hand in the place of power and coming back on the clouds of heaven."

Then the high priest tore his clothing to show his horror, shouting, "Blasphemy! Why do we need other witnesses? You have all heard his blasphemy. What is your verdict?"

"Guilty!" they shouted. "He must die!"

Then they spit in Jesus' face and hit him with their fists. And some slapped him, saying, "Prophesy to us, you Messiah! Who hit you that time?"

Peter Denies Jesus

Meanwhile, as Peter was sitting outside in the courtyard, a servant girl came over and said to him, "You were one of those with Jesus the Galilean."

But Peter denied it in front of everyone. "I don't know what you are talking about," he said.

Later, out by the gate, another servant girl noticed him and said to those standing around, "This man was with Jesus of Nazareth."

Again Peter denied it, this time with an oath. "I don't even know the man," he said.

A little later some other bystanders came over to him and said, "You must be one of them; we can tell by your Galilean accent."

Peter said, "I swear by God, I don't know the man." And immediately the rooster crowed. Suddenly, Jesus' words flashed through Peter's mind: "Before the rooster crows, you will deny me three times." And he went away, crying bitterly.

Take ANOTHER LOOK

During the Last Supper, Jesus talked about Peter's denial. The Gospel of Luke has that story. While Peter couldn't imagine doing such a thing, the story above proves that Jesus was right. As you read this next story, put yourself in Peter's place. What would you have done? Has there ever been a time when someone asked you about your faith and you found yourself answering as Peter did?

Luke 22:31-34, NLT

[Jesus said,] "Simon, Simon, Satan has asked to have all of you, to sift you like wheat. But I have pleaded in prayer for you, Simon, that your faith should not fail. So when you have repented and turned to me again, strengthen and build up your brothers."

Peter said, "Lord, I am ready to go to prison with you, and even to die with you."

But Jesus said, "Peter, let me tell you something. The rooster will not crow tomorrow morning until you have denied three times that you even know me."

Here's What I Think

Mike, age 19

It has happened to all of us at one time or another. We are surrounded by non-Christian friends, and someone makes a joke or insult about Jesus. Then, instead of standing up for Jesus and our faith, we sit back and remain quiet. Sounds like Peter, right? In this story, Peter denies Jesus three times.

I can only imagine how much pressure Peter felt and how scared he was about possibly being arrested. But Peter still shouldn't have denied Jesus, and neither should we. If our friends make jokes about Jesus and we say nothing, our silence is a form of denial. Think about it. If someone said something bad about one of your friends, would you let it happen? It should be the same when someone talks bad about Jesus. Speak up!

Mike

Speak up for Jesus and your faith!

A TRIAL AND
A TRADE

Introduction

Jesus' court trials continued as Jesus was taken before Pilate, the Roman governor. According to the laws of the land, the people of Israel could not put a person to death. Only the Romans, who ruled the region, had the power to impose a death sentence. Little did Pilate know that the God of Israel had the real power over life and death.

John 18:28-40, NLT

Jesus' trial before Caiaphas ended in the early hours of the morning. Then he was taken to the headquarters of the Roman governor. His accusers didn't go in themselves because it would defile them, and they wouldn't be allowed to celebrate the Passover feast. So Pilate, the governor, went out to them and asked, "What is your charge against this man?"

"We wouldn't have handed him over to you if he weren't a criminal!" they retorted.

"Then take him away and judge him by your own laws," Pilate told them.

"Only the Romans are permitted to execute someone," the Jewish leaders replied. This fulfilled Jesus' prediction about the way he would die.

Then Pilate went back inside and called for Jesus to be brought to him. "Are you the King of the Jews?" he asked him.

Jesus replied, "Is this your own question, or did others tell you about me?"

"Am I a Jew?" Pilate asked. "Your own people and their leading priests brought you here. Why? What have you done?"

Then Jesus answered, "I am not an earthly king. If I were, my followers would have fought when I was arrested by the Jewish leaders. But my Kingdom is not of this world."

Pilate replied, "You are a king then?"

"You say that I am a king, and you are right," Jesus said. "I was born for that purpose. And I came to bring truth to the world. All who love the truth recognize that what I say is true."

"What is truth?" Pilate asked. Then he went out again to the people and told them, "He is not guilty of any crime. But you have a custom of asking me to release someone from prison each year at Passover. So if you want me to, I'll release the King of the Jews."

But they shouted back, "No! Not this man, but Barabbas!" (Barabbas was a criminal.)

Take ANOTHER LOOK

Pilate didn't know that "truth" stood before him. Before this trial, Jesus had a lot to say about truth. Jesus said that he was the truth. The Word of God also is the truth. As the truth, Jesus sets people free from doing the wrong things.

John 8:31-36, NLT

Jesus said to the people who believed in him, "You are truly my disciples if you keep obeying my teachings. And you will know the truth, and the truth will set you free."

"But we are descendants of Abraham," they said. "We have never been slaves to anyone on earth. What do you mean, 'set free'?"

Jesus replied, "I assure you that everyone who sins is a slave of sin. A slave is not a permanent member of the family, but a son is part of the family forever. So if the Son sets you free, you will indeed be free."

John 14:6, NLT

Jesus told him, "I am the way, the truth, and the life. No one can come to the Father except through me."

Here's What I Think

Nicee, age 14

How do you define yourself?" That was the question a speaker once asked during a school assembly. I thought long and hard about his question, then came up with my answer. I am a child of God! Since my Father is a King, I'm royalty! And my job is to tell as many people as I can about my Father and how they, too, can become a child of God. Because I know who I am, I know exactly how I am supposed to act and think.

Jesus knew exactly who he was and how he was suppose to act. When on trial, Jesus didn't try to cover up or come up with excuses or lie about who he was. So when it was time for judgment, Pilate couldn't find anything to pin on Jesus. Jesus *was* the King—but not of this world. And Pilate didn't have any power over Jesus' kingdom.

So how do you define yourself?

Nicee

Live like a child of the King.

IT IS FINISHED

Introduction

Crucifixion—a common way to kill criminals in New Testament times—was the worst possible way for someone to die. Death came by suffocation as the person lost strength and the weight of the body made breathing more and more difficult. It seems an especially horrible death for someone who is innocent of any crime. But Jesus went to the cross, not for himself, but for each one of us.

Matthew 27:32-66, NLT

As they were on the way, they came across a man named Simon, who was from Cyrene, and they forced him to carry Jesus' cross. Then they went out to a place called Golgotha (which means Skull Hill). The soldiers gave him wine mixed with bitter gall, but when he had tasted it, he refused to drink it.

After they had nailed him to the cross, the soldiers gambled for his clothes by throwing dice. Then they sat around and kept guard as he hung there. A signboard was fastened to the cross above Jesus' head, announcing the charge against him. It read: "This is Jesus, the King of the Jews."

Two criminals were crucified with him, their crosses on either side of his. And the people passing by shouted abuse, shaking their heads in mockery. "So! You can destroy the Temple and build it again in three days, can you? Well then, if you are the Son of God, save yourself and come down from the cross!"

The leading priests, the teachers of religious law, and the other leaders also mocked Jesus. "He saved others," they scoffed, "but he can't save himself! So he is the king of Israel, is he? Let him come down from the cross, and we will believe in him! He trusted God—let God show his approval by delivering him! For he said, 'I am the Son of God.'" And the criminals who were crucified with him also shouted the same insults at him.

The Death of Jesus

At noon, darkness fell across the whole land until three o'clock. At about three o'clock, Jesus called out with a loud voice, *"Eli, Eli, lema sabachthani?"* which means, "My God, my God, why have you forsaken me?"

Some of the bystanders misunderstood and thought he was calling for the prophet Elijah. One of them ran and filled a sponge with sour wine, holding it up to him on a stick so he could drink. But the rest said, "Leave him alone. Let's see whether Elijah will come and save him."

Then Jesus shouted out again, and he gave up his spirit. At that moment the curtain in the Temple was torn in two, from top to bottom. The earth shook, rocks split apart, and tombs opened. The bodies of many godly men and women who had died were raised from the dead after Jesus' resurrection. They left the cemetery, went into the holy city of Jerusalem, and appeared to many people.

The Roman officer and the other soldiers at the crucifixion were terrified by the earthquake and all that had happened. They said, "Truly, this was the Son of God!"

And many women who had come from Galilee with Jesus to care for him were watching from a distance. Among them were Mary Magdalene, Mary (the mother of James and Joseph), and Zebedee's wife, the mother of James and John.

The Burial of Jesus

As evening approached, Joseph, a rich man from Arimathea who was one of Jesus' followers, went to Pilate and asked for Jesus' body. And Pilate issued an order to release it to him. Joseph took the body and wrapped it in a long linen cloth. He placed it in his own new tomb, which had been carved out of the rock. Then he rolled a great stone across the entrance as he left. Both Mary Magdalene and the other Mary were sitting nearby watching.

The Guard at the Tomb

The next day—on the first day of the Passover ceremonies—the leading priests and Pharisees went to see Pilate. They told him, "Sir, we remember what that deceiver once said while he was still alive: 'After three days I will be raised from the dead.' So we request that you seal the tomb until the third day. This will prevent his disciples from coming and stealing his body and then telling everyone he came back to life! If that happens, we'll be worse off than we were at first."

Pilate replied, "Take guards and secure it the best you can." So they sealed the tomb and posted guards to protect it.

Hundreds of years before Jesus died on the cross, a prophet wrote all about the event. That prophet was Isaiah. As you read this passage from Isaiah 53, compare it to the story above. God helped Isaiah know exactly what would happen. Although Jesus isn't mentioned by name below, he made this prophecy come true.

Isaiah 53:3-12, NLT

He was despised and rejected—a man of sorrows, acquainted with bitterest grief. We turned our backs on him and looked the other way when he went by. He was despised, and we did not care.

Yet it was our weaknesses he carried; it was our sorrows that weighed him down. And we thought his troubles were a punishment from God for his own sins! But he was wounded and crushed for our sins. He was beaten that we might have peace. He was whipped, and we were healed! All of us have strayed away like sheep. We have left God's paths to follow our own. Yet the LORD laid on him the guilt and sins of us all.

He was oppressed and treated harshly, yet he never said a word. He was led as a lamb to the slaughter. And as a sheep is silent before the shearers, he did not open his mouth. From prison and trial they led him away to his death. But who among the people realized that he was dying for their sins—that he was suffering their punishment? He had done no wrong, and he never deceived anyone. But he was buried like a criminal; he was put in a rich man's grave.

But it was the LORD's good plan to crush him and fill him with grief. Yet when his life is made an offering for sin, he will have a multitude of children, many heirs. He will enjoy a long life, and the LORD's plan will prosper in his hands. When he sees all that is accomplished by his anguish, he will be satisfied. And because of what he has experienced, my righteous servant will make it possible for many to be counted righteous, for he will bear all their sins. I will give him the honors of one who is mighty and great, because he exposed himself to death. He was counted among those who were sinners. He bore the sins of many and interceded for sinners.

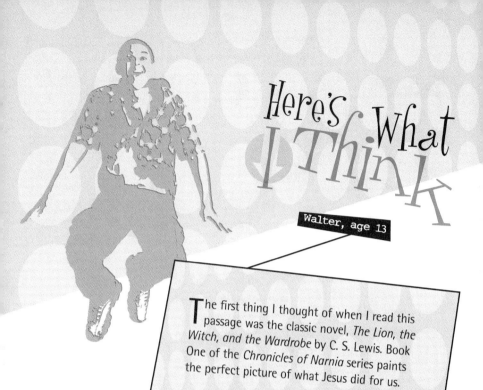

Here's What I Think

Walter, age 13

The first thing I thought of when I read this passage was the classic novel, *The Lion, the Witch, and the Wardrobe* by C. S. Lewis. Book One of the *Chronicles of Narnia* series paints the perfect picture of what Jesus did for us.

In the book, Aslan (a big lion who represents Jesus) lets the evil witch (who symbolizes the devil) kill him. When Aslan comes back, the evil witch is destroyed. This is exactly what Jesus did for us. He willingly died on the cross for our sins. And in doing so, our sins were forgiven and Satan was defeated forever. Jesus gave up his life for us. So in dying, he actually saved us; something that I am very grateful for. (By the way, I *highly* recommend reading this book!)

Walter

The end result of Jesus' death on the cross is eternal life.

AN EMPTY TOMB

Introduction

It was over. Jesus was dead. His enemies had won. All of the disciples' hopes had died with him. But was it really the end? Jesus' enemies thought so. The disciples thought so. But God knew otherwise.

John 20:1-23, NLT

Early Sunday morning, while it was still dark, Mary Magdalene came to the tomb and found that the stone had been rolled away from the entrance. She ran and found Simon Peter and the other disciple, the one whom Jesus loved. She said, "They have taken the Lord's body out of the tomb, and I don't know where they have put him!"

Peter and the other disciple ran to the tomb to see. The other disciple outran Peter and got there first. He stooped and looked in and saw the linen cloth lying there, but he didn't go in. Then Simon Peter arrived and went inside. He also noticed the linen wrappings lying there, while the cloth that had covered Jesus' head was folded up and lying to the side. Then the other disciple also went in, and he saw and believed—for until then they hadn't realized that the Scriptures said he would rise from the dead. Then they went home.

Jesus Appears to Mary Magdalene

Mary was standing outside the tomb crying, and as she wept, she stooped and looked in. She saw two white-robed angels sitting at the head and foot of the place where the body of Jesus had been lying. "Why are you crying?" the angels asked her.

"Because they have taken away my Lord," she replied, "and I don't know where they have put him."

She glanced over her shoulder and saw someone standing behind her. It was Jesus, but she didn't recognize him. "Why are you crying?" Jesus asked her. "Who are you looking for?"

She thought he was the gardener. "Sir," she said, "if you have taken him away, tell me where you have put him, and I will go and get him."

"Mary!" Jesus said.

She turned toward him and exclaimed, "Teacher!"

"Don't cling to me," Jesus said, "for I haven't yet ascended to the Father. But go find my brothers and tell them that I am ascending to my Father and your Father, my God and your God."

Mary Magdalene found the disciples and told them, "I have seen the Lord!" Then she gave them his message.

Jesus Appears to His Disciples

That evening, on the first day of the week, the disciples were meeting behind locked doors because they were afraid of the Jewish leaders. Suddenly, Jesus was standing there among them! "Peace be with you," he said. As he spoke, he held out his hands for them to see, and he showed them his side. They were filled with joy when they saw their Lord! He spoke to them again and said, "Peace be with you. As the Father has sent me, so I send you." Then he breathed on them and said to them, "Receive the Holy Spirit. If you forgive anyone's sins, they are forgiven. If you refuse to forgive them, they are unforgiven."

Take ANOTHER LOOK

In his first letter to Corinthian believers, Paul wrote about Jesus' resurrection. Although Paul became a follower of Jesus after Jesus returned to heaven, he heard all about Jesus' resurrection from Peter and the other disciples. He wanted others to know about it too. Whom have you told about Jesus' resurrection?

1 Corinthians 15:1-6, NLT

Now let me remind you, dear brothers and sisters, of the Good News I preached to you before. You welcomed it then and still do now, for your faith is built on this wonderful message. And it is this Good News that saves you if you firmly believe it—unless, of course, you believed something that was never true in the first place.

I passed on to you what was most important and what had also been passed on to me—that Christ died for our sins, just as the Scriptures said. He was buried, and he was raised from the dead on the third day, as the Scriptures said. He was seen by Peter and then by the twelve apostles. After that, he was seen by more than five hundred of his followers at one time, most of whom are still alive, though some have died by now.

Here's What I Think

Jammeshia, age 17

He has risen, he has risen indeed! Just imagine all Jesus' followers on that day when he appeared after being dead for three days. Imagine their thoughts, their feelings, their reactions. It's so cool to see that the God we love and serve is *alive* and working in our lives.

What's even better is that Jesus freely gives us the gift of salvation. By accepting this gift we get to live with Jesus forever! Because he lives, I live. Because he lives, so will you! Jesus says, "I will come and get you, so that you will always be with me where I am" (John 14:3). He's gonna come and get us. I can't wait till the day when I am able to sit and talk with him face-to-face. Just imagine.

Jammeshia

One day we'll be with
Jesus forever. Imagine!

»»» STRANGER ON THE ROAD «««

Ontroduction

Although Mary saw Jesus, there were others who didn't know that Jesus was alive. Some of Jesus' followers still believed that they would never see him again. Two of his followers sadly mourned that fact on their way home to Emmaus. But the sudden appearance of a stranger as they walked this road would change their lives forever.

Luke 24:13-34, NLT

That same day two of Jesus' followers were walking to the village of Emmaus, seven miles out of Jerusalem. As they walked along they were talking about everything that had happened. Suddenly, Jesus himself came along and joined them and began walking beside them. But they didn't know who he was, because God kept them from recognizing him.

"You seem to be in a deep discussion about something," he said. "What are you so concerned about?"

They stopped short, sadness written across their faces. Then one of them, Cleopas, replied, "You must be the only person in Jerusalem who hasn't heard about all the things that have happened there the last few days."

"What things?" Jesus asked.

"The things that happened to Jesus, the man from Nazareth," they said. "He was a prophet who did wonderful miracles. He was a mighty teacher, highly regarded by both God and all the people. But our leading priests and other religious leaders arrested him and handed him over to be condemned to death, and they crucified him. We had thought he was the Messiah who had come to rescue Israel. That all happened three days ago. Then some women from our group of his followers were at his tomb early this morning, and they came back with an amazing report. They said his body was missing, and they had seen angels who told them Jesus is alive! Some of our men ran out to see, and sure enough, Jesus' body was gone, just as the women had said."

Then Jesus said to them, "You are such foolish people! You find it so hard to believe all that the prophets wrote in the Scriptures. Wasn't it clearly predicted by the prophets that the Messiah would have to suffer all these things before entering his time of glory?" Then Jesus quoted passages from the writings of Moses and all the prophets, explaining what all the Scriptures said about himself.

By this time they were nearing Emmaus and the end of their journey. Jesus would have gone on, but they begged him to stay the night with them, since it was getting late. So he went home with them. As they sat down to eat, he took a small loaf of bread, asked God's blessing on it, broke it, then gave it to them. Suddenly, their eyes were opened, and they recognized him. And at that moment he disappeared!

They said to each other, "Didn't our hearts feel strangely warm as he talked with us on the road and explained the Scriptures to us?" And within the hour they were on their way back to Jerusalem, where the eleven disciples and the other followers of Jesus were gathered. When they arrived, they were greeted with the report, "The Lord has really risen! He appeared to Peter!"

Take ANOTHER LOOK

David wrote a psalm which showed what would happen to Jesus. David didn't know at the time that he was prophesying about the Messiah to come. This is one of the Scriptures that Jesus might have shared with the two disciples on the road to Emmaus.

Psalm 16:9-11, NLT

No wonder my heart is filled with joy,
  and my mouth shouts his praises!
  My body rests in safety.
For you will not leave my soul among the dead
  or allow your godly one to rot in the grave.
You will show me the way of life,
  granting me the joy of your presence
  and the pleasures of living with you forever.

Here's What I Think

I love detective stories. It's fun to put together bits and pieces of information and eventually figure out the solution to a mystery as I read. I find investigating irresistible! Unfortunately, sometimes I come across "mystery" situations that seem impossible to understand and solve.

These situations might be in a novel, a math problem . . . or even in my relationship with God. I often have hard questions for God—sometimes I simply can't figure him out!

I could use advice from the disciples in this Bible story. They couldn't understand the mystery of Jesus' death and resurrection. But who came to help them? Jesus himself! Jesus first showed them clues in Scripture to help them solve the mystery. Guess what? I can read the Bible to help me solve my problems too. As the disciples investigated, they realized that Jesus was always there helping them—just like he's always there helping me!

Julie

Jesus is always ready to "walk"
with you and help you.

SEEING IS BELIEVING

Introduction

Ever doubted something you heard about Jesus? Thomas doubted that Jesus was alive. But Jesus had big news for him. He was alive—and he could prove it without a doubt!

John 20:24-31, NLT

One of the disciples, Thomas (nicknamed the Twin), was not with the others when Jesus came. They told him, "We have seen the Lord!" But he replied, "I won't believe it unless I see the nail wounds in his hands, put my fingers into them, and place my hand into the wound in his side."

Eight days later the disciples were together again, and this time Thomas was with them. The doors were locked; but suddenly, as before, Jesus was standing among them. He said, "Peace be with you." Then he said to Thomas, "Put your finger here and see my hands. Put your hand into the wound in my side. Don't be faithless any longer. Believe!"

"My Lord and my God!" Thomas exclaimed.

Then Jesus told him, "You believe because you have seen me. Blessed are those who haven't seen me and believe anyway."

Purpose of the Book

Jesus' disciples saw him do many other miraculous signs besides the ones recorded in this book. But these are written so that you may believe that Jesus is the Messiah, the Son of God, and that by believing in him you will have life.

Take ANOTHER Look

Peter later wrote a letter describing what faith in Jesus is like. The Christians that he wrote to never saw Jesus. Yet they believed in him. As you read this passage from 1 Peter, consider whether you, like the first-century Christians, "love him even though you have never seen him."

1 Peter 1:8-12, NLT

You love him even though you have never seen him. Though you do not see him, you trust him; and even now you are happy with a glorious, inexpressible joy. Your reward for trusting him will be the salvation of your souls.

This salvation was something the prophets wanted to know more about. They prophesied about this gracious salvation prepared for you, even though they had many questions as to what it all could mean. They wondered what the Spirit of Christ within them was talking about when he told them in advance about Christ's suffering and his great glory afterward. They wondered when and to whom all this would happen.

They were told that these things would not happen during their lifetime, but many years later, during yours. And now this Good News has been announced by those who preached to you in the power of the Holy Spirit sent from heaven. It is all so wonderful that even the angels are eagerly watching these things happen.

Here's What I Think

Verity, age 14

Don't you ever wish you could physically see God? I do. Sometimes I feel like I just need some real face-to-face reassurance to know for sure that God is with me. Thomas felt like that too. But we know that God wants always to be with us. Though we cannot see him, he is always there. If ever we feel doubtful, we can pick up the Bible and read it as a source of reassurance that God is with us. He may not be face-to-face with you, but even though you cannot see him, God is always there.

Verity

God is with you! Believe it!

BREAKFAST WITH THE SAVIOR

Introduction

Now that Jesus was alive, the disciples still weren't sure what to do with themselves. After all, they had followed Jesus everywhere for three years. Now they weren't sure when they would see him next, if at all. There was only one thing they could do—go back to their old predictable jobs. But with a risen Savior around, life was anything but boring or predictable.

John 21:1-14, NLT

Later Jesus appeared again to the disciples beside the Sea of Galilee. This is how it happened. Several of the disciples were there—Simon Peter, Thomas (nicknamed the Twin), Nathanael from Cana in Galilee, the sons of Zebedee, and two other disciples.

Simon Peter said, "I'm going fishing."

"We'll come, too," they all said. So they went out in the boat, but they caught nothing all night.

At dawn the disciples saw Jesus standing on the beach, but they couldn't see who he was. He called out, "Friends, have you caught any fish?"

"No," they replied.

Then he said, "Throw out your net on the right-hand side of the boat, and you'll get plenty of fish!" So they did, and they couldn't draw in the net because there were so many fish in it.

Then the disciple whom Jesus loved said to Peter, "It is the Lord!" When Simon Peter heard that it was the Lord, he put on his tunic (for he had stripped for work), jumped into the water, and swam ashore. The others stayed with the boat and pulled the loaded net to the shore, for they were only out about three hundred feet. When they got there, they saw that a charcoal fire was burning and fish were frying over it, and there was bread.

"Bring some of the fish you've just caught," Jesus said. So Simon Peter went aboard and dragged the net to the shore. There were 153 large fish, and yet the net hadn't torn.

"Now come and have some breakfast!" Jesus said. And no one dared ask him if he really was the Lord because they were sure of it. Then Jesus served them the bread and the fish. This was the third time Jesus had appeared to his disciples since he had been raised from the dead.

TAKE ANOTHER LOOK

Remember when Peter denied Jesus three times? (Check back on page 324.) Well, Jesus gave Peter a chance to make up for that. The next story took place right after the story you just read.

John 21:15-19, NLT

After breakfast Jesus said to Simon Peter, "Simon son of John, do you love me more than these?"

"Yes, Lord," Peter replied, "you know I love you."

"Then feed my lambs," Jesus told him.

Jesus repeated the question: "Simon son of John, do you love me?"

"Yes, Lord," Peter said, "you know I love you."

"Then take care of my sheep," Jesus said.

Once more he asked him, "Simon son of John, do you love me?"

Peter was grieved that Jesus asked the question a third time. He said, "Lord, you know everything. You know I love you."

Jesus said, "Then feed my sheep." The truth is, when you were young, you were able to do as you liked and go wherever you wanted to. But when you are old, you will stretch out your hands, and others will direct you and take you where you don't want to go." Jesus said this to let him know what kind of death he would die to glorify God. Then Jesus told him, "Follow me."

Here's What I Think

Jammeshia, age 17

I love you, Lord, but I can't sit with that girl at lunch. I love you, Lord, but I can't give up my bad habits. So many times in my life I find myself saying those words, but I deny God when I don't give in totally. I realized I was just like Peter. He claimed he truly loved Jesus, but denied him three times.

Just like Peter, I truly love Jesus but sometimes my sinful ways cause me to reject him. In this story, we see how Jesus continues to confront Peter and question him about his intentions. Like it did with Peter, it took a lot of confrontations with Jesus before I realized that I need to live totally for him. What will it take for you to realize that Jesus wants all of you?

Jammeshia

Give Jesus your all.

>>>>> # THE
ASSIGNMENT <<<

Introduction

Imagine how you would feel if your best friend suddenly moved away. As you watch the moving truck pull away, you might feel horribly sad and lonely. Now, if you can imagine that, you know how the disciples might have felt. Their best friend, Jesus, was about to move away. He wasn't just moving to a new town or a new state. He was moving off the planet! They would never see him again . . . at least not in this life. But as bad as that news seemed, there was also some good news from an unexpected source.

Acts 1:3-12, NLT

During the forty days after his crucifixion, he appeared to the apostles from time to time and proved to them in many ways that he was actually alive. On these occasions he talked to them about the Kingdom of God.

In one of these meetings as he was eating a meal with them, he told them, "Do not leave Jerusalem until the Father sends you what he promised. Remember, I have told you about this before. John baptized with water, but in just a few days you will be baptized with the Holy Spirit."

The Ascension of Jesus

When the apostles were with Jesus, they kept asking him, "Lord, are you going to free Israel now and restore our kingdom?"

"The Father sets those dates," he replied, "and they are not for you to know. But when the Holy Spirit has come upon you, you will receive power and will tell people about me everywhere—in Jerusalem, throughout Judea, in Samaria, and to the ends of the earth."

It was not long after he said this that he was taken up into the sky while they were watching, and he disappeared into a cloud. As they were straining their eyes to see him, two white-robed men suddenly stood there among them. They said, "Men of Galilee, why are you standing here staring at the sky? Jesus has been taken away from you into heaven. And someday, just as you saw him go, he will return!"

The apostles were at the Mount of Olives when this happened, so they walked the half mile back to Jerusalem.

Take ANOTHER Look

At the Last Supper, Jesus talked about the coming of the Holy Spirit. Jesus knew how sad his followers would be when he returned to heaven. That's why he would send the Holy Spirit to take his place. And what was even cooler about the Holy Spirit is that he could be everywhere at once! The following passage from the book of John is Jesus' promise to send the Holy Spirit.

John 14:25-29, NLT

"I am telling you these things now while I am still with you. But when the Father sends the Counselor as my representative—and by the Counselor I mean the Holy Spirit—he will teach you everything and will remind you of everything I myself have told you.

"I am leaving you with a gift—peace of mind and heart. And the peace I give isn't like the peace the world gives. So don't be troubled or afraid. Remember what I told you: I am going away, but I will come back to you again. If you really love me, you will be very happy for me, because now I can go to the Father, who is greater than I am. I have told you these things before they happen so that you will believe when they do happen."

Here's What I Think

Daniel, age 15

I think I have mentioned before that I love to fish. The last time I was out I tried to cast to a specific spot. Soon after I had casted out, I realized I had totally missed the mark and got my fishing line hung up on the bank. You see, I had stopped watching where the lure should go and started thinking what lure I should use next.

Similarly, I think we get hung up by wondering what God is going to do next. We miss the mark when we do that. We should keep our eyes on Jesus and where *he* wants us to aim for right now. As with fishing, I can recast and try to do what God wants me to do. It may take a few bad casts to get there, but that's OK. God is patient; he'll give us another go.

Daniel

Keep your eyes on Jesus so you'll hit the mark.

THE BIRTH
OF A CHURCH

Introduction

The Holy Spirit's arrival happened exactly the way Jesus said it would. And with the coming of the Holy Spirit, a new group of people—the church—had begun. Nearly 3,000 people became believers that first day after hearing Peter's powerful testimony to the risen and living Savior, Jesus Christ.

Acts 2:1-24, 36-42, NLT

On the day of Pentecost, seven weeks after Jesus' resurrection, the believers were meeting together in one place. Suddenly, there was a sound from heaven like the roaring of a mighty windstorm in the skies above them, and it filled the house where they were meeting. Then, what looked like flames or tongues of fire appeared and settled on each of them. And everyone present was filled with the Holy Spirit and began speaking in other languages, as the Holy Spirit gave them this ability.

Godly Jews from many nations were living in Jerusalem at that time. When they heard this sound, they came running to see what it was all about, and they were bewildered to hear their own languages being spoken by the believers.

They were beside themselves with wonder. "How can this be?" they exclaimed. "These people are all from Galilee, and yet we hear them speaking the languages of the lands where we were born! Here we are—Parthians, Medes, Elamites, people from Mesopotamia, Judea, Cappadocia, Pontus, the province of Asia, Phrygia, Pamphylia, Egypt, and the areas of Libya toward Cyrene, visitors from Rome (both Jews and converts to Judaism), Cretans, and Arabians. And we all hear these people speaking in our own languages about the wonderful things God has done!" They stood there amazed and perplexed. "What can this mean?" they asked each other.

But others in the crowd were mocking. "They're drunk, that's all!" they said.

Peter Preaches to a Crowd

Then Peter stepped forward with the eleven other apostles and shouted to the crowd, "Listen carefully, all of you, fellow Jews and residents of Jerusalem! Make no mistake about this. Some of you are saying these people are drunk. It isn't true! It's much too early for that. People don't get drunk by nine o'clock in the morning. No, what you see this morning was predicted centuries ago by the prophet Joel:

'In the last days, God said,
    I will pour out my Spirit upon all people.
    Your sons and daughters will prophesy,
    your young men will see visions,
    and your old men will dream dreams.
In those days I will pour out my Spirit
    upon all my servants, men and women alike,
    and they will prophesy.
And I will cause wonders in the heavens above
    and signs on the earth below—
    blood and fire and clouds of smoke.
The sun will be turned into darkness,
    and the moon will turn bloodred,
    before that great and glorious day of the Lord arrives.
And anyone who calls on the name of the Lord
    will be saved.'

"People of Israel, listen! God publicly endorsed Jesus of Nazareth by doing wonderful miracles, wonders, and signs through him, as you well know. But you followed God's prearranged plan. With the help of lawless Gentiles, you nailed him to the cross and murdered him. However, God released him from the horrors of death and raised him back to life again, for death could not keep him in its grip."

2:36-42

"So let it be clearly known by everyone in Israel that God has made this Jesus whom you crucified to be both Lord and Messiah!"

Peter's words convicted them deeply, and they said to him and to the other apostles, "Brothers, what should we do?"

Peter replied, "Each of you must turn from your sins and turn to God, and be baptized in the name of Jesus Christ for the forgiveness of your sins. Then you will receive the gift of the Holy Spirit. This promise is to you and to your children, and even to the Gentiles—all who have been called by the Lord our God." Then Peter continued preaching for a long time, strongly urging all his listeners, "Save yourselves from this generation that has gone astray!"

Those who believed what Peter said were baptized and added to the church—about three thousand in all. They joined with the other believers and devoted themselves to the apostles' teaching and fellowship, sharing in the Lord's Supper and in prayer.

The apostle Paul included a description of the church in his first letter to the Corinthians. He called the church "the body of Christ." It was made up of different "parts" like a body. The Holy Spirit holds this body together.

1 Corinthians 12:12-20, NLT

The human body has many parts, but the many parts make up only one body. So it is with the body of Christ. Some of us are Jews, some are Gentiles, some are slaves, and some are free. But we have all been baptized into Christ's body by one Spirit, and we have all received the same Spirit.

Yes, the body has many different parts, not just one part. If the foot says, "I am not a part of the body because I am not a hand," that does not make it any less a part of the body. And if the ear says, "I am not part of the body because I am only an ear and not an eye," would that make it any less a part of the body? Suppose the whole body were an eye—then how would you hear? Or if your whole body were just one big ear, how could you smell anything?

But God made our bodies with many parts, and he has put each part just where he wants it. What a strange thing a body would be if it had only one part! Yes, there are many parts, but only one body.

Here's What I Think

Janna, age 14

God put the Holy Spirit into the believers, and they started talking about God and praising him in other languages! At first, many people thought they were drunk! But God used Peter to prove them wrong. Peter preached to the people and told them of Christ's love. About 3,000 people were saved that day!

God can use an unlikely circumstance and turn it into something awesome. About five years ago, my brother's friend died. She was such a cool girl, and nobody could understand why God would let her die. But as a result of her death, some people came to believe in Jesus. It wasn't a mass of people, but even that small number was important to God. Trust God. He can use anything—and anyone—for his glory.

Janna

God is at work in all you do.

»» SAUL SEES THE LIGHT ««

Ôntroduction

If you recall from the previous stories, the high priests and other leaders didn't exactly like Jesus. They wanted his disappearance from the tomb covered up. And they certainly didn't approve of the apostles' messages about Jesus. So they sent their number-one agent, Saul, to hunt down all followers of Jesus. But instead of finding believers, Saul found more than he bargained for—a whole new identity.

Acts 9:1-25, NLT

Meanwhile, Saul was uttering threats with every breath. He was eager to destroy the Lord's followers, so he went to the high priest. He requested letters addressed to the synagogues in Damascus, asking their cooperation in the arrest of any followers of the Way he found there. He wanted to bring them—both men and women—back to Jerusalem in chains.

As he was nearing Damascus on this mission, a brilliant light from heaven suddenly beamed down upon him! He fell to the ground and heard a voice saying to him, "Saul! Saul! Why are you persecuting me?"

"Who are you, sir?" Saul asked.

And the voice replied, "I am Jesus, the one you are persecuting! Now get up and go into the city, and you will be told what you are to do."

The men with Saul stood speechless with surprise, for they heard the sound of someone's voice, but they saw no one! As Saul picked himself up off the ground, he found that he was blind. So his companions led him by the hand to Damascus. He remained there blind for three days. And all that time he went without food and water.

Now there was a believer in Damascus named Ananias. The Lord spoke to him in a vision, calling, "Ananias!"

"Yes, Lord!" he replied.

The Lord said, "Go over to Straight Street, to the house of Judas. When you arrive, ask for Saul of Tarsus. He is praying to me right now. I have shown him a vision of a man named Ananias coming in and laying his hands on him so that he can see again."

"But Lord," exclaimed Ananias, "I've heard about the terrible things this man has done to the believers in Jerusalem! And we hear that he is authorized by the leading priests to arrest every believer in Damascus."

But the Lord said, "Go and do what I say. For Saul is my chosen instrument to take my message to the Gentiles and to kings, as well as to the people of Israel. And I will show him how much he must suffer for me."

So Ananias went and found Saul. He laid his hands on him and said, "Brother Saul, the Lord Jesus, who appeared to you on the road, has sent me so that you may get your sight back and be filled with the Holy Spirit." Instantly something like scales fell from Saul's eyes, and he regained his sight. Then he got up and was baptized. Afterward he ate some food and was strengthened.

Saul in Damascus and Jerusalem

Saul stayed with the believers in Damascus for a few days. And immediately he began preaching about Jesus in the synagogues, saying, "He is indeed the Son of God!"

All who heard him were amazed. "Isn't this the same man who persecuted Jesus' followers with such devastation in Jerusalem?" they asked. "And we understand that he came here to arrest them and take them in chains to the leading priests."

Saul's preaching became more and more powerful, and the Jews in Damascus couldn't refute his proofs that Jesus was indeed the Messiah. After a while the Jewish leaders decided to kill him. But Saul was told about their plot, and that they were watching for him day and night at the city gate so they could murder him. So during the night, some of the other believers let him down in a large basket through an opening in the city wall.

Take ANOTHER LOOK

Saul, who became known as Paul, later regretted what he had done before he became a believer. While he was a member of the Jewish council, Paul believed that he was right to treat Christians harshly. But Jesus changed his attitude and his life. Paul talked about this in a letter he wrote to the Philippian church.

Philippians 3:5-11, NLT

For I was circumcised when I was eight days old, having been born into a pure-blooded Jewish family that is a branch of the tribe of Benjamin. So I am a real Jew if there ever was one! What's more, I was a member of the Pharisees, who demand the strictest obedience to the Jewish law. And zealous? Yes, in fact, I harshly persecuted the church. And I obeyed the Jewish law so carefully that I was never accused of any fault.

I once thought all these things were so very important, but now I consider them worthless because of what Christ has done. Yes, everything else is worthless when compared with the priceless gain of knowing Christ Jesus my Lord. I have discarded everything else, counting it all as garbage, so that I may have Christ and become one with him. I no longer count on my own goodness or my ability to obey God's law, but I trust Christ to save me. For God's way of making us right with himself depends on faith. As a result, I can really know Christ and experience the mighty power that raised him from the dead. I can learn what it means to suffer with him, sharing in his death, so that, somehow, I can experience the resurrection from the dead!

Here's What I Think

Kali, age 18

The story of Saul/Paul and his conversion always amazes me. It reminds me that nothing is impossible with God. God changed the life of one of the early church's greatest enemies to one of the most influential apostles in the Bible. Saul had persecuted Christians everywhere. He was feared above all people. Then Jesus appeared to him, and within days, Saul/Paul was preaching about Jesus in the synagogues. What an amazing transformation! I have friends whom I pray for continually to find Christ, but they refuse to have anything to do with Jesus. Reading this story gives me hope that God can change the most stubborn and difficult people to further his kingdom. It gives me the strength to press on. As Luke 1:37 says, "For nothing is impossible with God."

Kali

With God, anything is possible!

))))) ALL IN THE FAMILY (((((

Introduction

For centuries, the people of Israel were taught that Jews and non-Jewish people, called Gentiles, didn't mix. That was the law Peter lived by and obeyed. He even considered Gentiles to be unclean. For most of his life, Peter would never have dreamed of entering the home of a Gentile. But all that was about to change.

Acts 10:1-33, NLT

In Caesarea there lived a Roman army officer named Cornelius, who was a captain of the Italian Regiment. He was a devout man who feared the God of Israel, as did his entire household. He gave generously to charity and was a man who regularly prayed to God. One afternoon about three o'clock, he had a vision in which he saw an angel of God coming toward him. "Cornelius!" the angel said.

Cornelius stared at him in terror. "What is it, sir?" he asked the angel.

And the angel replied, "Your prayers and gifts to the poor have not gone unnoticed by God! Now send some men down to Joppa to find a man named Simon Peter. He is staying with Simon, a leatherworker who lives near the shore. Ask him to come and visit you."

As soon as the angel was gone, Cornelius called two of his household servants and a devout soldier, one of his personal attendants. He told them what had happened and sent them off to Joppa.

Peter Visits Cornelius

The next day as Cornelius's messengers were nearing the city, Peter went up to the flat roof to pray. It was about noon, and he was hungry. But while lunch was being prepared, he fell into a trance. He saw the sky open, and something like a large sheet was let down by its four corners. In the sheet were all sorts of animals, reptiles, and birds. Then a voice said to him, "Get up, Peter; kill and eat them."

"Never, Lord," Peter declared. "I have never in all my life eaten anything forbidden by our Jewish laws."

The voice spoke again, "If God says something is acceptable, don't say it isn't." The same vision was repeated three times. Then the sheet was pulled up again to heaven.

Peter was very perplexed. What could the vision mean? Just then the men sent by Cornelius found the house and stood outside at the gate. They asked if this was the place where Simon Peter was staying. Meanwhile, as Peter was puzzling over the vision, the Holy Spirit said to him, "Three men have come looking for you. Go down and go with them without hesitation. All is well, for I have sent them."

So Peter went down and said, "I'm the man you are looking for. Why have you come?"

They said, "We were sent by Cornelius, a Roman officer. He is a devout man who fears the God of Israel and is well respected by all the Jews. A holy angel instructed him to send for you so you can go to his house and give him a message." So Peter invited the men to be his guests for the night. The next day he went with them, accompanied by some other believers from Joppa.

They arrived in Caesarea the following day. Cornelius was waiting for him and had called together his relatives and close friends to meet Peter. As Peter entered his home, Cornelius fell to the floor before him in worship. But Peter pulled him up and said, "Stand up! I'm a human being like you!" So Cornelius got up, and they talked together and went inside where the others were assembled.

Peter told them, "You know it is against the Jewish laws for me to come into a Gentile home like this. But God has shown me that I should never think of anyone as impure. So I came as soon as I was sent for. Now tell me why you sent for me."

Cornelius replied, "Four days ago I was praying in my house at three o'clock in the afternoon. Suddenly, a man in dazzling clothes was standing in front of me. He told me, 'Cornelius, your prayers have been heard, and your gifts to the poor have been noticed by God! Now send some men to Joppa and summon Simon Peter. He is staying in the home of Simon, a leatherworker who lives near the shore.' So I sent for you at once, and it was good of you to come. Now here we are, waiting before God to hear the message the Lord has given you."

Take ANOTHER LOOK

After hearing Cornelius' story, Peter at once realized that God did not show partiality to any people. The Gospel was meant for all people to hear. So he proceeded to tell Cornelius and his household the Good News of Jesus Christ. Read below to what Peter said and how Cornelius and his family responded.

Acts 10:44-48, NLT

Even as Peter was saying these things, the Holy Spirit fell upon all who had heard the message. The Jewish believers who came with Peter were amazed that the gift of the Holy Spirit had been poured out upon the Gentiles, too. And there could be no doubt about it, for they heard them speaking in tongues and praising God.

Then Peter asked, "Can anyone object to their being baptized, now that they have received the Holy Spirit just as we did?" So he gave orders for them to be baptized in the name of Jesus Christ. Afterward Cornelius asked him to stay with them for several days.

Here's What I Think

Mike, age 19

Many times we get caught up in the events of our lives and forget that at any moment we might be called to share the gospel with someone. There have been times when I wasn't thinking about God and I let opportunities pass when I could have told someone about Jesus.

In this story, God asks Peter to share the gospel with some Gentiles. Up to that point, Jews did not associate with Gentiles. But Peter didn't worry about that. He trusted that God had a plan for taking him to see Cornelius. We also must be ready and willing to share God's good news to an unlikely audience—whenever and wherever.

Michel

Always be ready to share your faith with whomever—whenever and wherever.

THE GREAT ESCAPE

Introduction

These were dangerous times for Christians. Many were killed or imprisoned simply because they believed in Jesus. Such was the case for Peter, about 10 years after Jesus returned to heaven. His friend James had already been killed for his faith. Would Peter be next?

Acts 12:1-17, NLT

About that time King Herod Agrippa began to persecute some believers in the church. He had the apostle James (John's brother) killed with a sword. When Herod saw how much this pleased the Jewish leaders, he arrested Peter during the Passover celebration and imprisoned him, placing him under the guard of four squads of four soldiers each. Herod's intention was to bring Peter out for public trial after the Passover. But while Peter was in prison, the church prayed very earnestly for him.

Peter's Miraculous Escape from Prison

The night before Peter was to be placed on trial, he was asleep, chained between two soldiers, with others standing guard at the prison gate. Suddenly, there was a bright light in the cell, and an angel of the Lord stood before Peter. The angel tapped him on the side to awaken him and said, "Quick! Get up!" And the chains fell off his wrists. Then the angel told him, "Get dressed and put on your sandals." And he did. "Now put on your coat and follow me," the angel ordered.

So Peter left the cell, following the angel. But all the time he thought it was a vision. He didn't realize it was really happening. They passed the first and second guard posts and came to the iron gate to the street, and this opened to them all by itself. So they passed through and started walking down the street, and then the angel suddenly left him.

Peter finally realized what had happened. "It's really true!" he said to himself.

"The Lord has sent his angel and saved me from Herod and from what the Jews were hoping to do to me!"

After a little thought, he went to the home of Mary, the mother of John Mark, where many were gathered for prayer. He knocked at the door in the gate, and a servant girl named Rhoda came to open it. When she recognized Peter's voice, she was so overjoyed that, instead of opening the door, she ran back inside and told everyone, "Peter is standing at the door!"

"You're out of your mind," they said. When she insisted, they decided, "It must be his angel."

Meanwhile, Peter continued knocking. When they finally went out and opened the door, they were amazed. He motioned for them to quiet down and told them what had happened and how the Lord had led him out of jail. "Tell James and the other brothers what happened," he said. And then he went to another place.

Take ANOTHER LOOK

The writer of Hebrews describes what life was like for the believers in the first century. Horrible things happened to them because of their faith in Jesus. Some weren't rescued from prison like Peter was. Yet they're in the "Hebrews Hall of Faith" because of their faithful examples.

Hebrews 11:35-40, NLT

But others trusted God and were tortured, preferring to die rather than turn from God and be free. They placed their hope in the resurrection to a better life. Some were mocked, and their backs were cut open with whips. Others were chained in dungeons. Some died by stoning, and some were sawed in half; others were killed with the sword. Some went about in skins of sheep and goats, hungry and oppressed and mistreated. They were too good for this world. They wandered over deserts and mountains, hiding in caves and holes in the ground.

All of these people we have mentioned received God's approval because of their faith, yet none of them received all that God had promised. For God had far better things in mind for us that would also benefit them, for they can't receive the prize at the end of the race until we finish the race.

Here's What I Think

Nicee, age 14

On Wednesday, July 23, 2003, my youth church was scheduled to go to Florida. That same day my grandfather went into the hospital after suffering a massive heart attack with other serious problems. When I went to the hospital to see him, he was lying on the bed in a light sleep.

I sat down beside him and began to cry and pray until it was time to go to church and board the bus. When I arrived at the church, my pastor and friends began to pray for him and encourage me. We continued to pray for my grandfather while in Florida. By Sunday I got the call that he was home from the hospital and was feeling better than before.

My grandfather is living proof that there is power in praying for others in need. God is awesome! Just as he heard the prayers of the church for Peter, he heard all the prayers for my grandfather and healed him.

Nicee

Never doubt the power of prayer.

»» WHO'S GOT THE POWER? ««

Introduction

What comes to mind when you think of a missionary's life? Someone who travels around a lot? Someone who stays in the same place (a foreign land) all the time preaching to the same people? Paul and Barnabas were sent as missionaries to take the gospel of Jesus everywhere. They traveled with a young man who would someday write the Gospel of Mark. Unfortunately, they quickly ran into trouble.

Acts 13:4-12, NLT

Sent out by the Holy Spirit, Saul and Barnabas went down to the seaport of Seleucia and then sailed for the island of Cyprus. There, in the town of Salamis, they went to the Jewish synagogues and preached the word of God. (John Mark went with them as their assistant.)

Afterward they preached from town to town across the entire island until finally they reached Paphos, where they met a Jewish sorcerer, a false prophet named Bar-Jesus. He had attached himself to the governor, Sergius Paulus, a man of considerable insight and understanding. The governor invited Barnabas and Saul to visit him, for he wanted to hear the word of God. But Elymas, the sorcerer (as his name means in Greek), interfered and urged the governor to pay no attention to what Saul and Barnabas said. He was trying to turn the governor away from the Christian faith.

Then Saul, also known as Paul, filled with the Holy Spirit, looked the sorcerer in the eye and said, "You son of the Devil, full of every sort of trickery and villainy, enemy of all that is good, will you never stop perverting the true ways of the Lord? And now the Lord has laid his hand of punishment upon you, and you will be stricken awhile with blindness." Instantly mist and darkness fell upon him, and he began wandering around begging for someone to take his hand and lead him. When the governor saw what had happened, he believed and was astonished at what he learned about the Lord.

Take ANOTHER LOOK

If you think what God did through Barnabas and Paul was exciting, check out this story from chapter 14 of the book of Acts. Paul and Barnabas had been sent to tell people about Jesus and to remind them to worship the true God. But some people in the city of Lystra wanted to worship Paul and Barnabas!

Acts 14:8-18, NLT

While they were at Lystra, Paul and Barnabas came upon a man with crippled feet. He had been that way from birth, so he had never walked. He was listening as Paul preached, and Paul noticed him and realized he had faith to be healed. So Paul called to him in a loud voice, "Stand up!" And the man jumped to his feet and started walking.

When the listening crowd saw what Paul had done, they shouted in their local dialect, "These men are gods in human bodies!" They decided that Barnabas was the Greek god Zeus and that Paul, because he was the chief speaker, was Hermes. The temple of Zeus was located on the outskirts of the city. The priest of the temple and the crowd brought oxen and wreaths of flowers, and they prepared to sacrifice to the apostles at the city gates.

But when Barnabas and Paul heard what was happening, they tore their clothing in dismay and ran out among the people, shouting, "Friends, why are you doing this? We are merely human beings like yourselves! We have come to bring you the Good News that you should turn from these worthless things to the living God, who made heaven and earth, the sea, and everything in them. In earlier days he permitted all the nations to go their own ways, but he never left himself without a witness. There were always his reminders, such as sending you rain and good crops and giving you food and joyful hearts." But even so, Paul and Barnabas could scarcely restrain the people from sacrificing to them.

Here's What I Think

Walter, age 13

This passage reminds me of the fact that there is a very big spiritual battle going on—God vs. Satan. God wants us to spend time in his Word, to focus on him, and to talk to him. On the other hand, Satan works hard to stop us from doing those things. All Satan wants to do is blind and deceive us from God's truth.

Now if I had to guess, I would say that Satan probably isn't going to send a wizard into your life. But Satan will make sure to tempt you with all the things you could be doing instead of spending time with God—like goofing off with your friends, or watching TV, or playing basketball. Every time we make the effort to deepen our relationship with God, we frustrate Satan's battle plans a little more . . . and that's always a good thing!

Walter

Be alert to Satan's attempts to distract you from God's truth.

AN EARTHSHAKING
EXPERIENCE

Introduction

How do you react when you are treated unfairly? Sometimes missionaries were treated unfairly. Paul and his traveling partner, Silas, learned that firsthand. When they tried to do good, they found themselves in trouble. But their reaction when in trouble changed one man's life.

Acts 16:16-34, NLT

One day as we were going down to the place of prayer, we met a demon-possessed slave girl. She was a fortune-teller who earned a lot of money for her masters. She followed along behind us shouting, "These men are servants of the Most High God, and they have come to tell you how to be saved."

This went on day after day until Paul got so exasperated that he turned and spoke to the demon within her. "I command you in the name of Jesus Christ to come out of her," he said. And instantly it left her.

Her masters' hopes of wealth were now shattered, so they grabbed Paul and Silas and dragged them before the authorities at the marketplace. "The whole city is in an uproar because of these Jews!" they shouted. "They are teaching the people to do things that are against Roman customs."

A mob quickly formed against Paul and Silas, and the city officials ordered them stripped and beaten with wooden rods. They were severely beaten, and then they were thrown into prison. The jailer was ordered to make sure they didn't escape. So he took no chances but put them into the inner dungeon and clamped their feet in the stocks.

Around midnight, Paul and Silas were praying and singing hymns to God, and the other prisoners were listening. Suddenly, there was a great earthquake, and the prison was shaken to its foundations. All the doors flew open, and the chains of every prisoner fell off! The jailer woke up to see the prison doors wide open. He assumed the prisoners had escaped, so he drew his sword to kill himself. But Paul shouted to him, "Don't do it! We are all here!"

Trembling with fear, the jailer called for lights and ran to the dungeon and fell down before Paul and Silas. He brought them out and asked, "Sirs, what must I do to be saved?"

They replied, "Believe on the Lord Jesus and you will be saved, along with your entire household." Then they shared the word of the Lord with him and all who lived in his household. That same hour the jailer washed their wounds, and he and everyone in his household were immediately baptized. Then he brought them into his house and set a meal before them. He and his entire household rejoiced because they all believed in God.

Take ANOTHER LOOK

While in Philippi, Paul and Silas told the good news of Jesus to another person—someone who welcomed them into her home. As missionaries, they depended on the kindness of strangers. This passage from Acts tells you all about that meeting.

Acts 16:11-15, NLT

We boarded a boat at Troas and sailed straight across to the island of Samothrace, and the next day we landed at Neapolis. From there we reached Philippi, a major city of the district of Macedonia and a Roman colony; we stayed there several days.

On the Sabbath we went a little way outside the city to a riverbank, where we supposed that some people met for prayer, and we sat down to speak with some women who had come together. One of them was Lydia from Thyatira, a merchant of expensive purple cloth. She was a worshiper of God. As she listened to us, the Lord opened her heart, and she accepted what Paul was saying. She was baptized along with other members of her household, and she asked us to be her guests. "If you agree that I am faithful to the Lord," she said, "come and stay at my home." And she urged us until we did.

Here's What I Think

Daniel, age 15

This passage is a great lesson about respecting the authority that God has placed over each one of us—whether it's parents, teachers, or anyone. Consider Paul and Silas's situation. To begin with, Paul and Silas did a good thing in casting out a demon from that oppressed woman. As a reward for their good deed, they were brutally beaten.

They went to jail, and even with an easy escape, Paul and Silas remained obedient and didn't leave. Then, the officials tried to get Paul and Silas to leave town in secret, cheating them out of the formal apology they deserved by being Roman citizens. In all of this, Paul and Silas acted with respect. They even left town respectfully and without incident. God wants us to respect those he has put in authority to be over us. We all have problems following authority from time to time, but God calls us not only to obey, but also to respect those in charge. The story of Paul and Silas is certainly one to learn from.

Daniel

Respect and obey those who are in charge.

A PLOT
PREVENTED

Introduction

Paul had many enemies, simply because he was a Christian. Some of his bitterest enemies were his own people! Many of the Jewish leaders couldn't decide what to do with Paul. But there was one group who had decided to get rid of Paul once and for all.

Acts 23:12-24, NLT

The next morning a group of Jews got together and bound themselves with an oath to neither eat nor drink until they had killed Paul. There were more than forty of them. They went to the leading priests and other leaders and told them what they had done. "We have bound ourselves under oath to neither eat nor drink until we have killed Paul. You and the high council should tell the commander to bring Paul back to the council again," they requested. "Pretend you want to examine his case more fully. We will kill him on the way."

But Paul's nephew heard of their plan and went to the fortress and told Paul. Paul called one of the officers and said, "Take this young man to the commander. He has something important to tell him."

So the officer did, explaining, "Paul, the prisoner, called me over and asked me to bring this young man to you because he has something to tell you."

The commander took him by the arm, led him aside, and asked, "What is it you want to tell me?"

Paul's nephew told him, "Some Jews are going to ask you to bring Paul before the Jewish high council tomorrow, pretending they want to get some more information. But don't do it! There are more than forty men hiding along the way ready to jump him and kill him. They have vowed not to eat or drink until they kill him. They are ready, expecting you to agree to their request."

"Don't let a soul know you told me this," the commander warned the young man as he sent him away.

Paul Is Sent to Caesarea

Then the commander called two of his officers and ordered, "Get two hundred soldiers ready to leave for Caesarea at nine o'clock tonight. Also take two hundred spearmen and seventy horsemen. Provide horses for Paul to ride, and get him safely to Governor Felix."

Then he wrote this letter to the governor:

"From Claudius Lysias, to his Excellency, Governor Felix. Greetings! This man was seized by some Jews, and they were about to kill him when I arrived with the troops. When I learned that he was a Roman citizen, I removed him to safety. Then I took him to their high council to try to find out what he had done. I soon discovered it was something regarding their religious law—certainly nothing worthy of imprisonment or death. But when I was informed of a plot to kill him, I immediately sent him on to you. I have told his accusers to bring their charges before you."

So that night, as ordered, the soldiers took Paul as far as Antipatris. They returned to the fortress the next morning, while the horsemen took him on to Caesarea. When they arrived in Caesarea, they presented Paul and the letter to Governor Felix. He read it and then asked Paul what province he was from. "Cilicia," Paul answered.

"I will hear your case myself when your accusers arrive," the governor told him. Then the governor ordered him kept in the prison at Herod's headquarters.

Take Another Look

Paul wasn't afraid to die. He knew where he would wind up after death—with Jesus in heaven. In the letter to the Philippians, Paul talked about his trust in Jesus.

Philippians 1:20-26, NLT

For I live in eager expectation and hope that I will never do anything that causes me shame, but that I will always be bold for Christ, as I have been in the past, and that my life will always honor Christ, whether I live or I die. For to me, living is for Christ, and dying is even better. Yet if I live, that means fruitful service for Christ. I really don't know which is better. I'm torn between two desires: Sometimes I want to live, and sometimes I long to go and be with Christ. That would be far better for me, but it is better for you that I live.

I am convinced of this, so I will continue with you so that you will grow and experience the joy of your faith. Then when I return to you, you will have even more reason to boast about what Christ Jesus has done for me.

Here's What I Think

Julie, age 18

Someone else will help. That's what I thought when I saw my classmate drop all his books in the middle of the busy middle-school hallway. I dropped my gaze and hurried by, rushing off to get settled in class. The late bell sounded.

Just as class was starting, the boy who had dropped his books in the hallway hurried in late, eyes filled with tears and obviously upset. *Oh, no!* I thought. *No one stopped to help him.*

What would have happened if Paul's nephew had thought, *Someone else will help?* If he hadn't gone out of his comfort zone to take action and help Paul by talking with the Roman commander, his uncle might have been killed. Next time you see someone who needs help, don't think, *Someone else will do it.* Step up. Take action. God has big plans to use *you* to help!

Julie

Take action when you have the chance.

»»» SHIPWRECKED!

Introduction

Like Jesus, Paul had to face a number of court trials. He appeared before two Roman governors and Agrippa, the king who was appointed by Rome. Finally, Paul asked to talk to the emperor in Rome. As a citizen of Rome, he had that right. But would Paul survive the sea voyage to Rome?

Acts 27:7-44, NLT

We had several days of rough sailing, and after great difficulty we finally neared Cnidus. But the wind was against us, so we sailed down to the leeward side of Crete, past the cape of Salmone. We struggled along the coast with great difficulty and finally arrived at Fair Havens, near the city of Lasea. We had lost a lot of time. The weather was becoming dangerous for long voyages by then because it was so late in the fall, and Paul spoke to the ship's officers about it.

"Sirs," he said, "I believe there is trouble ahead if we go on—shipwreck, loss of cargo, injuries, and danger to our lives." But the officer in charge of the prisoners listened more to the ship's captain and the owner than to Paul. And since Fair Havens was an exposed harbor—a poor place to spend the winter—most of the crew wanted to go to Phoenix, farther up the coast of Crete, and spend the winter there. Phoenix was a good harbor with only a southwest and northwest exposure.

The Storm at Sea

When a light wind began blowing from the south, the sailors thought they could make it. So they pulled up anchor and sailed along close to shore. But the weather changed abruptly, and a wind of typhoon strength (a "northeaster," they called it) caught the ship and blew it out to sea. They couldn't turn the ship into the wind, so they gave up and let it run before the gale.

We sailed behind a small island named Cauda, where with great difficulty we hoisted aboard the lifeboat that was being towed behind us. Then we banded the ship with ropes to strengthen the hull. The sailors were afraid of being driven across to the sandbars of Syrtis off the African coast, so they lowered the sea anchor and were thus driven before the wind.

The next day, as gale-force winds continued to batter the ship, the crew began throwing the cargo overboard. The following day they even threw out the ship's equipment and anything else they could lay their hands on. The terrible storm raged unabated for many days, blotting out the sun and the stars, until at last all hope was gone.

No one had eaten for a long time. Finally, Paul called the crew together and said, "Men, you should have listened to me in the first place and not left Fair Havens. You would have avoided all this injury and loss. But take courage! None of you will lose your lives, even though the ship will go down. For last night an angel of the God to whom I belong and whom I serve stood beside me, and he said, 'Don't be afraid, Paul, for you will surely stand trial before Caesar! What's more, God in his goodness has granted safety to everyone sailing with you.' So take courage! For I believe God. It will be just as he said. But we will be ship-wrecked on an island."

The Shipwreck

About midnight on the fourteenth night of the storm, as we were being driven across the Sea of Adria, the sailors sensed land was near. They took soundings and found the water was only 120 feet deep. A little later they sounded again and found only 90 feet. At this rate they were afraid we would soon be driven against the rocks along the shore, so they threw out four anchors from the stern and prayed for daylight. Then the sailors tried to abandon the ship; they lowered the lifeboat as though they were going to put out anchors from the prow. But Paul said to the commanding officer and the soldiers, "You will all die unless the sailors stay aboard." So the soldiers cut the ropes and let the boat fall off.

As the darkness gave way to the early morning light, Paul begged everyone to eat. "You haven't touched food for two weeks," he said. "Please eat something now for your own good. For not a hair of your heads will perish." Then he took some bread, gave thanks to God before them all, and broke off a piece and ate it. Then everyone was encouraged, and all 276 of us began eating—for that is the number we had aboard. After eating, the crew lightened the ship further by throwing the cargo of wheat overboard.

When morning dawned, they didn't recognize the coastline, but they saw a bay with a beach and wondered if they could get between the rocks and get the ship safely to shore. So they cut off the anchors and left them in the sea. Then they lowered the rudders, raised the foresail, and headed toward shore. But the ship hit a shoal and ran aground. The bow of the ship stuck fast, while the stern was repeatedly smashed by the force of the waves and began to break apart.

The soldiers wanted to kill the prisoners to make sure they didn't swim ashore and escape. But the commanding officer wanted to spare Paul, so he didn't let them carry out their plan. Then he ordered all who could swim to jump overboard first and make for land, and he told the others to try for it on planks and debris from the broken ship. So everyone escaped safely ashore!

Take ANOTHER LOOK

Paul had been shipwrecked more than once. In fact, many things happened to Paul during his missionary journeys. He wrote about his adventures (and mishaps) in 2 Corinthians.

2 Corinthians 11:23-27, NLT

They say they serve Christ? I know I sound like a madman, but I have served him far more! I have worked harder, been put in jail more often, been whipped times without number, and faced death again and again. Five different times the Jews gave me thirty-nine lashes. Three times I was beaten with rods. Once I was stoned. Three times I was shipwrecked. Once I spent a whole night and a day adrift at sea. I have traveled many weary miles. I have faced danger from flooded rivers and from robbers. I have faced danger from my own people, the Jews, as well as from the Gentiles. I have faced danger in the cities, in the deserts, and on the stormy seas. And I have faced danger from men who claim to be Christians but are not. I have lived with weariness and pain and sleepless nights. Often I have been hungry and thirsty and have gone without food. Often I have shivered with cold, without enough clothing to keep me warm.

Here's What I Think

Verity, age 13

When life get rough, do you ever doubt what God has planned? When Paul and the sailors were in the storm, they went to great lengths to save themselves; yet, they still were not safe. In the midst of the storm, God sent an angel to Paul with a message that everyone would survive.

Paul and his shipmates still endured rough weather and a frightening shipwreck, but Paul firmly trusted God to keep the crew safe just as he promised. And of course, God kept his word. When we go through "storms" in our lives, we should remember how God guided and reassured Paul. God will do the same for us. All we need to do is trust that God is in the middle of any storm we will experience. Believe, as Paul did, that God will see you through.

Verity

Trust God to help you weather the storms.

A PRISONER IN ROME

Introduction

Finally Paul arrived in Rome, but he wasn't a free man. He was still under arrest. But that didn't stop him from doing the job he came to do—spreading the good news of Jesus. Being guarded by soldiers 24/7 gave him a captive audience.

Acts 28:11-24, NLT

It was three months after the shipwreck that we set sail on another ship that had wintered at the island—an Alexandrian ship with the twin gods as its figurehead. Our first stop was Syracuse, where we stayed three days. From there we sailed across to Rhegium. A day later a south wind began blowing, so the following day we sailed up the coast to Puteoli. There we found some believers, who invited us to stay with them seven days. And so we came to Rome.

The brothers and sisters in Rome had heard we were coming, and they came to meet us at the Forum on the Appian Way. Others joined us at The Three Taverns. When Paul saw them, he thanked God and took courage.

When we arrived in Rome, Paul was permitted to have his own private lodging, though he was guarded by a soldier.

Paul Preaches at Rome Under Guard

Three days after Paul's arrival, he called together the local Jewish leaders. He said to them, "Brothers, I was arrested in Jerusalem and handed over to the Roman government, even though I had done nothing against our people or the customs of our ancestors. The Romans tried me and wanted to release me, for they found no cause for the death sentence. But when the Jewish leaders protested the decision, I felt it necessary to appeal to Caesar, even though I had no desire to press charges against my own people. I asked you to come here today so we could get acquainted and so I could tell you that I am bound with this chain because I believe that the hope of Israel—the Messiah—has already come."

They replied, "We have heard nothing against you. We have had no letters from Judea or reports from anyone who has arrived here. But we want to hear what you believe, for the only thing we know about these Christians is that they are denounced everywhere."

So a time was set, and on that day a large number of people came to Paul's house. He told them about the Kingdom of God and taught them about Jesus from the Scriptures—from the five books of Moses and the books of the prophets. He began lecturing in the morning and went on into the evening. Some believed and some didn't.

Take ANOTHER LOOK

While a prisoner in Rome, Paul wrote some of the letters you see in the New Testament. He wrote letters to the Ephesians, Philippians, Colossians, and to his associates, such as Timothy and Philemon during this time. Check out this passage from Ephesians. When Paul talked about the armor of God, he probably looked at the armor of his Roman guards for inspiration.

Ephesians 6:10-17, NLT

A final word: Be strong with the Lord's mighty power. Put on all of God's armor so that you will be able to stand firm against all strategies and tricks of the Devil. For we are not fighting against people made of flesh and blood, but against the evil rulers and authorities of the unseen world, against those mighty powers of darkness who rule this world, and against wicked spirits in the heavenly realms.

Use every piece of God's armor to resist the enemy in the time of evil, so that after the battle you will still be standing firm. Stand your ground, putting on the sturdy belt of truth and the body armor of God's righteousness. For shoes, put on the peace that comes from the Good News, so that you will be fully prepared. In every battle you will need faith as your shield to stop the fiery arrows aimed at you by Satan. Put on salvation as your helmet, and take the sword of the Spirit, which is the word of God.

Here's What I Think

Jammeshia, age 17

Sometimes it's funny to see how God puts me in a weird or uncomfortable situation. Someone is always asking me about Christ or something that has to do with God. Time after time I think, *Why me, Lord?* But then I remember Paul when he went to Rome.

Paul definitely was in an uneasy situation—under house arrest and in chains. But he never backed down from what he was called to do. Romans 8:28 says, "And we know that God causes everything to work together for the good of those who love God and are called according to his purpose for them." Paul used that time he was under arrest to preach the gospel to whomever would listen—whether it was his guards or visitors. So now when God gives me opportunities to share about him and his Son, I will not be afraid because I know that the Lord is working on my side.

Jammeshia

Share your faith with confidence because God is on your side!

A "FATHER'S" ADVICE

Introduction

Remember the story of Paul's adventures in Philippi? Paul and Silas traveled with a young preacher named Timothy. Timothy was like a son to Paul. And like any good father, Paul had advice for his spiritual "son."

2 Timothy 1:3–2:7, NLT

Timothy, I thank God for you. He is the God I serve with a clear conscience, just as my ancestors did. Night and day I constantly remember you in my prayers. I long to see you again, for I remember your tears as we parted. And I will be filled with joy when we are together again.

I know that you sincerely trust the Lord, for you have the faith of your mother, Eunice, and your grandmother, Lois. This is why I remind you to fan into flames the spiritual gift God gave you when I laid my hands on you. For God has not given us a spirit of fear and timidity, but of power, love, and self-discipline. So you must never be ashamed to tell others about our Lord. And don't be ashamed of me, either, even though I'm in prison for Christ. With the strength God gives you, be ready to suffer with me for the proclamation of the Good News.

It is God who saved us and chose us to live a holy life. He did this not because we deserved it, but because that was his plan long before the world began—to show his love and kindness to us through Christ Jesus.

And now he has made all of this plain to us by the coming of Christ Jesus, our Savior, who broke the power of death and showed us the way to everlasting life through the Good News. And God chose me to be a preacher, an apostle, and a teacher of this Good News.

And that is why I am suffering here in prison. But I am not ashamed of it, for I know the one in whom I trust, and I am sure that he is able to guard what I have entrusted to him until the day of his return.

Hold on to the pattern of right teaching you learned from me. And remember to live in the faith and love that you have in Christ Jesus. With the help of the Holy Spirit who lives within us, carefully guard what has been entrusted to you.

As you know, all the Christians who came here from the province of Asia have deserted me; even Phygelus and Hermogenes are gone. May the Lord show special kindness to Onesiphorus and all his family because he often visited and encouraged me. He was never ashamed of me because I was in prison. When he came to Rome, he searched everywhere until he found me. May the Lord show him special kindness on the day of Christ's return. And you know how much he helped me at Ephesus.

A Good Solider of Christ Jesus

Timothy, my dear son, be strong with the special favor God gives you in Christ Jesus. You have heard me teach many things that have been confirmed by many reliable witnesses. Teach these great truths to trustworthy people who are able to pass them on to others.

Endure suffering along with me, as a good soldier of Christ Jesus. And as Christ's soldier, do not let yourself become tied up in the affairs of this life, for then you cannot satisfy the one who has enlisted you in his army. Follow the Lord's rules for doing his work, just as an athlete either follows the rules or is disqualified and wins no prize. Hardworking farmers are the first to enjoy the fruit of their labor. Think about what I am saying. The Lord will give you understanding in all these things.

Take Another Look

Timothy was the leader of a church. That was a pretty big responsibility. But Timothy had doubts about his ability to do the job. So Paul had more advice for Timothy. His advice is good for you too.

1 Timothy 4:12-16, NLT

Don't let anyone think less of you because you are young. Be an example to all believers in what you teach, in the way you live, in your love, your faith, and your purity. Until I get there, focus on reading the Scriptures to the church, encouraging the believers, and teaching them.

Do not neglect the spiritual gift you received through the prophecies spoken to you when the elders of the church laid their hands on you. Give your complete attention to these matters. Throw yourself into your tasks so that everyone will see your progress. Keep a close watch on yourself and on your teaching. Stay true to what is right, and God will save you and those who hear you.

Here's What I Think

Daniel, age 15

There is one person in my life, though he may not know it, who has been a mentor to me. This man has taught me about family, relationships, integrity, and life. In this chapter, Paul is being a mentor—training, looking after, and trying to help Timothy.

I believe we should all have someone to mentor us as Paul did for Timothy, whether it's a parent, youth pastor, or friend of the family. I encourage you to reread this passage by Paul as if he were writing it to you. As believers we should work to surround ourselves with godly people, both younger and older, who will influence us to be like Jesus.

Daniel

Look for others who can train
you in the faith.

A HEAVENLY VISION

Introduction

Have you ever read the book of Revelation? It's sometimes thought of as the weird, scary book at the end of the Bible. But as you'll read in the story below, it's the best advertisement for heaven ever made. God allowed John, one of the original 12 disciples, to see a vision of heaven many years after Jesus returned there. What he saw amazed him.

Revelation 21:1-27, NLT

Then I saw a new heaven and a new earth, for the old heaven and the old earth had disappeared. And the sea was also gone. And I saw the holy city, the new Jerusalem, coming down from God out of heaven like a beautiful bride prepared for her husband.

I heard a loud shout from the throne, saying, "Look, the home of God is now among his people! He will live with them, and they will be his people. God himself will be with them. He will remove all of their sorrows, and there will be no more death or sorrow or crying or pain. For the old world and its evils are gone forever."

And the one sitting on the throne said, "Look, I am making all things new!" And then he said to me, "Write this down, for what I tell you is trustworthy and true." And he also said, "It is finished! I am the Alpha and the Omega—the Beginning and the End. To all who are thirsty I will give the springs of the water of life without charge! All who are victorious will inherit all these blessings, and I will be their God, and they will be my children. But cowards who turn away from me, and unbelievers, and the corrupt, and murderers, and the immoral, and those who practice witchcraft, and idol worshipers, and all liars—their doom is in the lake that burns with fire and sulfur. This is the second death."

Then one of the seven angels who held the seven bowls containing the seven last plagues came and said to me, "Come with me! I will show you the bride, the wife of the Lamb."

So he took me in spirit to a great, high mountain, and he showed me the holy city, Jerusalem, descending out of heaven from God. It was filled with the glory of God and sparkled like a precious gem, crystal clear like jasper. Its walls were broad and high, with twelve gates guarded by twelve angels. And the names of the twelve tribes of Israel were written on the gates. There were three gates on each side—east, north, south, and west. The wall of the city had twelve foundation stones, and on them were written the names of the twelve apostles of the Lamb.

The angel who talked to me held in his hand a gold measuring stick to measure the city, its gates, and its wall. When he measured it, he found it was a square, as wide as it was long. In fact, it was in the form of a cube, for its length and width and height were each 1,400 miles. Then he measured the walls and found them to be 216 feet thick (the angel used a standard human measure).

The wall was made of jasper, and the city was pure gold, as clear as glass. The wall of the city was built on foundation stones inlaid with twelve gems: the first was jasper, the second sapphire, the third agate, the fourth emerald, the fifth onyx, the sixth carnelian, the seventh chrysolite, the eighth beryl, the ninth topaz, the tenth chrysoprase, the eleventh jacinth, the twelfth amethyst.

The twelve gates were made of pearls—each gate from a single pearl! And the main street was pure gold, as clear as glass.

No temple could be seen in the city, for the Lord God Almighty and the Lamb are its temple. And the city has no need of sun or moon, for the glory of God illuminates the city, and the Lamb is its light. The nations of the earth will walk in its light, and the rulers of the world will come and bring their glory to it. Its gates never close at the end of day because there is no night. And all the nations will bring their glory and honor into the city. Nothing evil will be allowed to enter—no one who practices shameful idolatry and dishonesty—but only those whose names are written in the Lamb's Book of Life.

Paul also wrote about heaven and the new bodies we'll have once we arrive there (we can't take the old ones with us). Check out this passage from 2 Corinthians.

2 Corinthians 5:1-5, NLT

For we know that when this earthly tent we live in is taken down—when we die and leave these bodies—we will have a home in heaven, an eternal body made for us by God himself and not by human hands. We grow weary in our present bodies, and we long for the day when we will put on our heavenly bodies like new clothing. For we will not be spirits without bodies, but we will put on new heavenly bodies. Our dying bodies make us groan and sigh, but it's not that we want to die and have no bodies at all. We want to slip into our new bodies so that these dying bodies will be swallowed up by everlasting life. God himself has prepared us for this, and as a guarantee he has given us his Holy Spirit.

Here's What I Think

Janna, age 14

What do you imagine when you think of heaven? Is your view like what John describes in this passage from Revelation? I think when we get to heaven, it will be much more overwhelming than we can ever picture from these verses. Just think of the wonderful place that God is preparing for us. As John tells us, there will be no more pain and no more crying in heaven. That's a very comforting thought! But not all people will be able to rejoice in this great promise. First, you have to accept Jesus into your life. Jesus died on the cross for us, and we must ask him into our hearts so we can receive eternal life promised with him in heaven. If you are a Christian, you have an amazing assurance for when you die. Heaven will be a wonderful place—I can't wait to get there!

Janna

**Heaven awaits all who believe in Jesus.
Imagine!**

Teen Bios

Daniel Gill Lichtenberger

I was born in Alaska, grew up in Arizona, and love the outdoors. I enjoy paint-balling, rock climbing, backpacking, mountain biking, working on cars, and especially all types of fishing. I like hanging out with friends. I'm a junior at Peoria High School in Peoria, Arizona, and a leader in my youth group. I might go into youth work or possibly become a missionary to a Third World country, but I don't know for sure. I hope this Bible has made a positive impact on your walk with God and pray that God spoke to you through it.

Faith Tucker

My life in a nutshell would be described as "fun, yet hectic." School is crazy, and soccer is even crazier. I've played soccer for about nine years and I love it more every day. In March 2003, I was selected for the Northern California State soccer team. I was so excited! But my bubble was burst the next week when I tore some cartilage in my knee. I had to have surgery, and after four months of rehab, I am able to play again. God used this time to teach me so many things and bring me close to him. As a matter of fact, I got baptized that same summer.

I live with my parents and two older brothers in Los Altos, California.

Jammeshia Burgess

I attend Robert E. Lee High School in Tyler, Texas, where I am a senior. After I graduate I plan on attending Ouachita Baptist University in Arkansas and majoring in business with a minor in youth ministry. Once I graduate from college, I plan on attending seminary and then working in some field of full-time ministry, hopefully in an area dealing with youth. I am just seeking what the Lord wants out of my life.

In my free time, I enjoy hanging out at church, playing basketball, computers, and working out. At my high school I am involved in varsity basketball, Fellowship of Christian Athletes (I am vice president), and Bible Club. At church I am involved in many activities such as teaching discipleship groups, youth group, and doing various jobs around the church building.

Julie DeJager

I am from Naperville, Illinois, but I currently attend Gordon College in Massachusetts. I am studying to become a high school history teacher and hope eventually to be a published author as well (this is a good start!). Although I'm a full-time student during the school year and a camp counselor during the summer, I still find time to bike, hike, write, and have fun with friends and family.

Janna Riggs

I am a fourteen-year-old freshman at Pleasant View Christian School in Tennessee. I play volleyball and basketball, and am currently the volleyball captain. I am on the Principal's List at school. I have three great older brothers. My dad is the pastor of our church. I became a Christian at the age of six. I try to make God first in my life, though I fail often. God has done many wonderful things in my life. He deserves all the glory.

Kali Veerman

I am eighteen years old and a freshman at Bethel College in Minnesota. I have not decided on a major. I absolutely love music—singing, playing the guitar, and being in musical theater as well as plays. I also love to scrapbook, hang out with friends and family, and be spontaneous. I live in Chaska, Minnesota, with mom and dad, two younger brothers, and a dog named Moses. I am excited to see all that God has in store for me in the near future. It will be one incredible journey!

Michael Malone

I was born in Delaware, but I have spent most of my life living in Ft. Lauderdale, Florida. I currently am a biological science major at Florida State University, where I hope to develop a way for humans to use photosynthesis as a means of energy production.

Nicee M. Jones

Born and raised in Chicago, I am, above all else, a Christian. I enjoy spending time with my family and helping others deal with their problems. As a young writer, I enjoy writing poetry and songs. I find both to be an awesome means of self-expression. I am very active in the youth ministry of my church. I am an evangelistic counselor, a member of the youth choir, and an honor student at Gwendolyn Brooks College Preparatory Academy.

Verity Hamilton

I am 13 years old, and my passion is art. My favorite artists are Van Gogh and Picasso. I also spend my time exercising or just hanging out with friends. I love to write poetry, and I'm always striving to become a better writer. I take a lot influence and inspiration from my favorite bands. My hope is to be happy with life. I live with my family in Easton, Connecticut.

Walter L. Woods IV

I am an eighth grader at A.E. Phillips Laboratory School in Ruston, Louisiana. I was formerly the editor of our school newspaper, and now I'm serving as president of the student council and I'm also an officer in the Fellowship of Christian Athletes. In addition to my involvement in various theatrical productions, including *Peter Pan* and *The Lion, the Witch, and The Wardrobe*, I enjoy reading, writing, and making movies with my friends.